BÄUMER

30 YEARS OF ART

TEXTS PAUL-HENRY BIZON
PHOTOGRAPHS PHILIPPE GARCIA

BÄUMER

30 YEARS OF ART

ABRAMS | NEW YORK

ENCOUNTERS FOR ETERNITY

The first thirty years of the House of Bäumer have flown by.
That's why I wanted to collect them in a book, like an album
where good memories can be shared and we can prepare for the future.
When thinking about what form it might take, a sentence from
Paul Éluard sprang to mind: "There are no accidents, only encounters."
How true it is. What would have become of my conviction and desire
to create without these encounters? Without all the people that life
has allowed me to meet and spend time with? These loved ones, advisors,
partners, clients, colleagues—and now friends—have always been
there for me and I wanted to take this opportunity to show their vital
importance in my work. If I've created with so much passion, it is
also—and above all—for them. To give them joy, happiness, and
delight. And while they have often been the recipients of my jewelry,
they have also been its co-creators. So, I decided to flip the mirror
by asking them about the importance of these jewelry pieces in
their lives, how they perceived them, and how they were inspired
by them in turn. Thirty friends have answered my questions based
on a piece that I chose for them. Their answers have painted a picture
of a living and ever-changing house. Their answers have given me
the greatest anniversary gift there is. I'd like to thank them.
This book is also their own.

DREAM AFTER DREAM

Cubist Garden ring
Diana Picasso

Ellipse Solitaire
Kelly Wearstler

Meteorite yellow diamond ring
Kamel Mennour

Writing bracelet "Les belles nuits…"
Philippe Labro

Titanium Ocean Crush earrings
Bénédicte Epinay

Extravagant Spider brooch
Chahan Minassian

Sumba hoops
Chris Burch

Treasure Island bracelet
Cyril Karaoglan

Love Bird hoops
Géraldine Bäumer

Diamonds Heartbeat bracelet
Artus, Carl and Alma Bäumer

Vanitas Diamonds ring
Philippe Pasqua

Black Magic Nébuleuse bracelet
Linda Pinto

Mikado architect bracelet
Hervé Van der Straeten

Sea Urchin ring
Cécilia and Jean-Conrad Hottinguer

À la folie ring
Alain Ducasse

Scarab brooch
François-Paul Journe

Tattoo diamond ring The key to my heart
Princesse Astrid von Liechtenstein

Friendship knife
Cédric Aumonier

Hedgehog ring
Jean-Norbert Salit

Gourmandise Winter bracelet
Évelyne Possémé

Metamorphose earrings
Alexandre Murat

Pense à moi Diamonds ring
Thierry Lhermitte

Morse Amour earrings
Hubert Le Gall

À la folie blossom ring
Vik Muniz

Vanitas daguerreotype watch
Jean-Pierre Brun

Damascus Rose NFT ring
Luc Ferry

Diamonds Foam tiara
H.S.H. Princess Charlène of Monaco

Academician's sword
Xavier Darcos

Gourmandise red jasper ring
François Perret

Surfer and Princess frames
Sloan Barnett

Tree of Life costume jewelry brooch
Marie-José Bäumer

BÄUMER DESIGN

Louis Vuitton, Soul of the Journey necklace
Pietro Beccari

Chanel, Camelia ring
Yves Béhar

Guerlain, Bee bottle
Laurent Boillot

Guerlain, Rouge G
Olivier Echaudemaison

Hennessy NBA, Paradise decanter
Renaud Fillioux de Gironde

Le beau est une promesse
de bonheur...

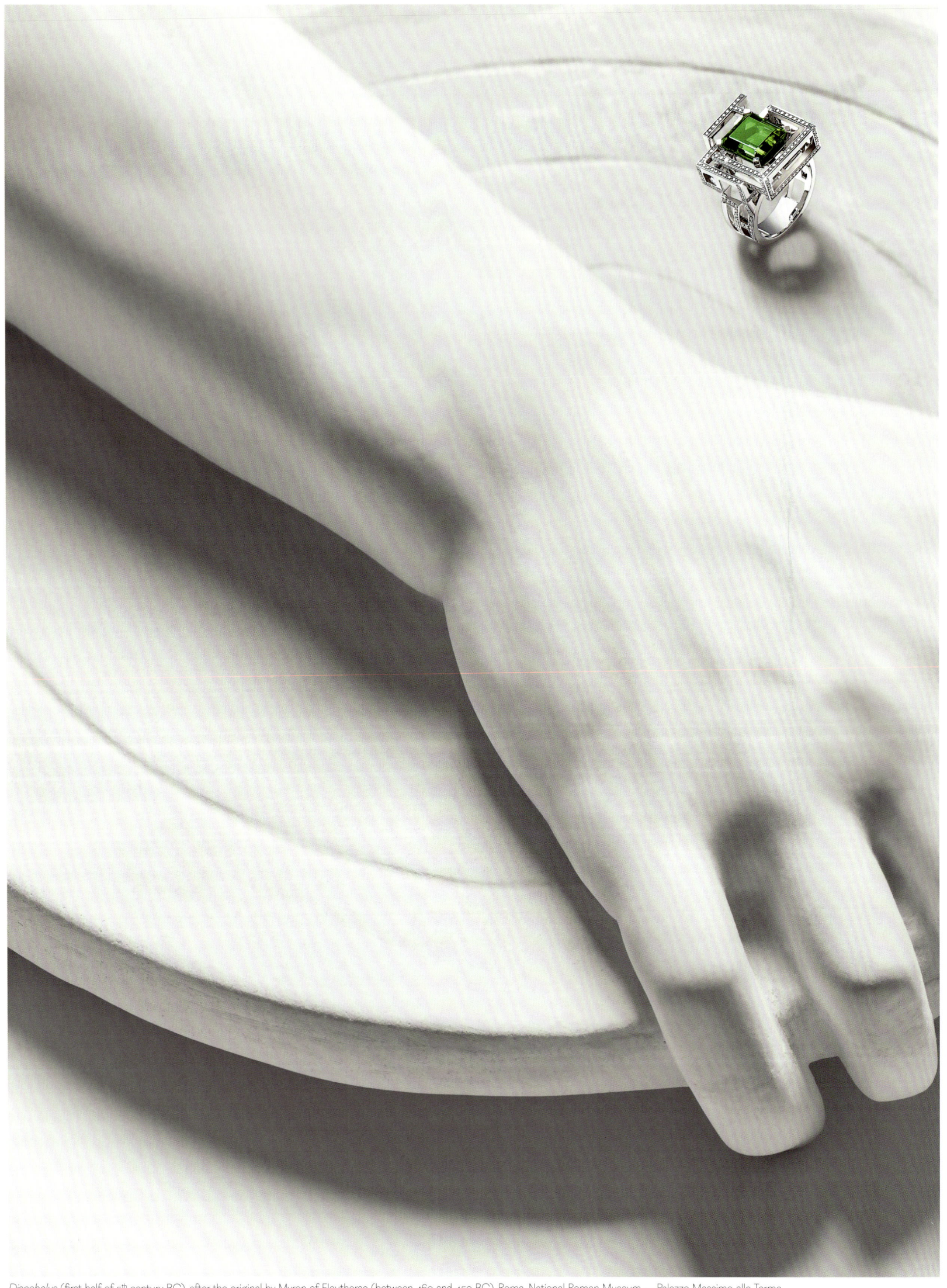

Discobolus (first half of 5th century BC), after the original by Myron of Eleutherae (between 460 and 450 BC), Roma, National Roman Museum — Palazzo Massimo alle Terme.

CUB
IST

GAR
DEN

When Lorenz introduced me to his world, I was impressed by his knowl-edge and curiosity, particularly for design, which is a shared passion. His creations are always highly lyrical, sumptuous, poetic, and original. They transport me to a very personal world, as I know how committed Lorenz is to satisfying his clients and adapting to their aspirations as far as he possibly can through his jewelry. This ring reminds me of Horta de Sant Joan, a charming Catalan village that played a key role in Picasso's life and his invention of Cubism. My grandfather depicted landscapes through interlocking geometric shapes captured from multiple perspectives and in different planes. Lorenz's ring is an ode to these Cubist compositions and the precious stones are in complete symbiosis with the sky and nature.

Diana Picasso
Art historian, curator
and jewelry designer

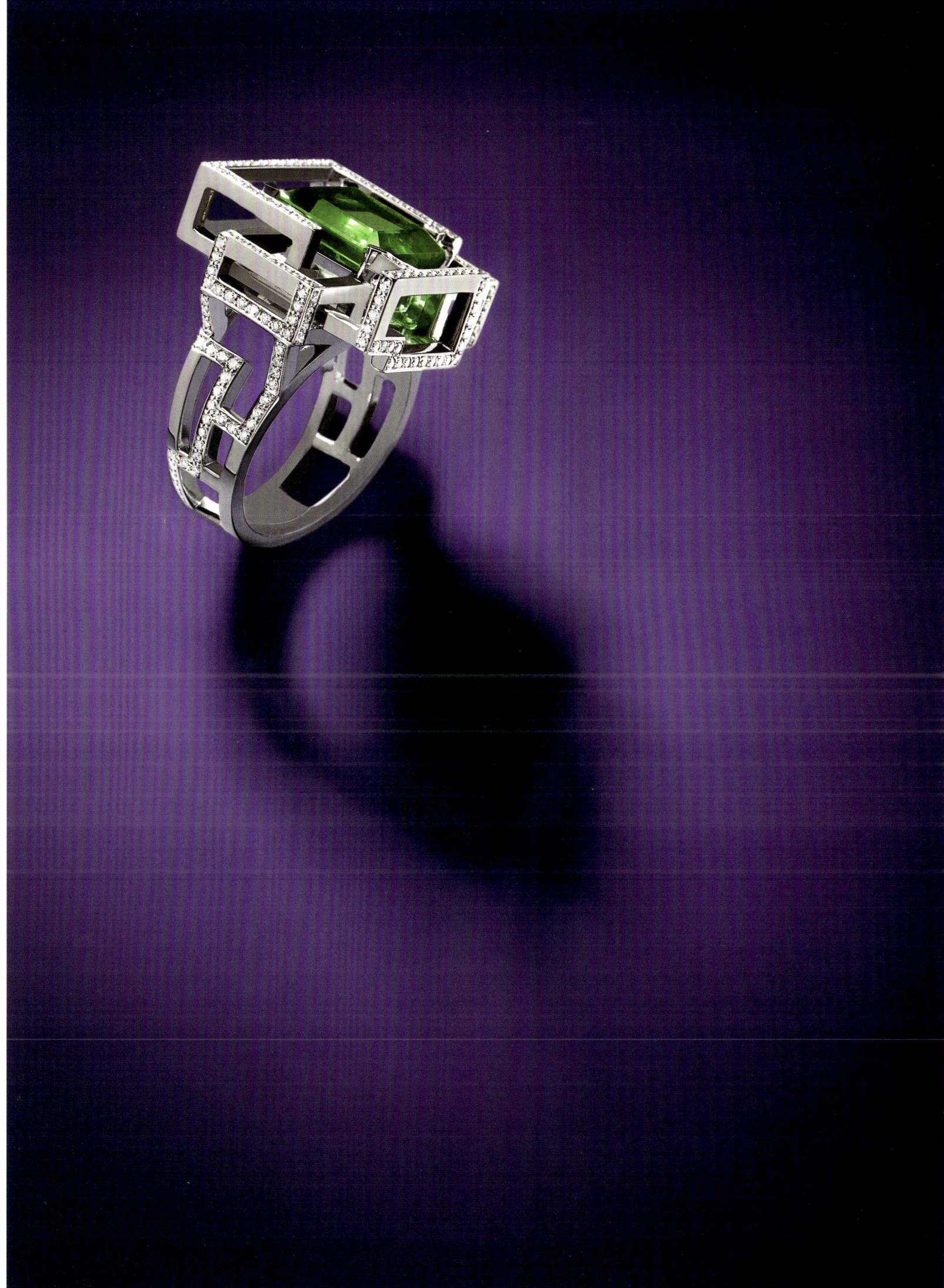

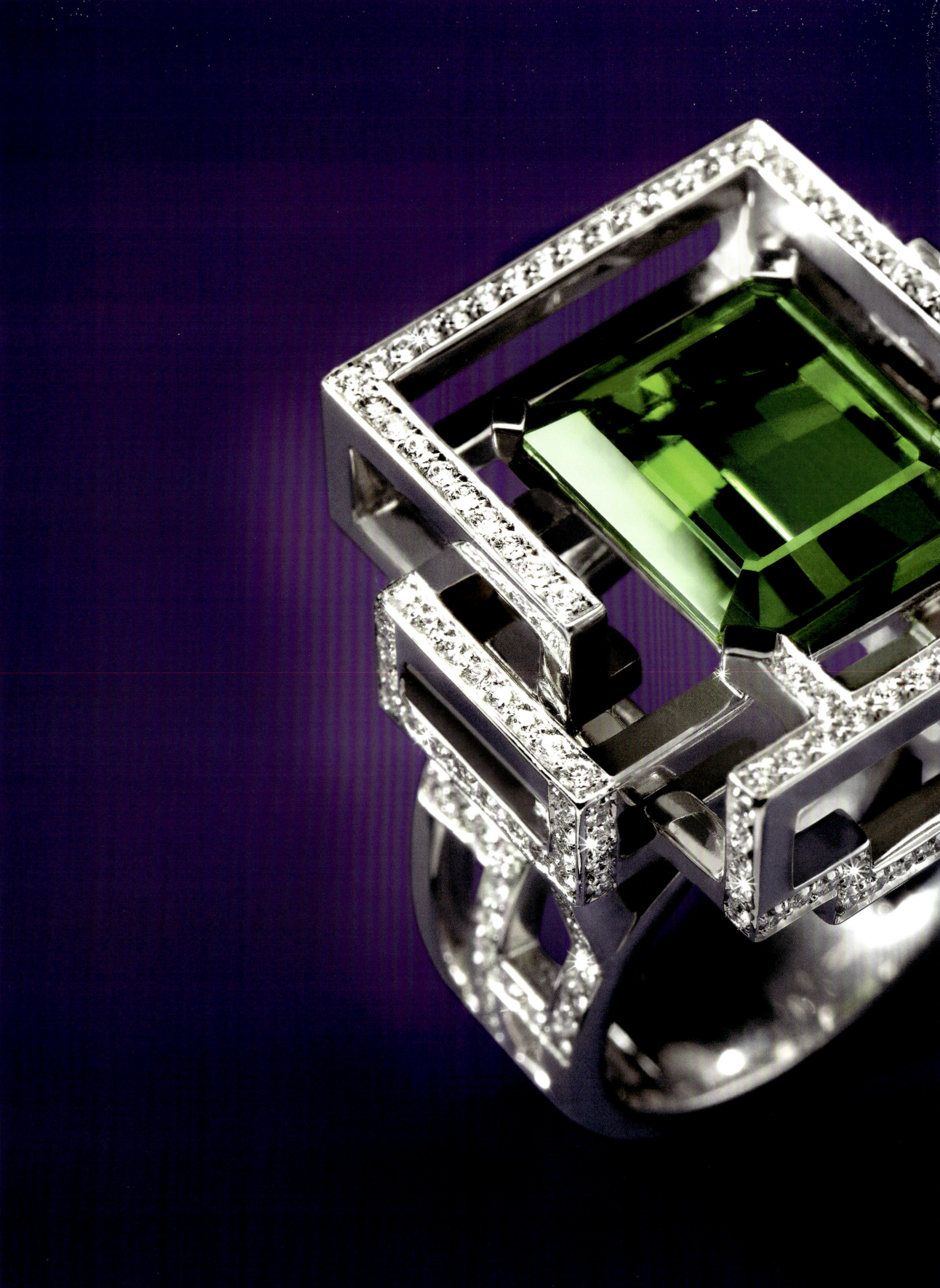

CUBIST GARDEN
RING

This piece is inspired by the Cubist
garden of Villa Noailles in Hyères, France;
it's a mineral depiction of plant life.

EL
LI
PSE

Lorenz and I met in Indonesia, on the island of Sumba. We had both come there with our families to recharge and enjoy the sea and incredible nature. It was special to connect with him there. I love Lorenz's work because it's full of joy—he has a strong sense of color, materiality and texture. And his approach to mixing these elements is similar to my own work. His jewelry-making skills are very French, very Parisian, but Lorenz is very curious and has a great sense of humor. He knows how to be serious without taking himself too seriously. His open-minded approach brings a unique style to even the most classic creations, as this *Ellipse* ring. We share this desire to create timelessly elegant objects for the people who place their trust in us, objects that will accompany them for a lifetime, thanks to the most amazing craftsmen and artisans who bring our dreams to life.

Kelly Wearstler
Interior designer

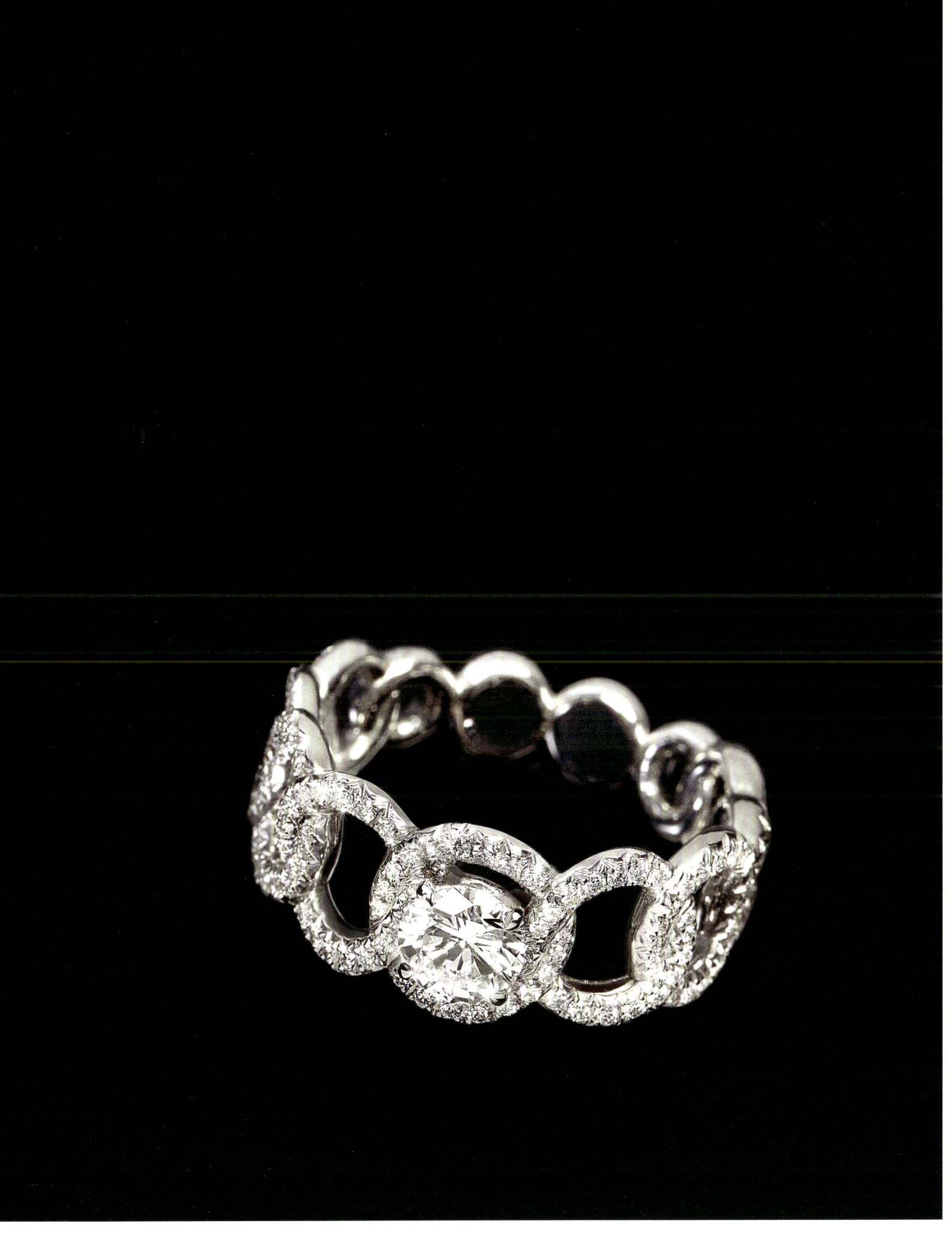

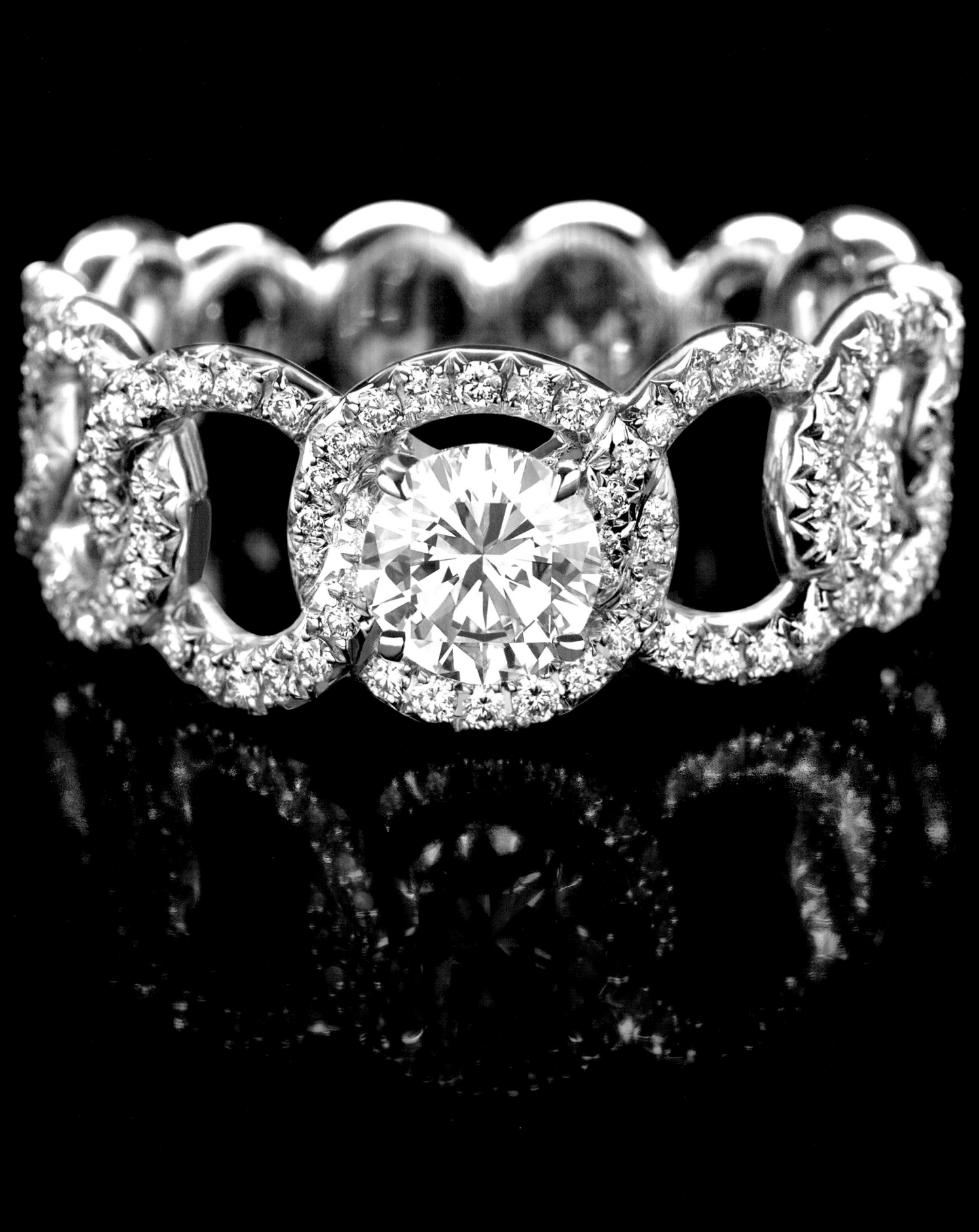

ELLIPSE
SOLITAIRE

The diamond links are like a glittering
bond that symbolizes a love story.

METE
O
RITE

Lorenz isn't a manufacturer, he's a creator. His ingenuity and ability to invent stories make him an author, a true artist in his field. We were initially brought together by our interest in photography, but the friendship that has developed between us since then goes far beyond that. We are from the same generation and share the same concerns about our role in society. Our mutual respect is also fueled by our respective commitments to causes that are close to our hearts. As good as he is in his field, Lorenz always needs to look at the world to find inspiration. I don't know the origins of this meteorite piece, but I can just picture Lorenz being inspired by a movie about a space mission or a night spent observing the stars! He himself is hungry for that wonder he inspires in us when he creates jewelry, which I personally experience whenever I watch him working in his studio.

Kamel Mennour
Gallery owner

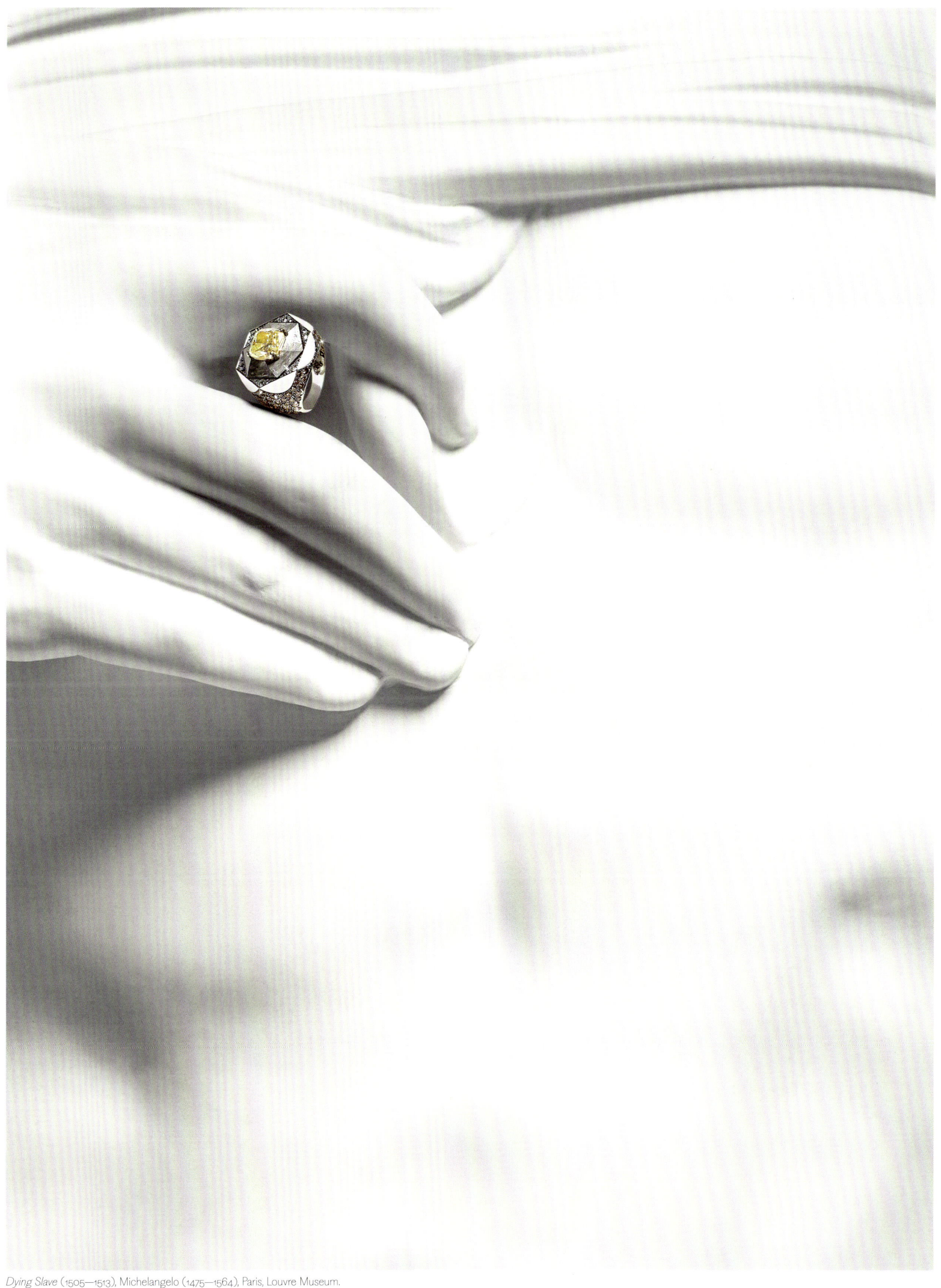

Dying Slave (1505—1513), Michelangelo (1475—1564), Paris, Louvre Museum.

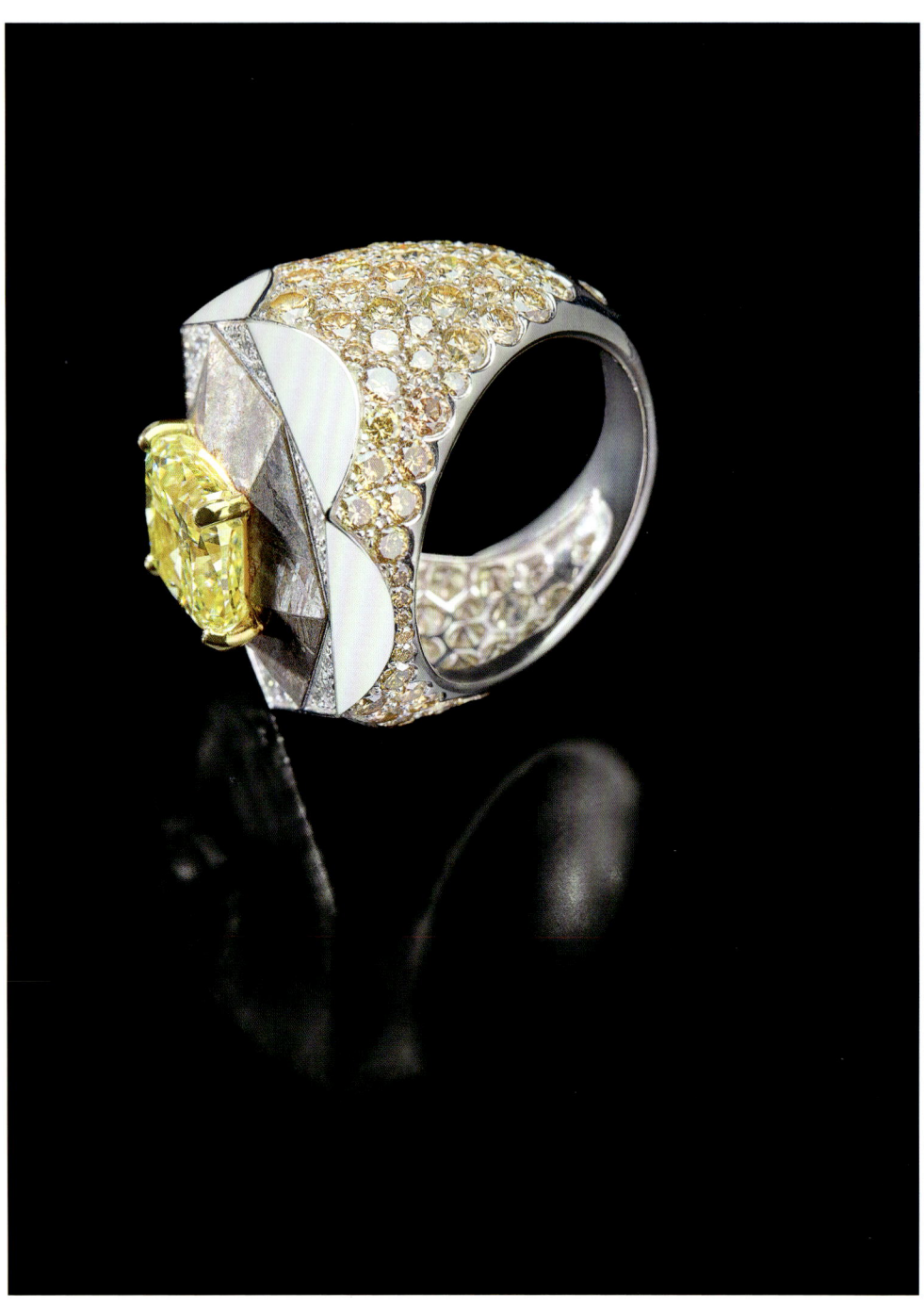

METEORITE
YELLOW DIAMOND
RING

Moving heaven and earth for a woman you
love is nothing when you can give her the stars...
On this ring, a sunny diamond sparkles
in the middle of this piece of a star.

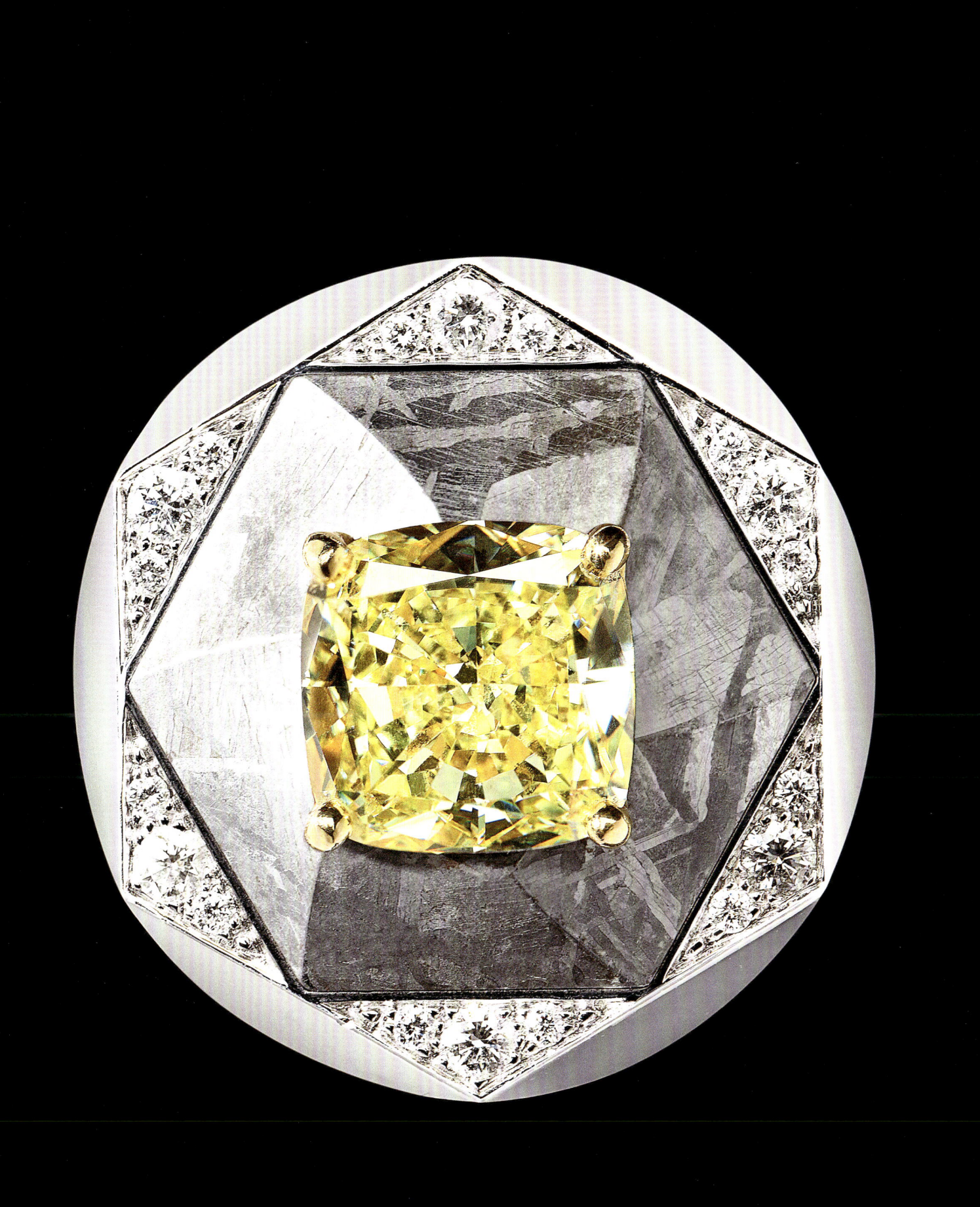

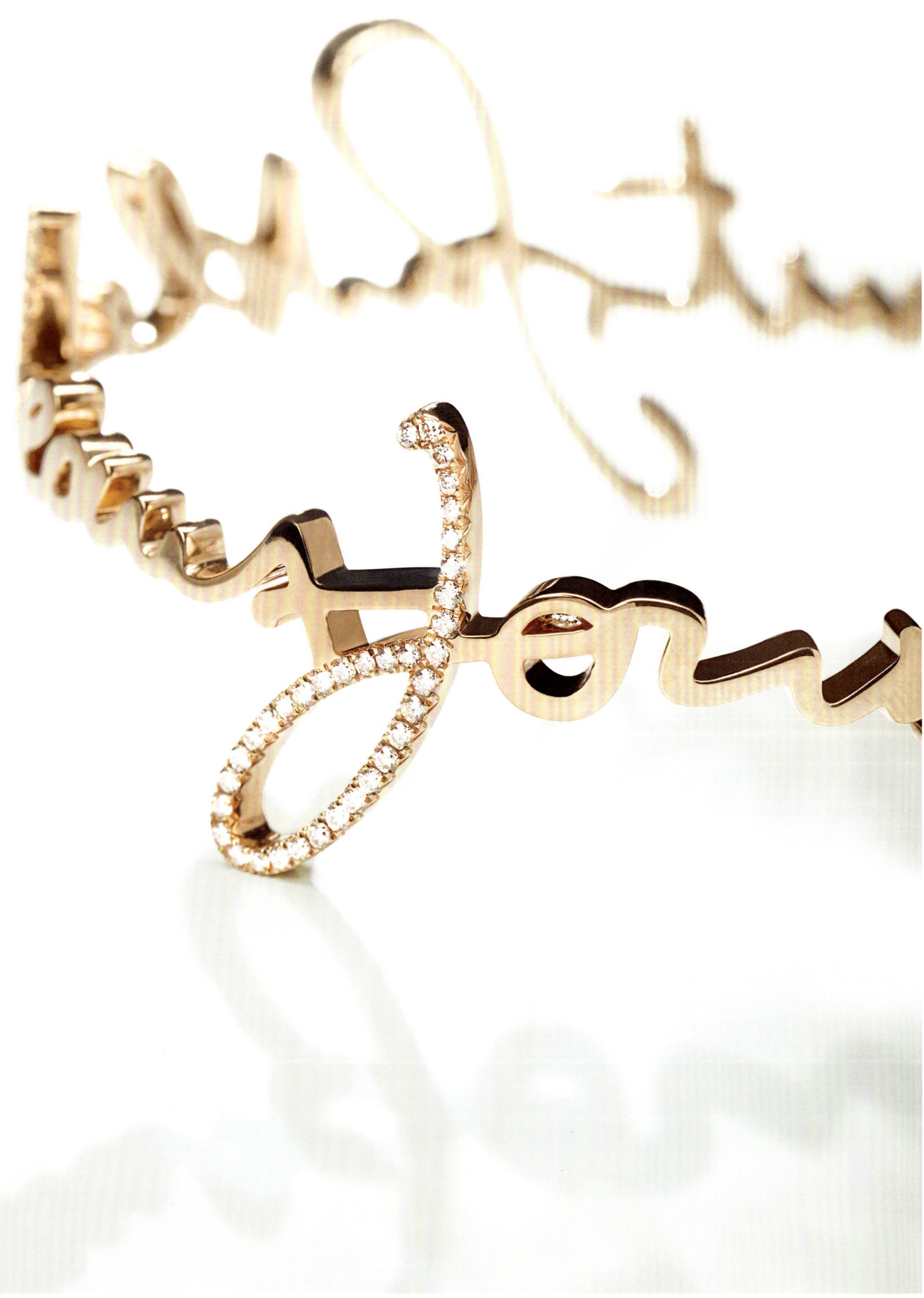

LES BELLES NUITS...

Jewelry is a field of excellence where there is no room for error. Lorenz's skill lies in taking it even further. There is something liberated and daring about his work that appeals to me. He's a free man who is sure of his decisions while remaining open to others. I like well-rounded people! He is very interested in literature, for example. I remember that one of the first times we met, he gave me a notebook. I kept it with me for a long time, like a talisman. For Lorenz, everything starts with words. The *Writing bracelet* is the perfect illustration of this. This piece pays homage to French literary culture.

Philippe Labro
Author, journalist and film director

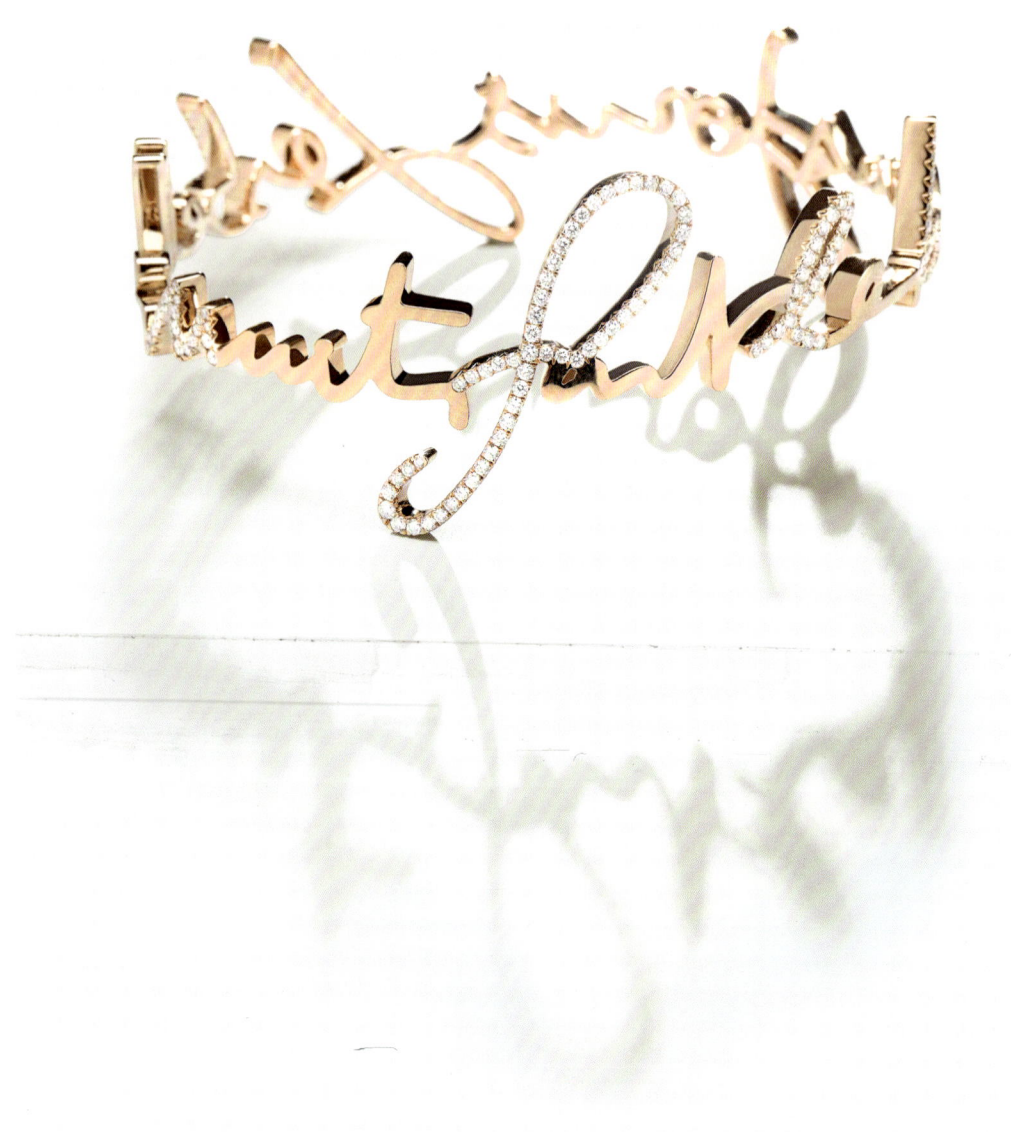

WRITING BRACELET
"LES BELLES NUITS..."

Turning words into jewelry and bringing them
to life in the most precious materials—a bracelet
that becomes a new declaration of love.

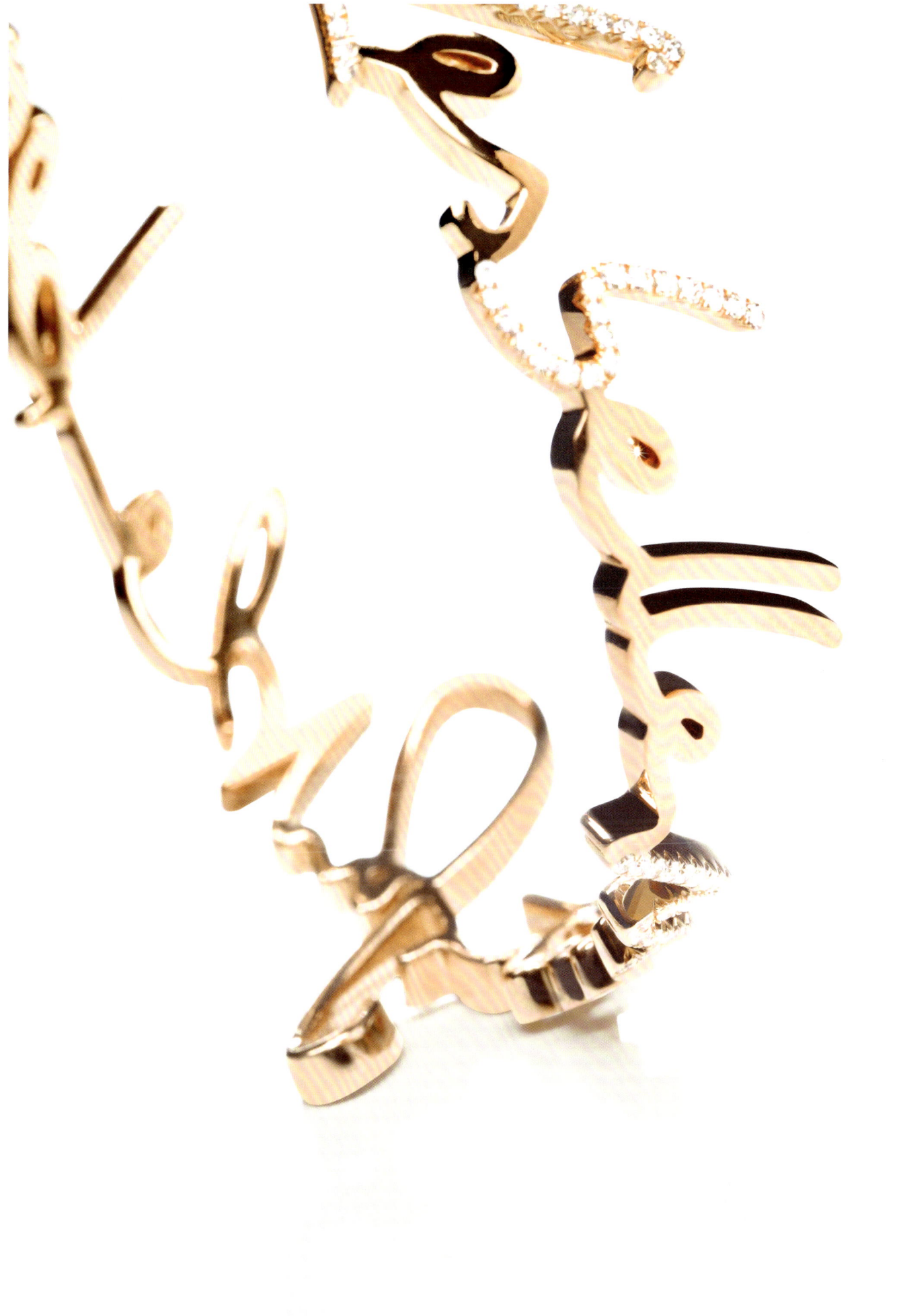

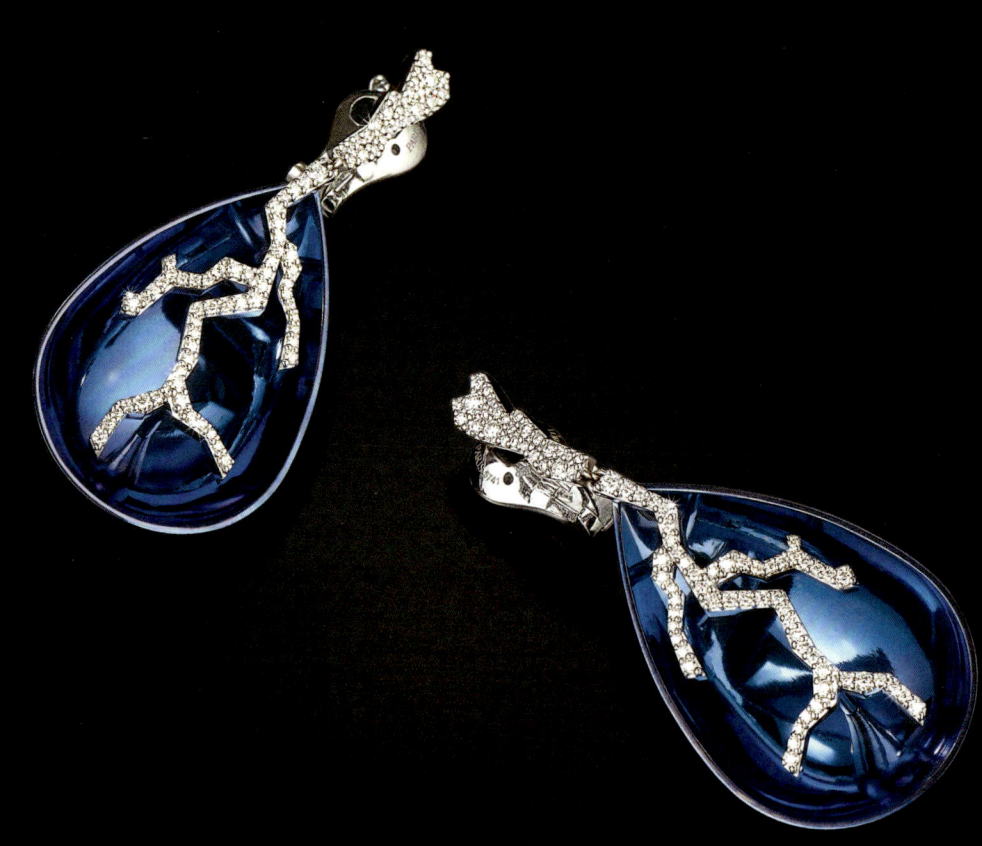

TITANIUM OCEAN CRUSH

I discovered Lorenz's work at a Chanel jewelry presentation nearly twenty years ago. Some of the creations I saw there, such as the carved stone *Camellia*, the *Coco* ring, and the Ultra line, which used black ceramic in jewelry for the first time, are still fantastically modern and their desirability has remained unchanged. They gave me an immediate impression of a different perspective—that of a sensitive engineer or a rational poet. Lorenz's work is unique, joyful, and romantic and I have a great deal of admiration for his journey. Firstly for his entrepreneurial spirit—I have none and I envy those who do! And secondly for his guts: designing costume jewelry at the age of 23, founding a jewelry company at 27, moving to Place Vendôme alongside the industry's behemoths, and ultimately seeing his work—including four pieces made for Chanel Fine Jewelry—exhibited in the permanent collection of the French Musée des Arts décoratifs. What a trajectory! He is an inventive and easy-going jeweler who designs unpretentious pieces. His creations conjure another world and demonstrate a real wealth of artistic inspiration. They tell of Lorenz's passion for fine objects, his sensitivity, and his romanticism. Such is the case with these *Ocean Crush* earrings. The blue titanium is simultaneously deep, bright, and metallic. Combined with diamonds and white gold, the result is a perfect, chic harmony.

Bénédicte Epinay
CEO of the Comité Colbert

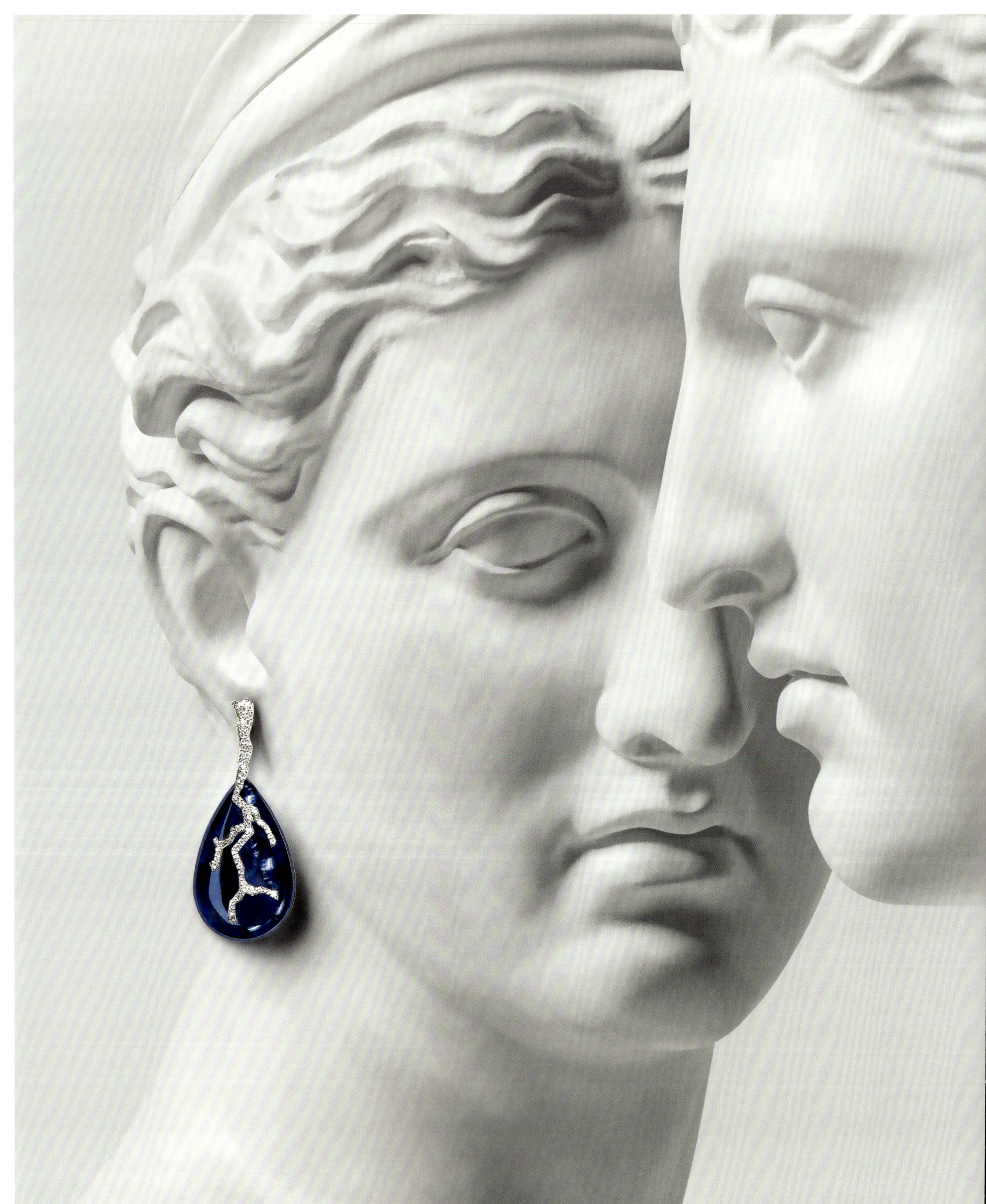

Diana Huntress, known as *Diana of Versailles* (2nd century CE), attributed to Leochares, Paris, Louvre Museum.

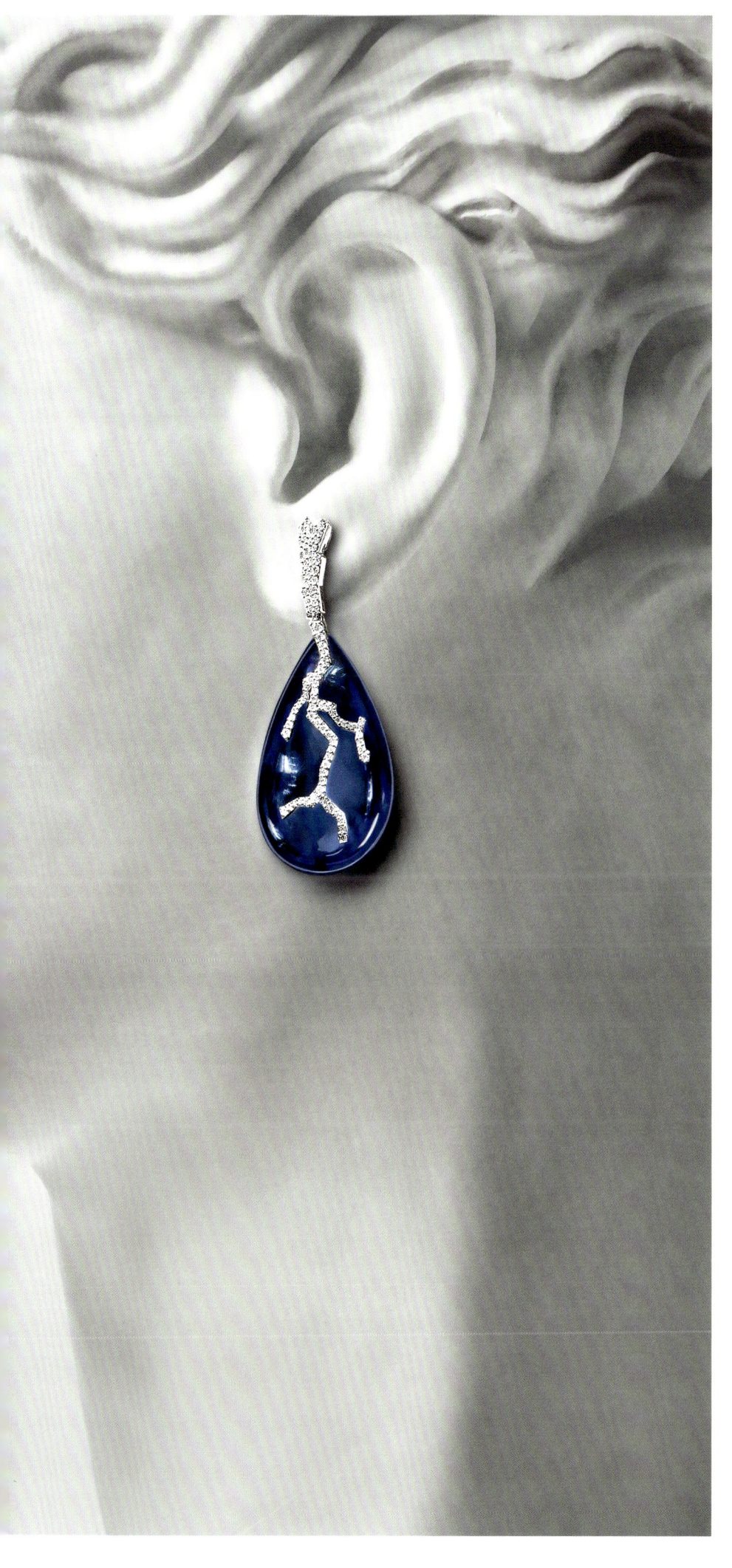

TITANIUM
OCEAN CRUSH
EARRINGS

These earrings call to mind a branch
of coral sparkling on the seabed, or the sun
reflecting like flashes of diamonds to accompany
Venus after she has left the water.

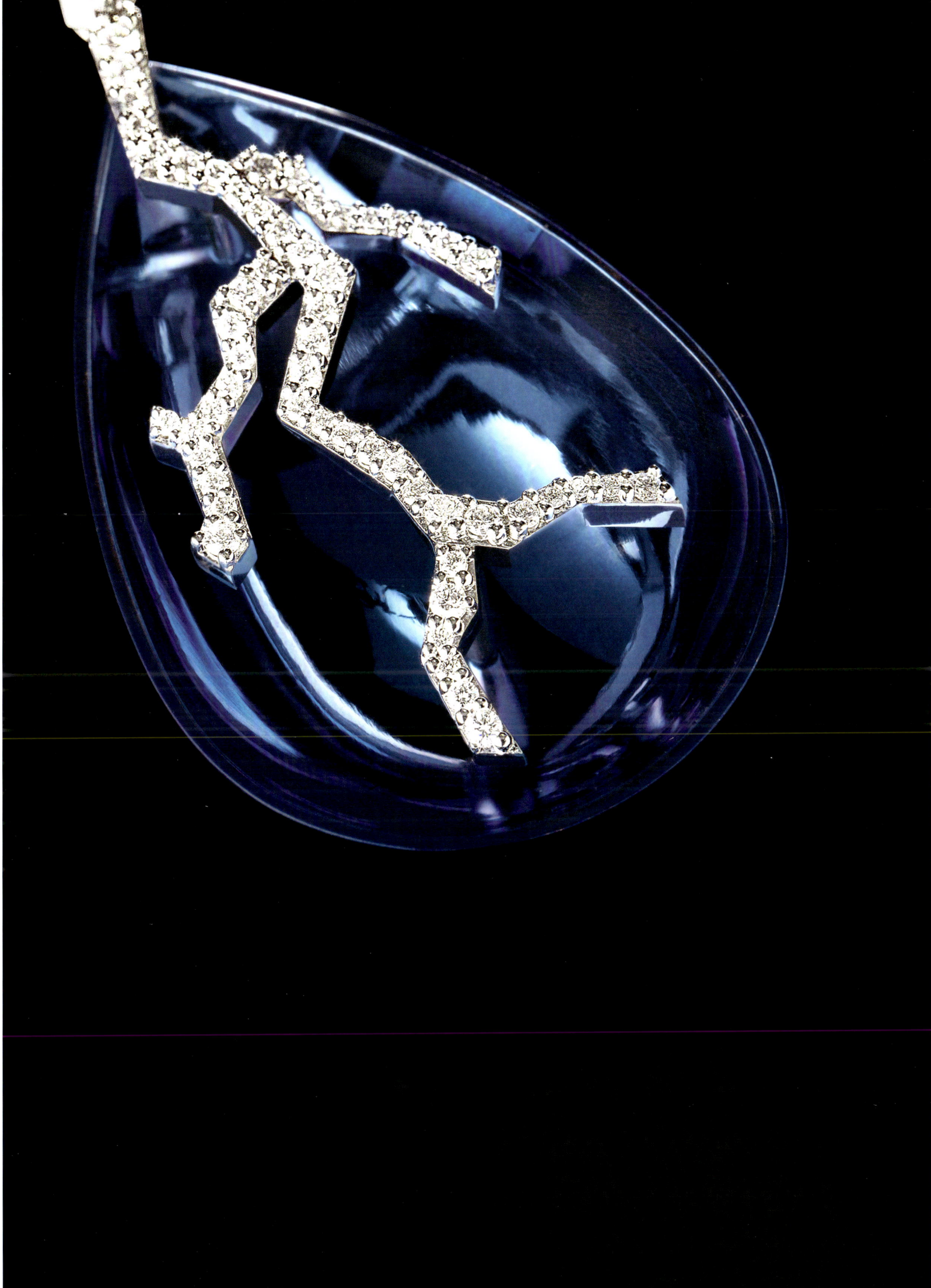

EXTRA VAGANT SPIDER

I met Lorenz when he was starting out, twenty-six years ago. I immediately related to his work because, even though the pieces he presented to me weren't yet quite fine jewelry, they were extremely precise. Lorenz is an architect in his field. His work is three-dimensional. He creates a narrative but not in a simple poetic or romantic sense, and that's what allows him to always stay very contemporary. He doesn't design "pretty" jewelry; he creates intelligent jewelry that tells a story. I wear a lot of jewelry and I am always pleasantly surprised by the subjects and shapes that Lorenz presents. He was one of the first to mix colors boldly and to incorporate calligraphy in a totally unique way. His jewelry gives a three-dimensional view of things that we usually see as flat shapes. I find that really fascinating. This completely diamond-studded spider with an iridescent center stone, for example, captivated me with its lightness and the transparency of the stones. Particularly as it is only attached by one leg, which gives it movement. It's extraordinary. Transparency, lightness, and movement. It's not just a representation; it's a three-dimensional recreation of the real thing. It's a spectacular approach to the object. Lorenz's jewelry is distinguished by this entirely novel approach to constructing frames. His jewelry isn't just a series of pavé-set forms, it is made up of overlapping planes. The relief is created through fascinating assembly and jewelry-making technique.

Chahan Minassian
Interior designer

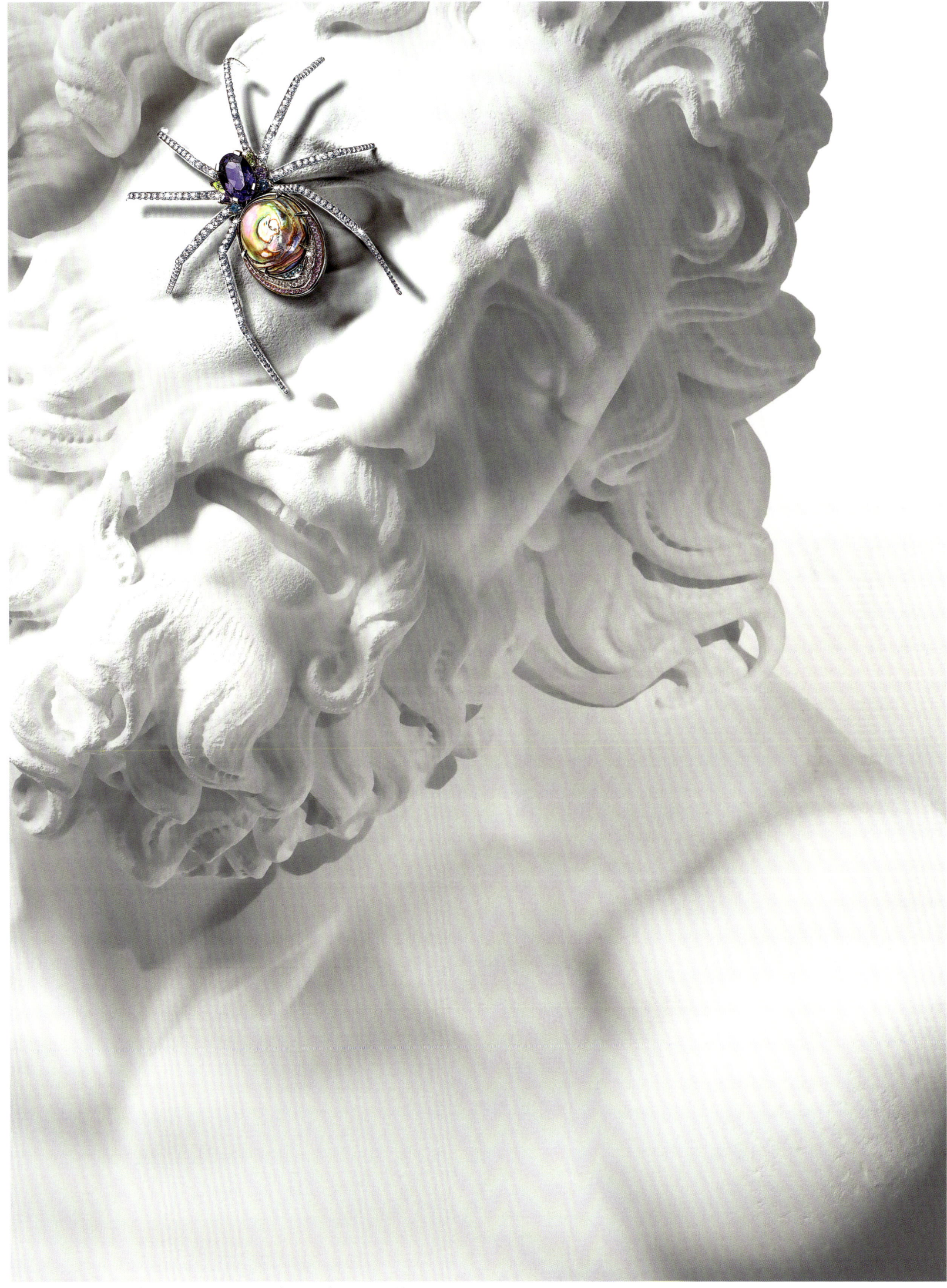

Bust of Laocoön (17th century), attributed to Giuliano Finelli (1601—1657), Paris, Louvre Museum.

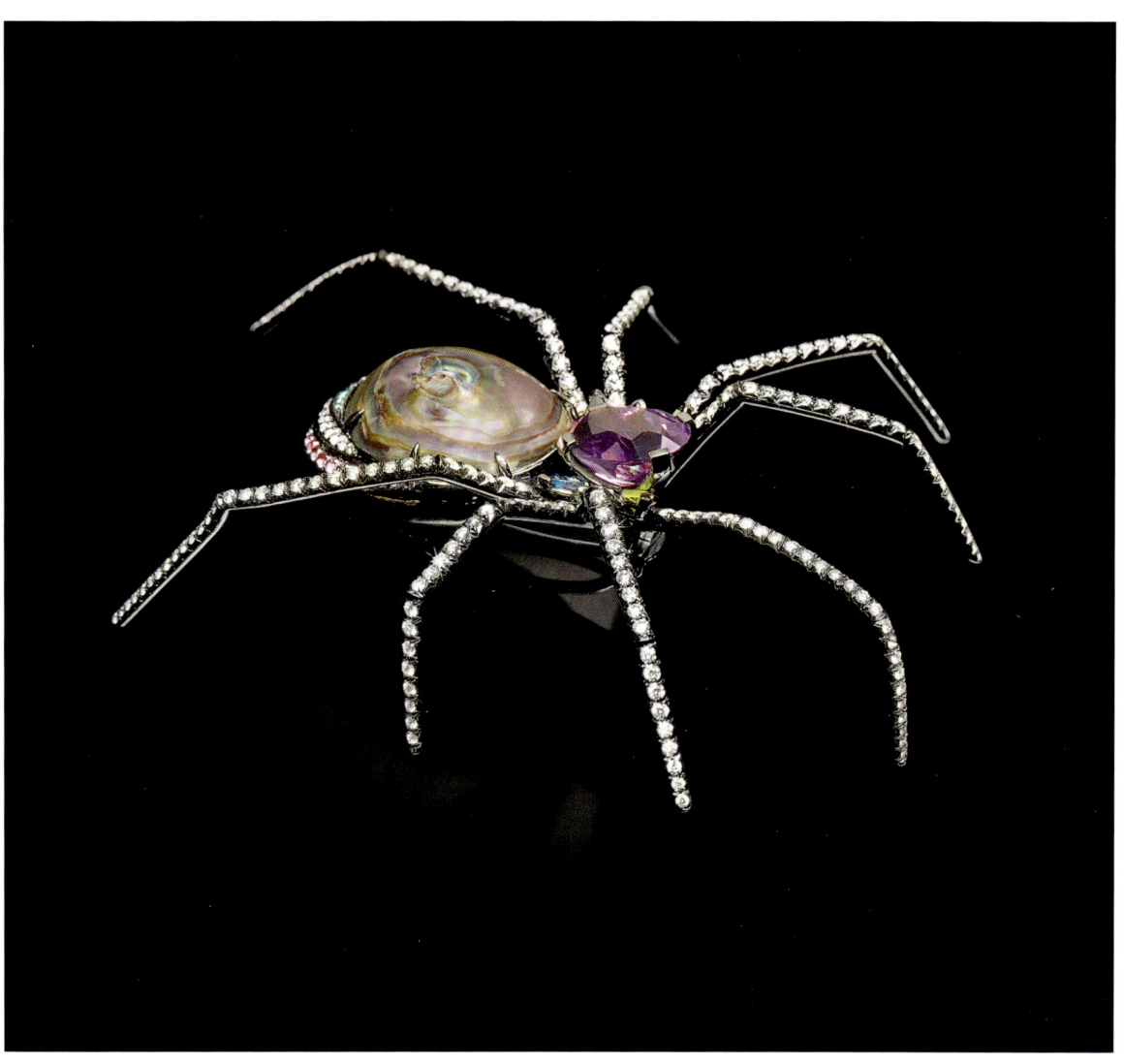

EXTRAVAGANT
SPIDER BROOCH

I love this beautiful, mysterious and
disconcerting spider designed around a natural
abalone pearl—nature's masterpiece.

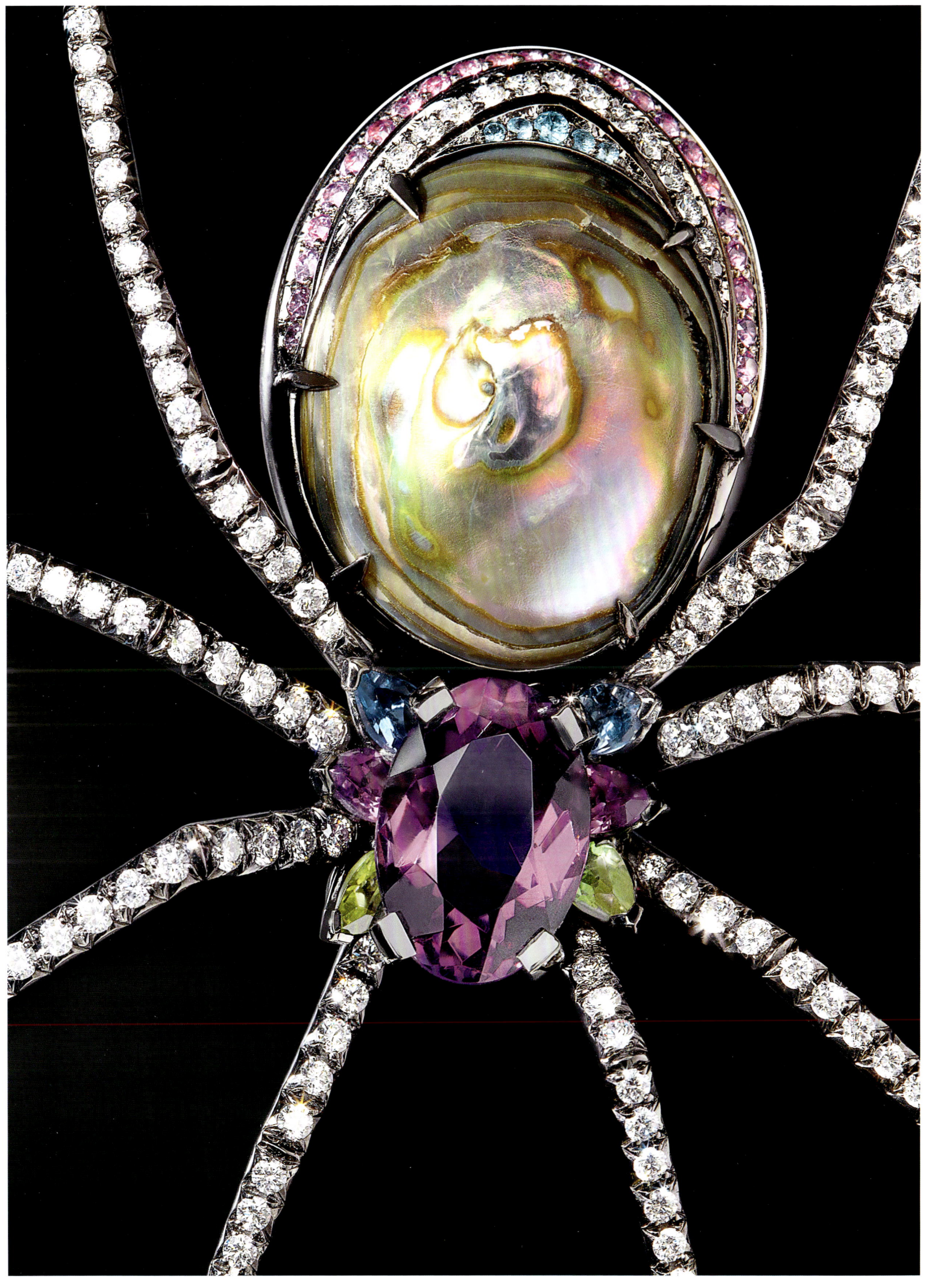

SUM BA

I met Lorenz when he brought his family on vacation to Nihi on the island of Sumba, in Indonesia. This hotel has a charitable foundation that supports local communities and Lorenz is one of its most generous and committed donors. This is why he created the *Sumba* jewelry piece, which is available to buy from our boutique in aid of the village's children. Lorenz excels in the art of combining stones and creating shapes. His work is unique, emotive, and always elegant.

Chris Burch
Entrepreneur and philanthropist

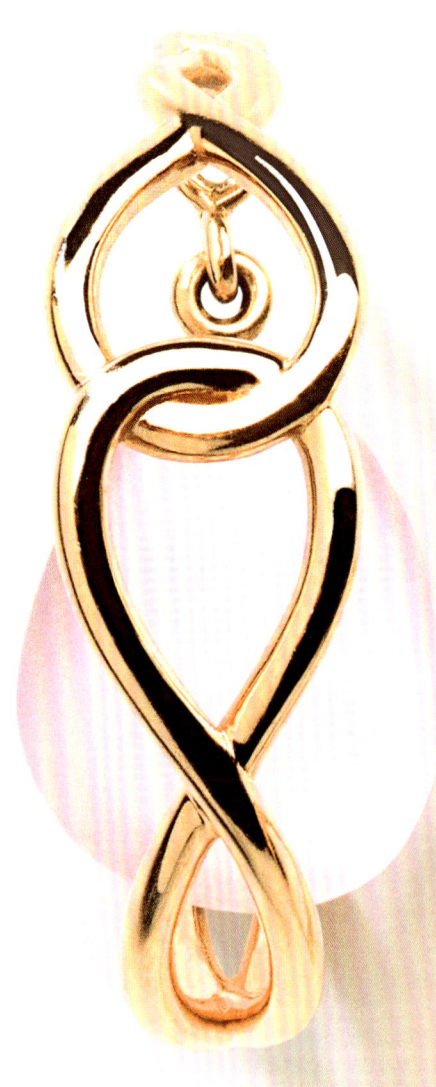
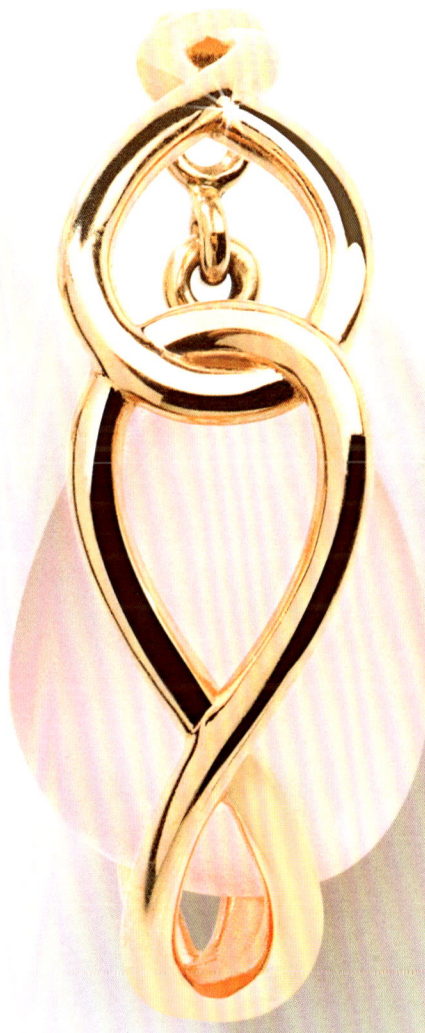

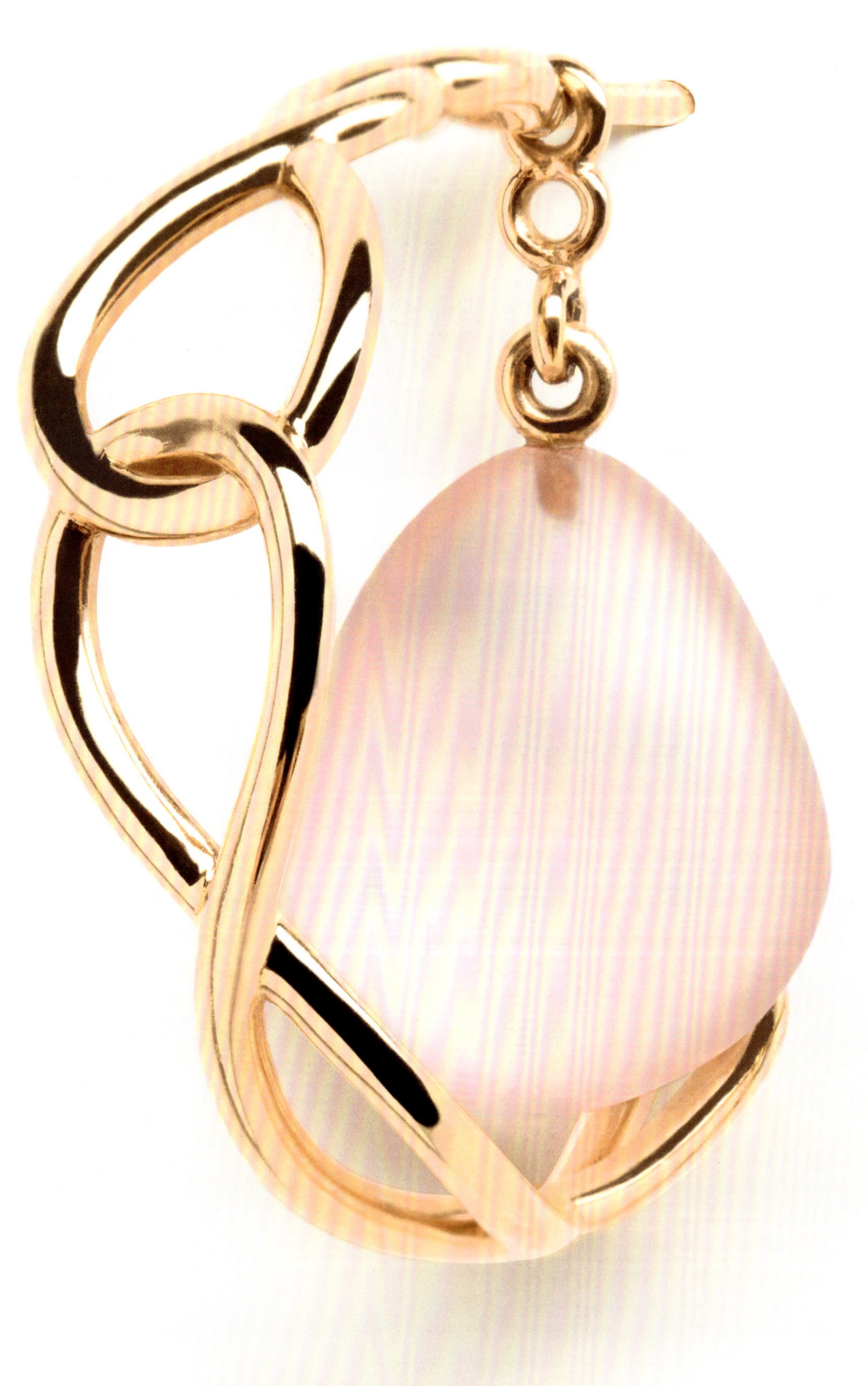

SUMBA
HOOPS

These earrings call to mind a pebble and
a piece of gold rope found on my favorite
beach on the island of Sumba in Indonesia.
And it was to support brighter futures
for the children of this island that I created
these hoops for the Fondation Sumba.

TREA
SURE
ISLAND

I met Lorenz at a dinner party hosted by some mutual friends, and later visited him in his rooms on Place Vendôme. I was immediately won over by his work and creativity. It was so much more than a showroom—it was his world. He works among his collections of art, in an environment I found fascinating. Lorenz has a very keen eye. He loves beautiful things and has the knack of finding the right place for them. You can see his passions and know-how in his designs. His jewelry and objects are extremely modern. They are poetic reflections of his curiosity and his love of beauty. They are extraordinary pieces because they're always executed with the greatest precision. Lorenz doesn't modernize things, he is constantly inventing and reinventing, without ever taking himself seriously. I think this *Treasure Island* bracelet is characteristic of his work. It is a thing of joy. You can sense the happiness that Lorenz feels when his marvelous objects speak to people. This passion and his quest for perfection, which goes far beyond aesthetic expression, inspire me and make me dream.

Cyril Karaoglan
Insurance expert and collector

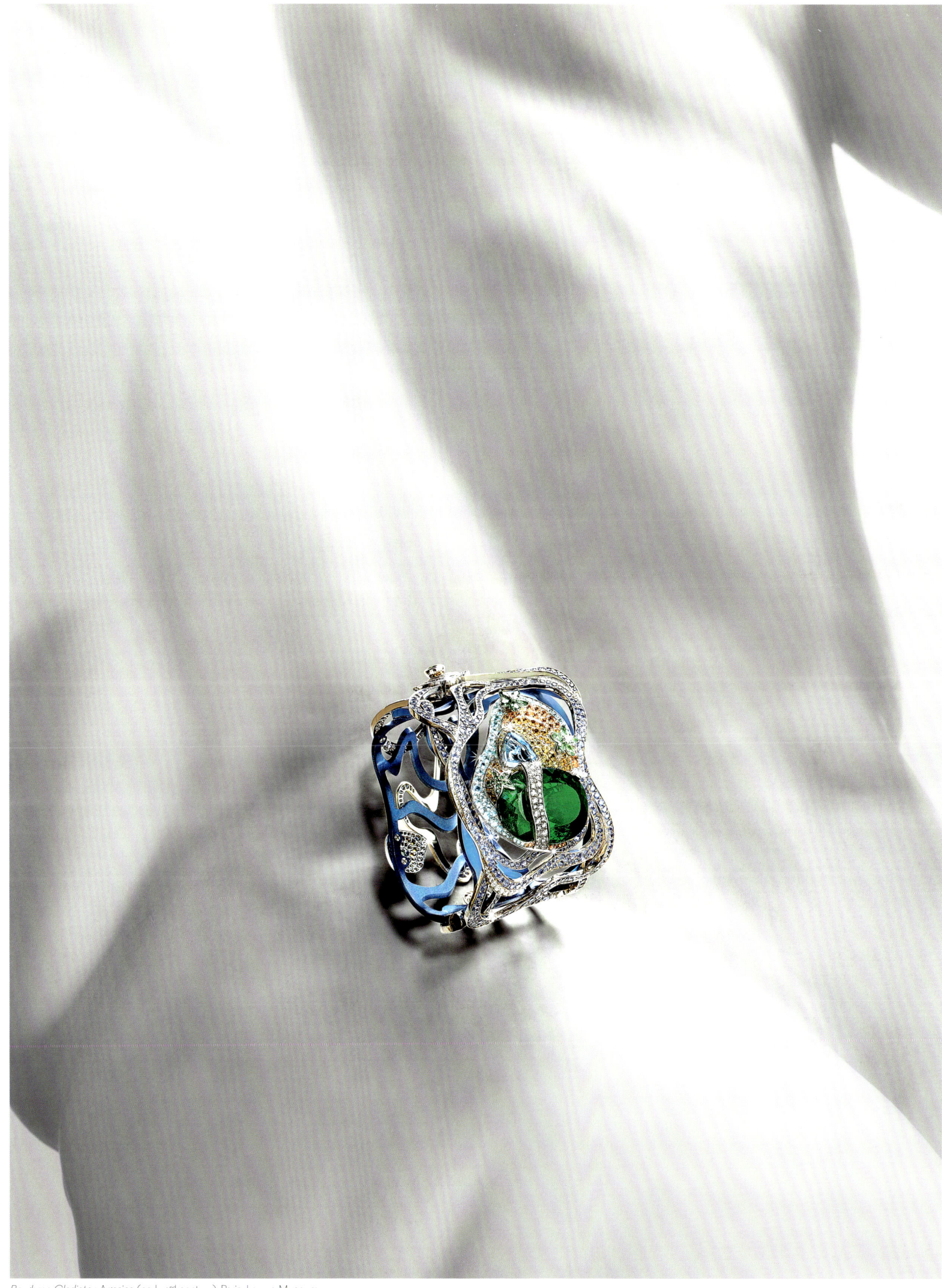

Borghese Gladiator, Agasias (early 2nd century), Paris, Louvre Museum.

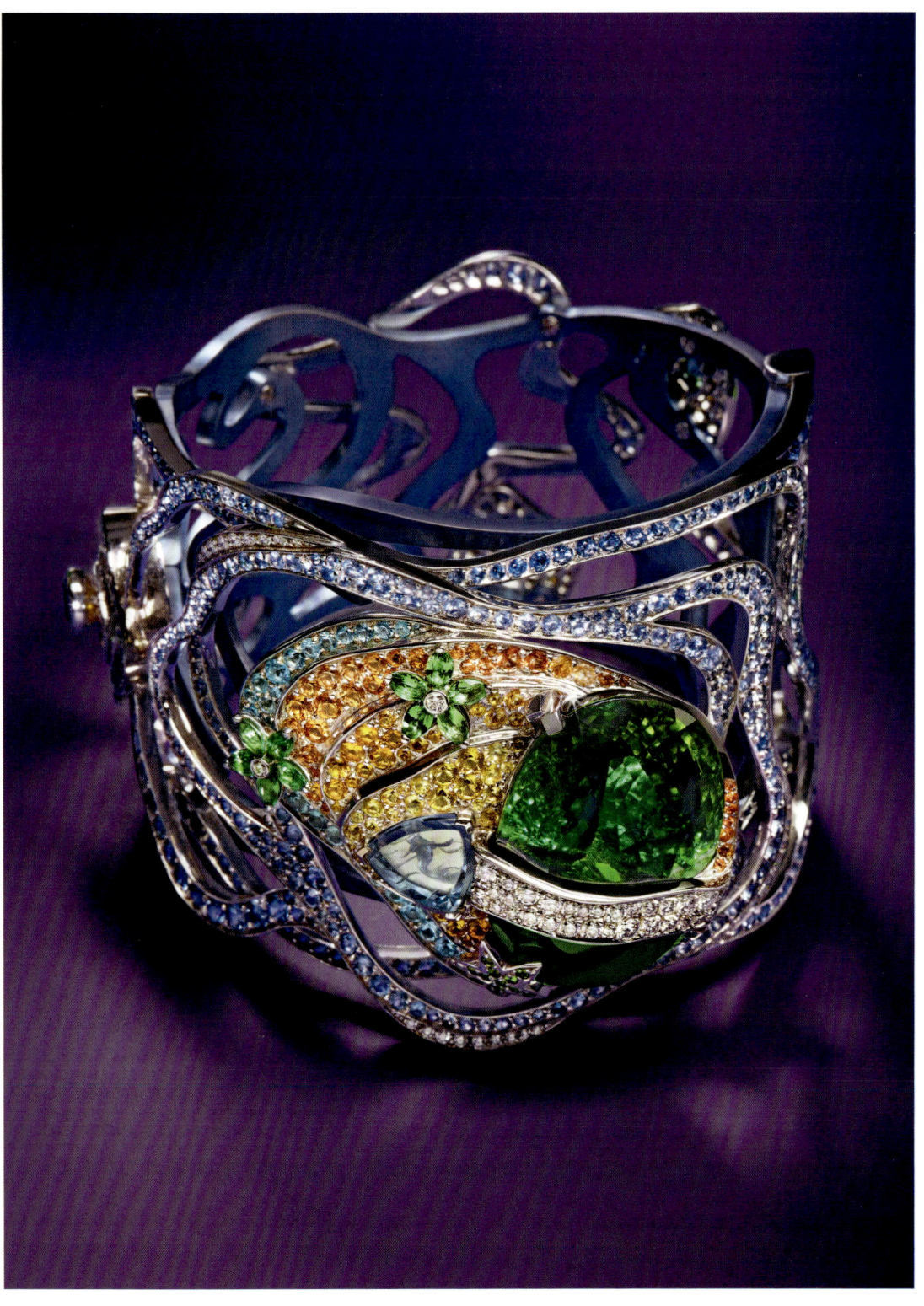

TREASURE ISLAND
BRACELET

This bracelet tells the story of Robert Louis
Stevenson's famous novel, *Treasure Island*, which
I grew up with. There is a secret mechanism
on the reverse for accessing the real treasure:
love—a precious heart-shaped pendant.

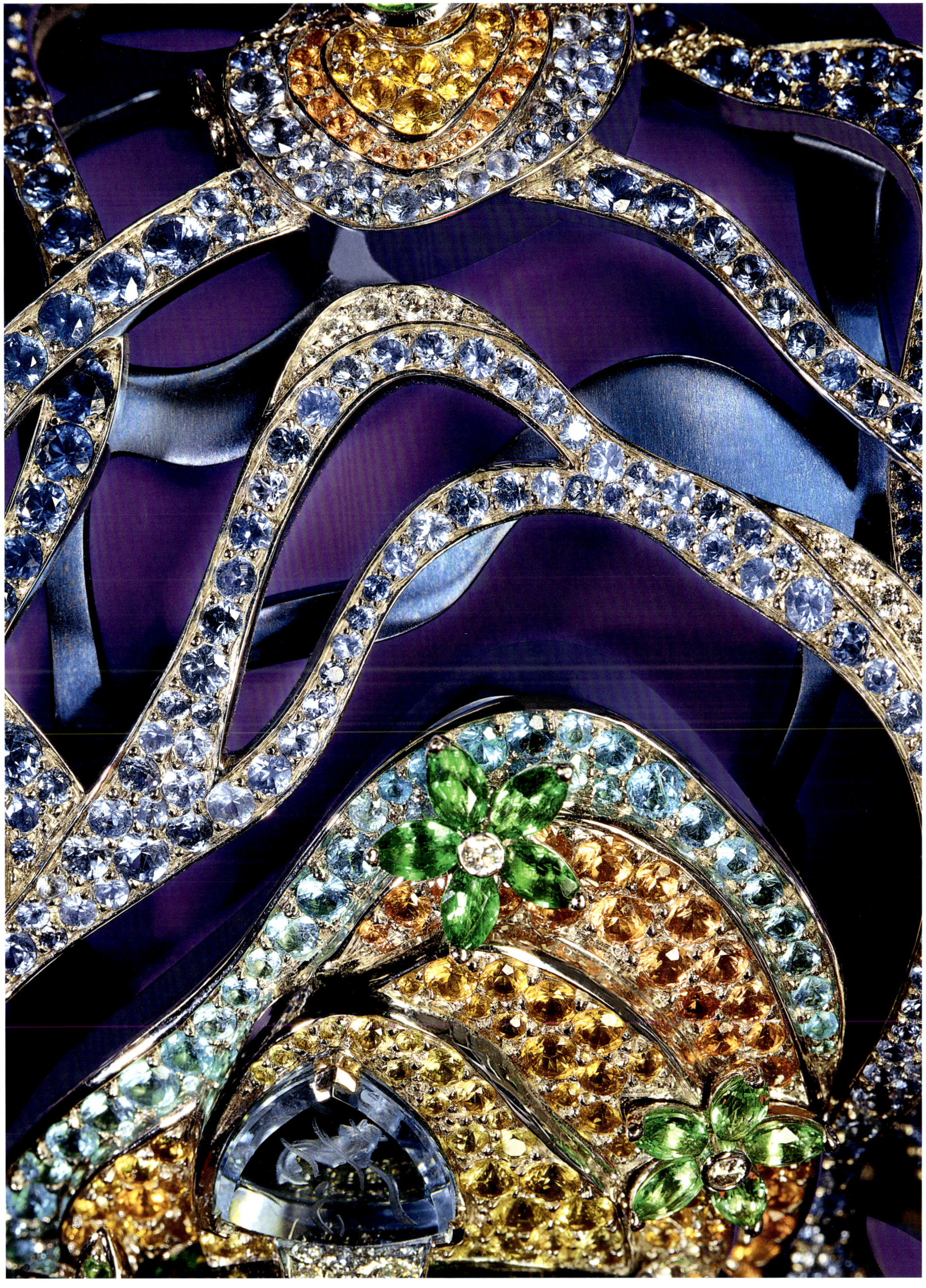

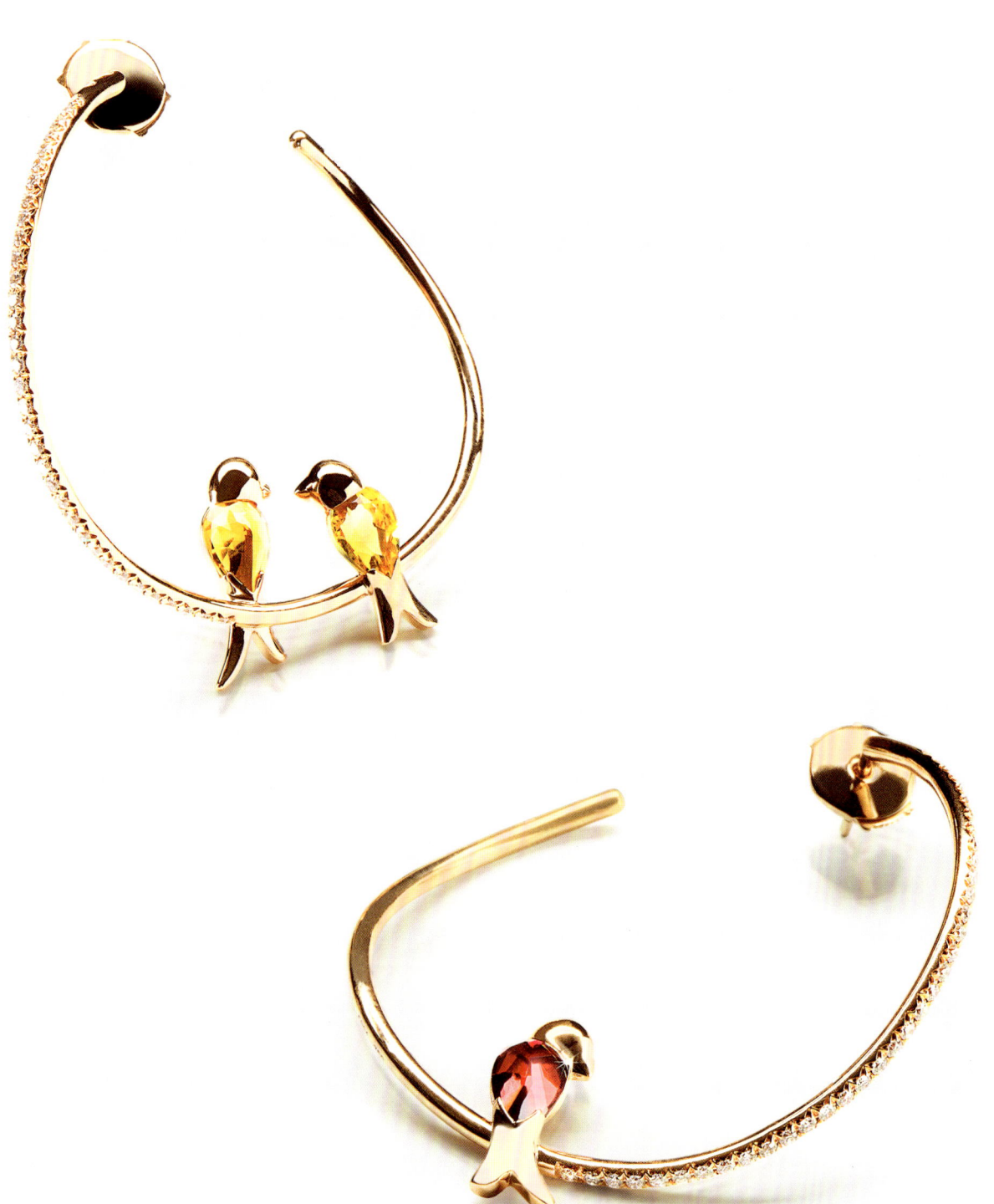

LOVE
BIRD
HO
OPS

The first time I met Lorenz, he showered me with jewelry! I was 23 years old and I was awestruck. The jewelry was magnificent, but it was his personality that made the greatest impression on me. He was very kind and attentive. I thought that his jewelry perfectly reflected his charm and way of being. Lorenz creates jewelry to make people happy. Each piece carries an aspect of their own personal story, sometimes almost imperceptibly—like my engagement ring, which is engraved with words that are ours and ours alone. This is also true of this pair of hoop earrings, which are linked to the birth of our daughter, Alma. They were a surprise that really touched me. Lorenz has the ability to convey a great deal of emotion and sensitivity through his jewelry—another thing that makes them beautiful.

Géraldine Bäumer
Muse

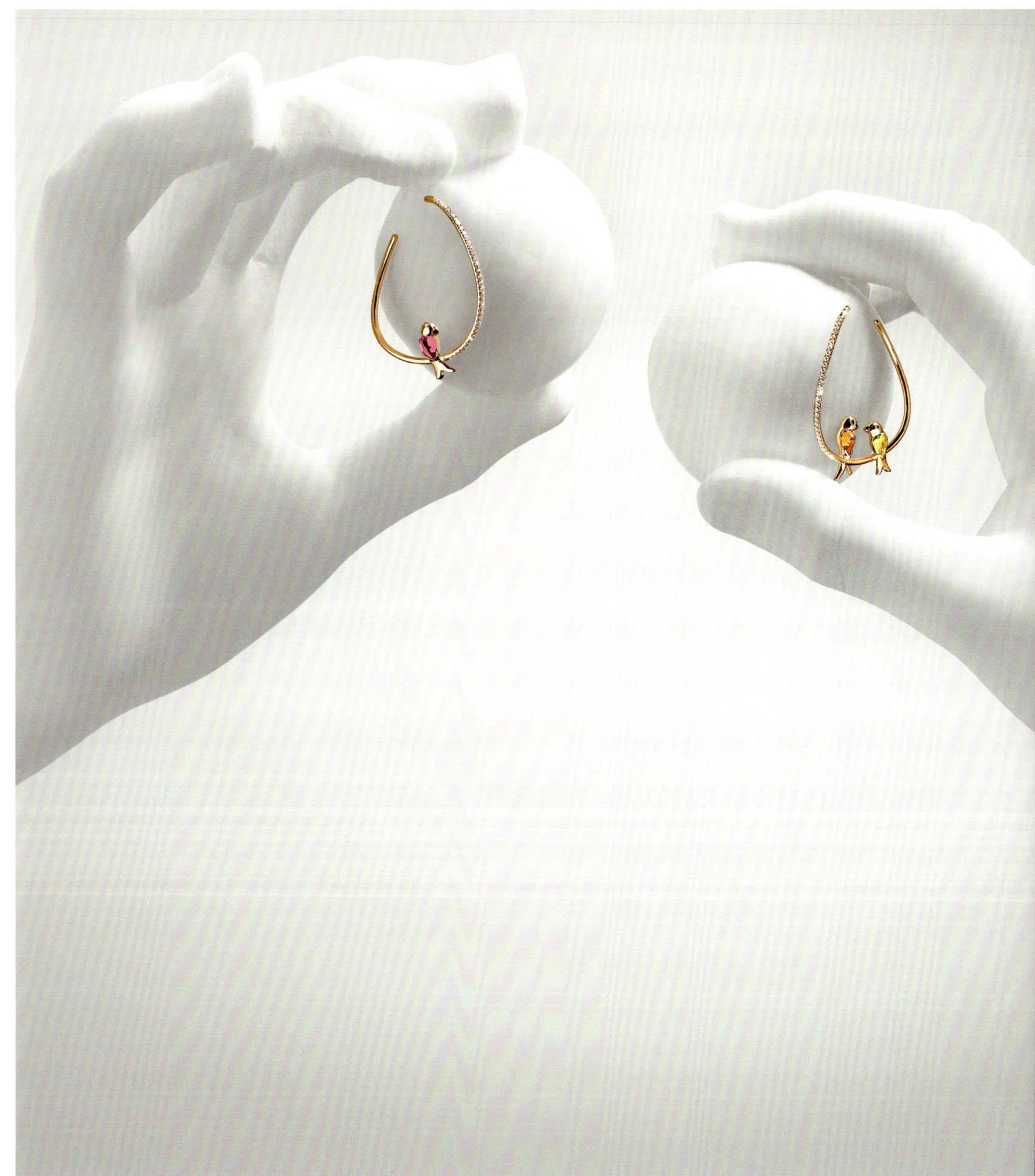

Venus of Arles (circa 360 BC), Paris, Louvre Museum.

LOVE BIRD HOOPS

When our daughter Alma was born,
I wanted to pay tribute to my wife
and celebrate love with these lovebirds,
our three children.

H ART
E
BEAT

His work is a big part of our lives. We don't have a home office, instead we normally all work together at the big dining table. He sits opposite us sketching while we do our homework, and he asks us what we think of pairings of colors or stones. We don't always have answers to his questions, but it's nice to be involved in his thinking. It says a lot about his way of being and creating. Papa is all about life and sharing. He asks us about the music we listen to and the things we like. That's how it's been ever since we were little. He gives us drawings that we display on the walls in our rooms. And we're even in his creations, as Artus' first heartbeat is immortalized in this piece. He always surprises us. There is passion and beauty in everything he does, and he passes this on to us.

Artus, Carl and Alma Bäumer
Muses

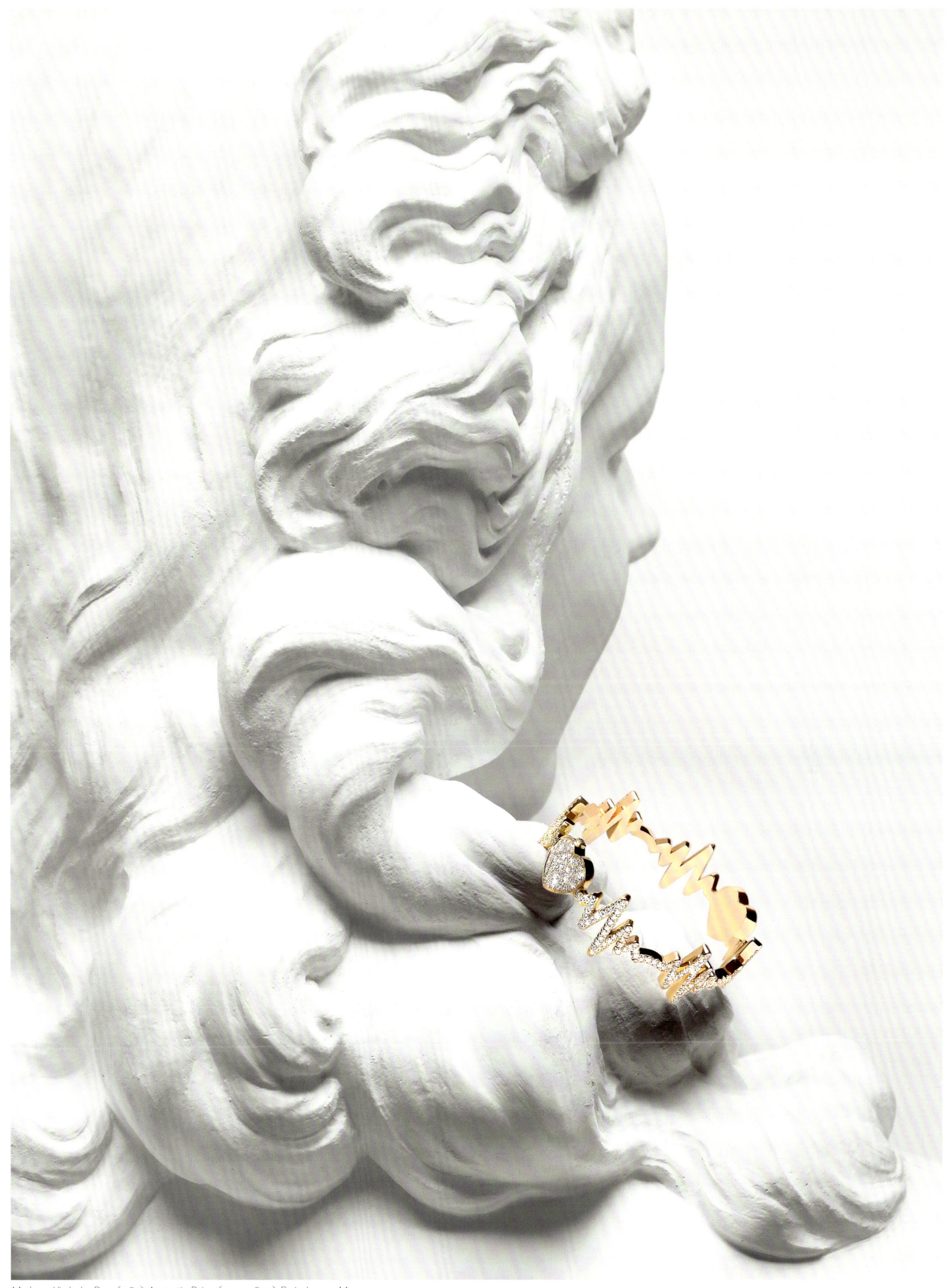

Madame Vigée Le Brun (1783), Augustin Pajou (1730—1809), Paris, Louvre Museum.

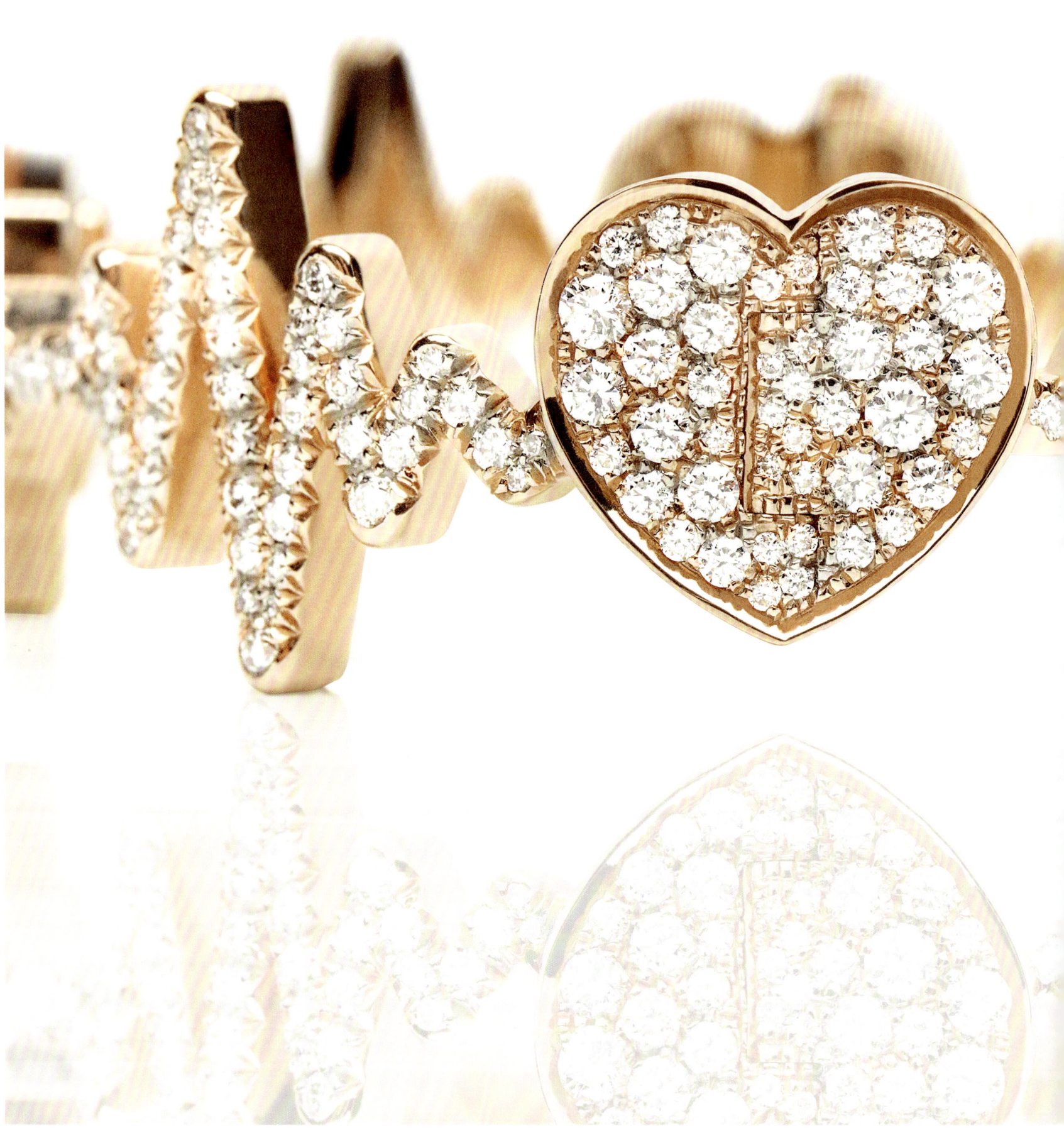

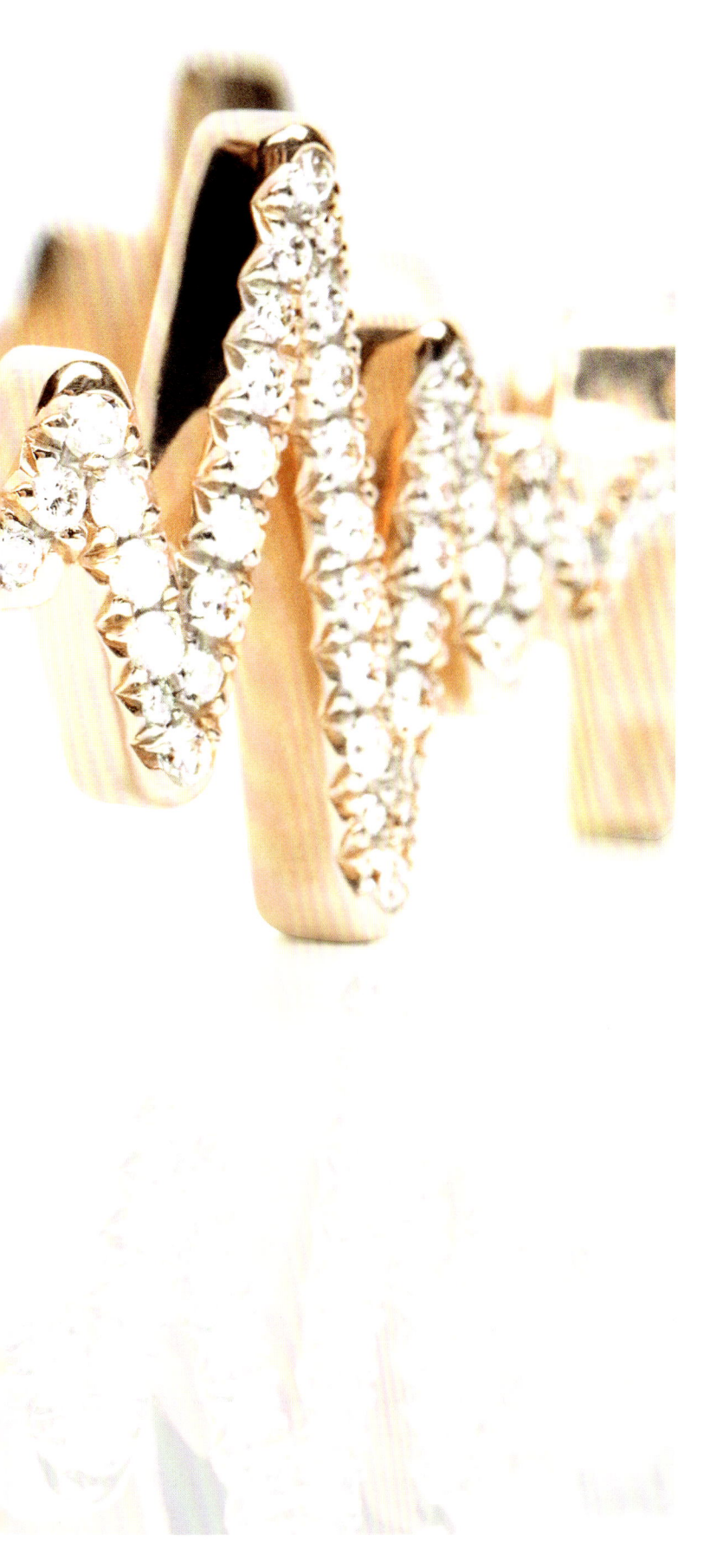

DIAMONDS
HEARTBEAT
BRACELET

When my son Artus was born,
I wanted to capture and share the most
precious thing in life: the heartbeat.

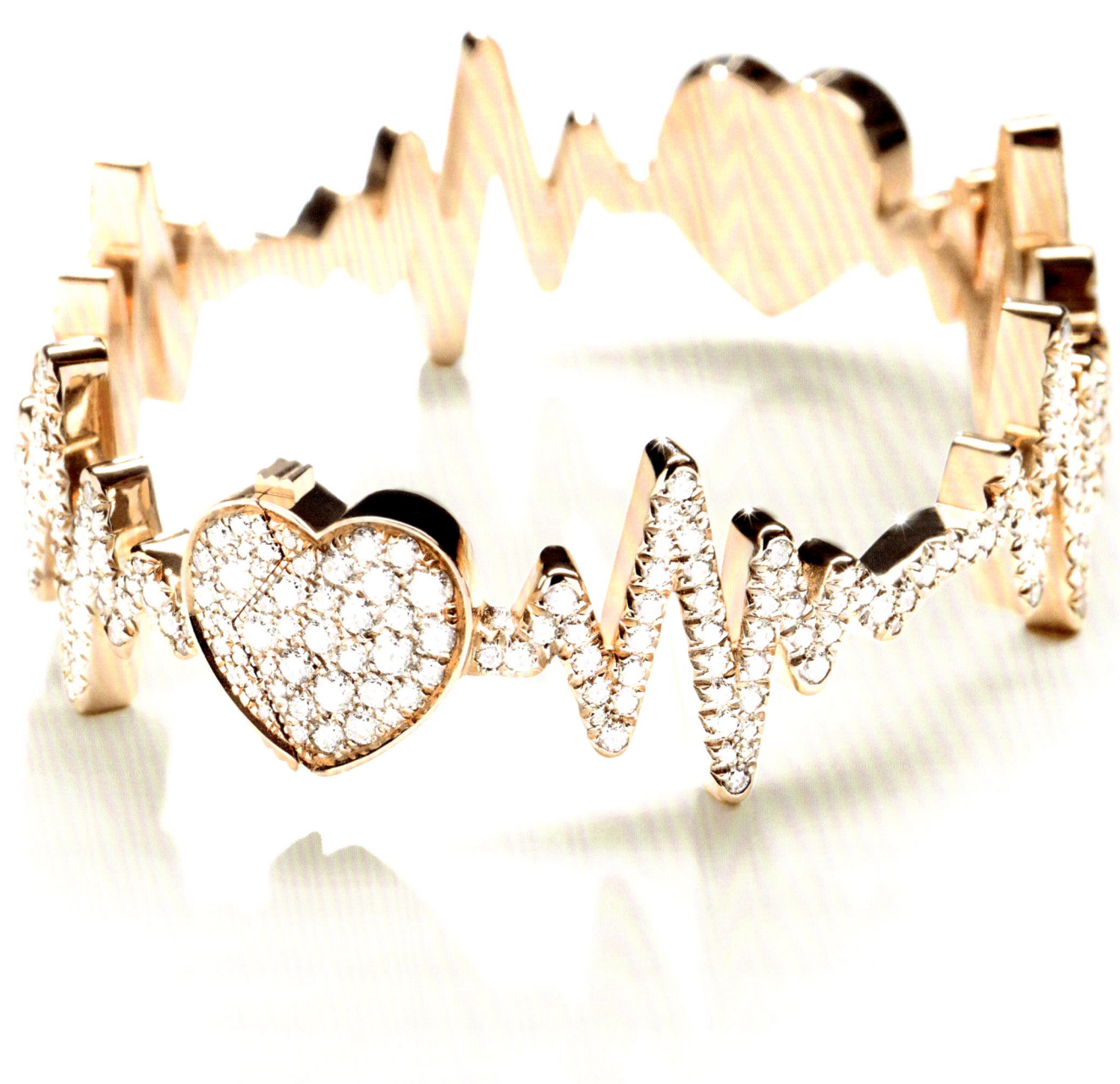

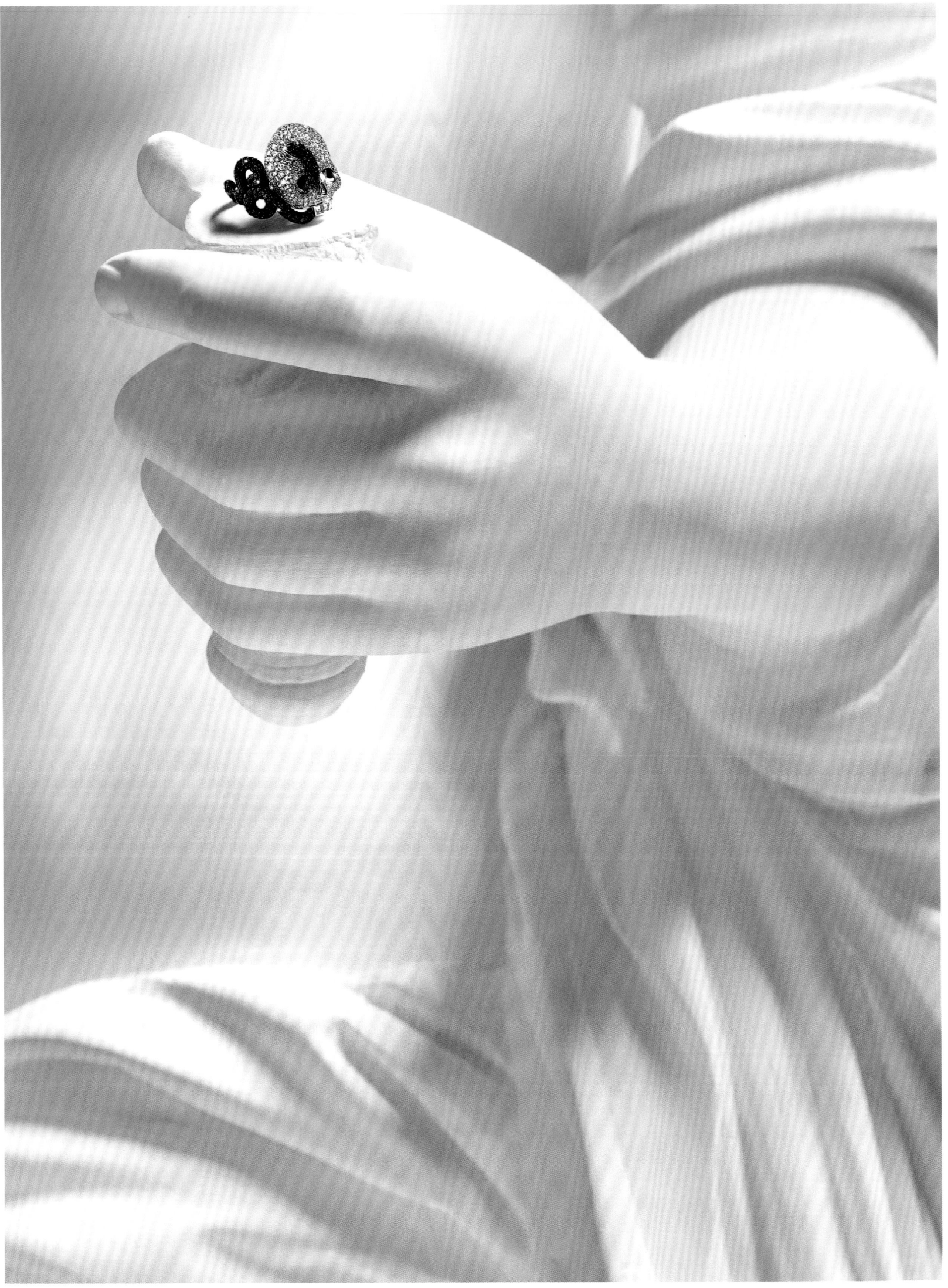

Venus of Arles (circa 360 BC), Paris, Louvre Museum.

VA
NI
TAS

I can't quite say what it is about Lorenz's work that I find so moving. There are some pieces I really love, like the *sea urchins* or the *Writing* pieces. Some of his creations mirror my own work perfectly, like a dialog. That's why we really enjoyed working together to design a rosary made from beads and skulls. Lorenz is a very open-minded designer. We have a lot of things in common: watches, knives, art... We have frequent conversations on a wide variety of topics. Like me, he loves to bring the old into the contemporary. He likes to create dialog between eras. The *Vanitas* ring is a perfect example of this. It's a theme that has stood the test of time.

Philippe Pasqua
Artist

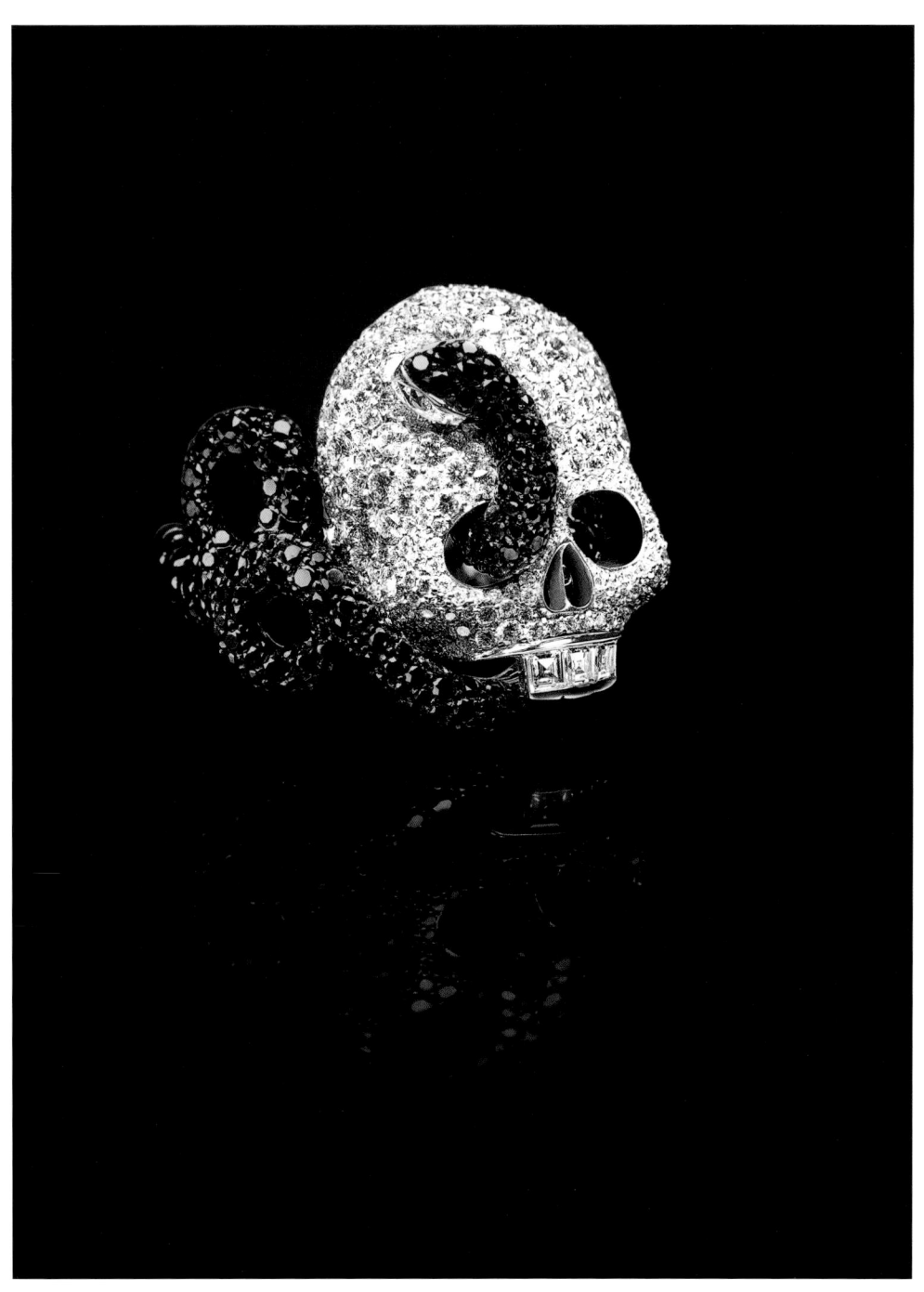

VANITAS
DIAMONDS RING

Snake and skull, life and death, angel or demon,
good girl or bad girl, black and white...
My jewelry speaks of this duality in all of us.

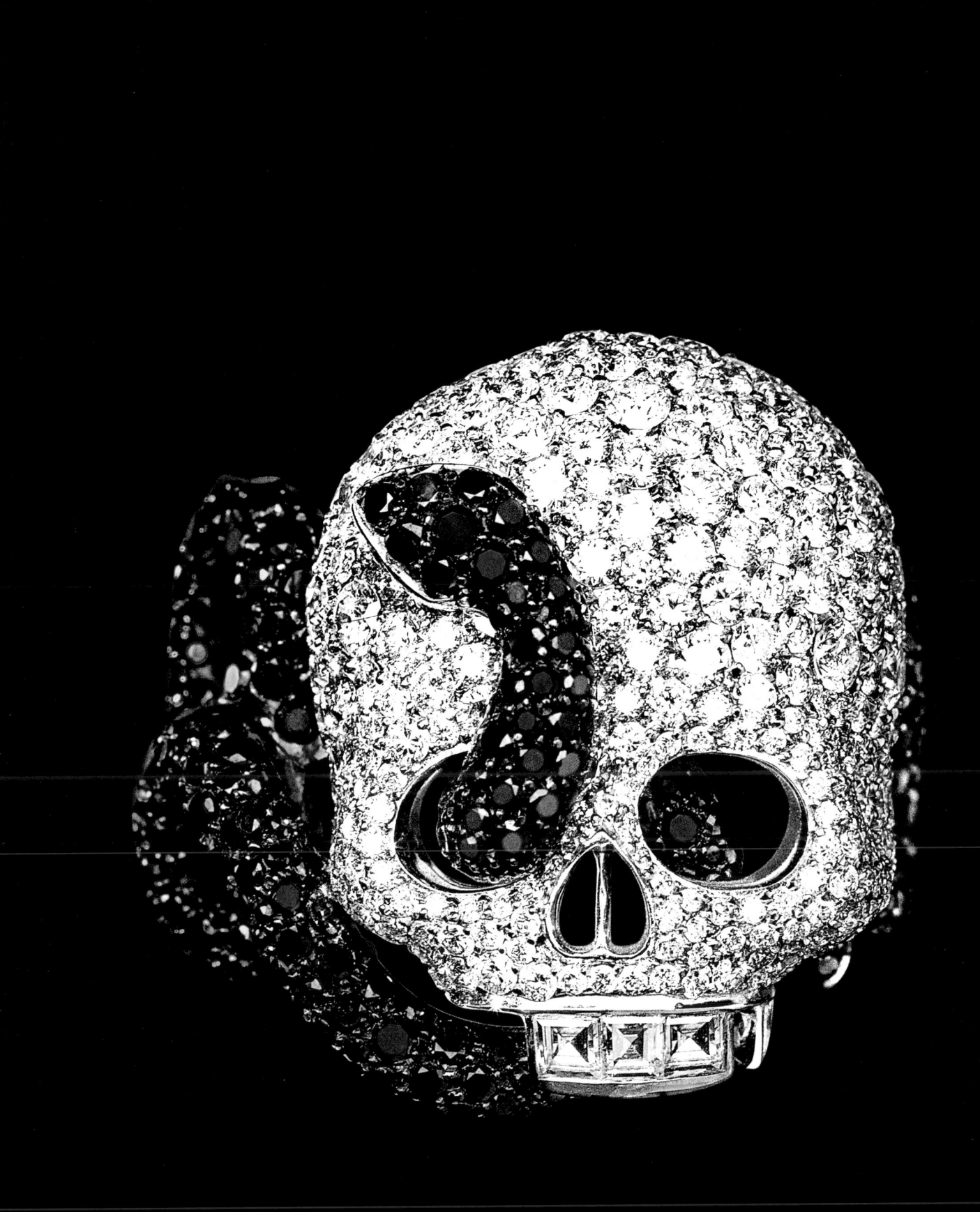

BLACK MAGIC NÉBU LEUSE

Lorenz has the eye of an architect. It is unique to him and that is what makes his approach to jewelry so different. In addition to being a perfectionist, he has the ability to design jewelry like works of art, with extraordinary details and mechanisms. His design skills are so perfect that he can create magnificent things to really simple effect or with extreme sophistication—like this bracelet, an ode to Soulages. It is characterized by its modernity, beauty, perfection, and attention to detail.

Linda Pinto
Interior designer

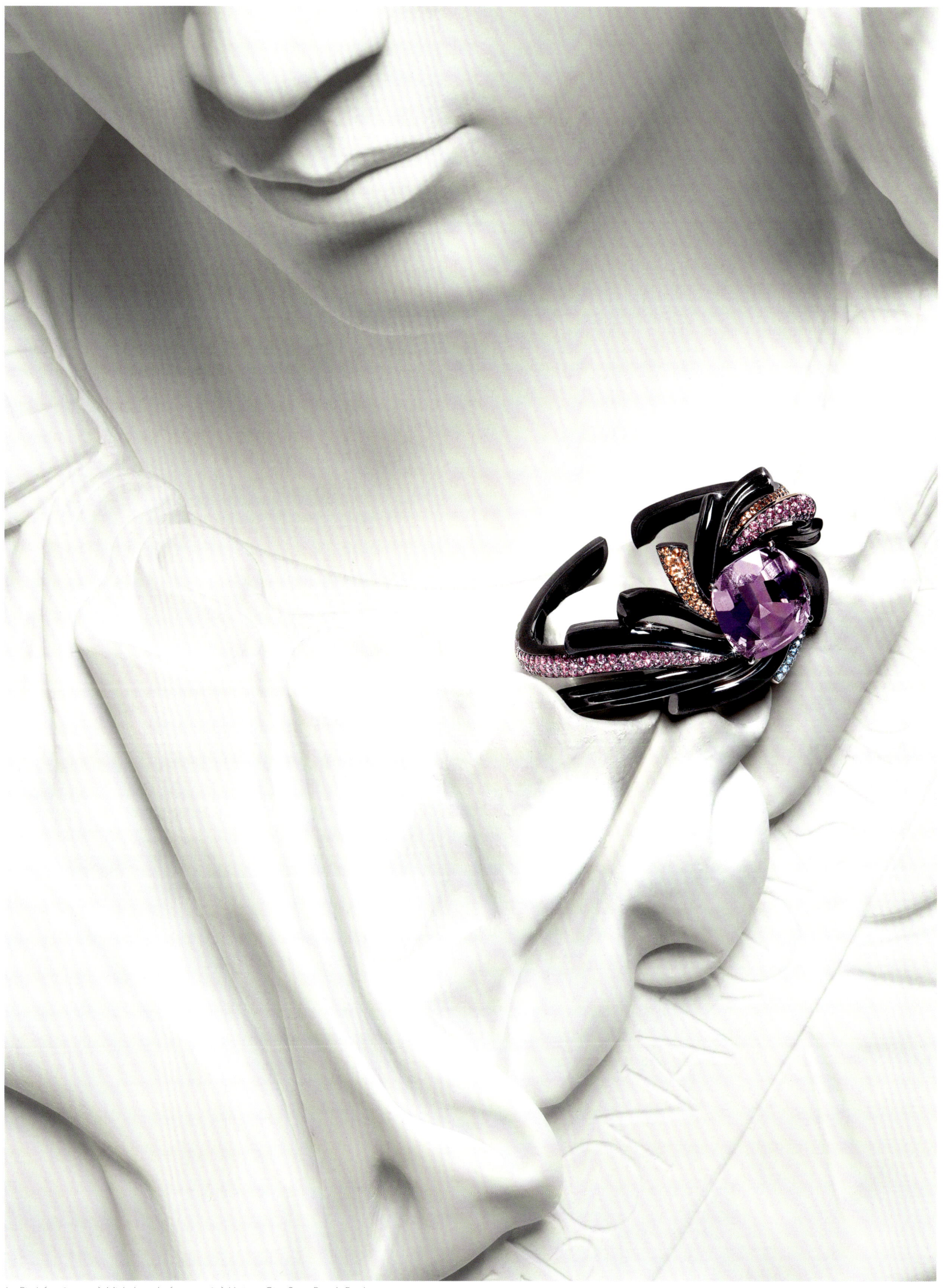

La Pietà (1498—1499), Michelangelo (1475—1564), Vatican City, Saint Peter's Basilica.

BLACK MAGIC NÉBULEUSE BRACELET

Painter Pierre Soulages knew that color was accentuated by black and all its shades: glossy, matte, smooth, engraved, lacquered, and onyx. This bracelet is a homage to his vision.

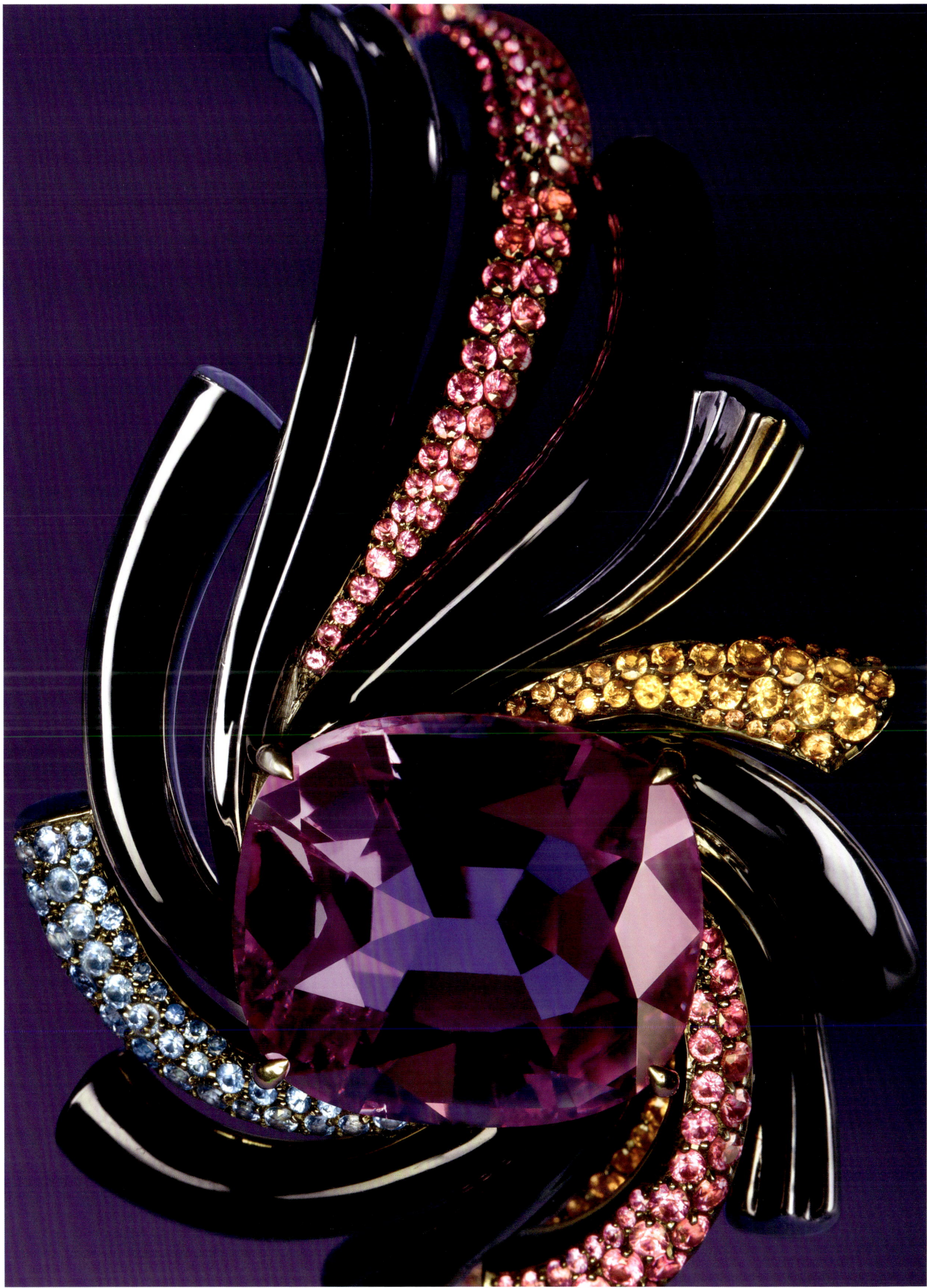

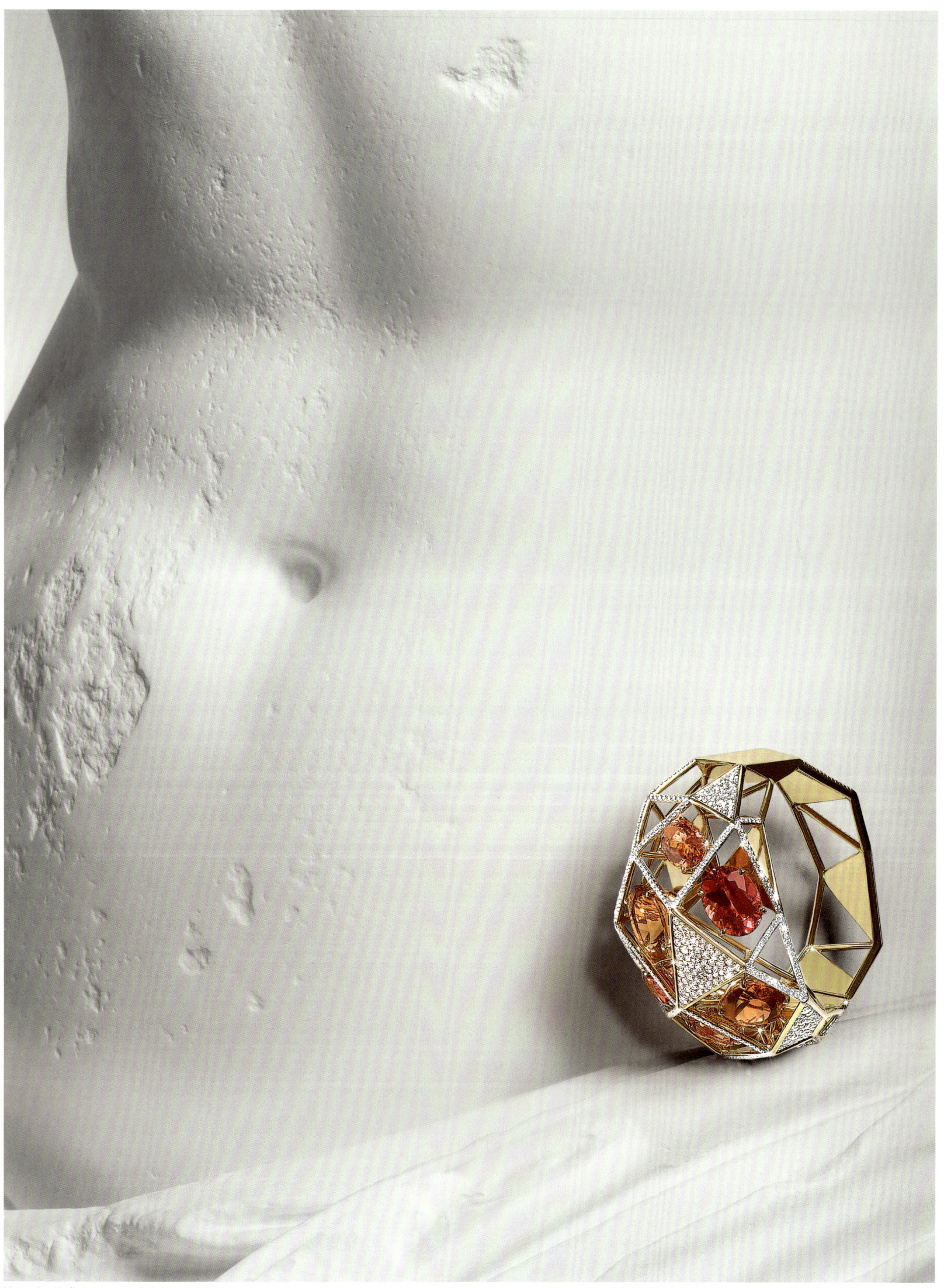

Venus de Milo (late 2nd century), Paris, Louvre Museum.

MI
KA
DO

From his early years in costume jewelry design, Lorenz has retained a very impactful aesthetic that is the product of completely free inspiration. In fine jewelry, he has managed to develop more precise and innovative techniques and use rarer materials while retaining the distinctive style and broad repertoire that characterize his work. He has always placed great emphasis on research, culture, and surprises. This Mikado bracelet is an excellent example—eye-catching, sculptural and designed like architecture made up of solid and empty space. Precious and playful, it epitomizes Lorenz's work.

Hervé Van der Straeten
Designer and furniture maker

MIKADO ARCHITECT
BRACELET

Architecture has always inspired me... and this bracelet
is like a palace made up of solid forms and empty
spaces, shadow and light, and diamonds and gold.

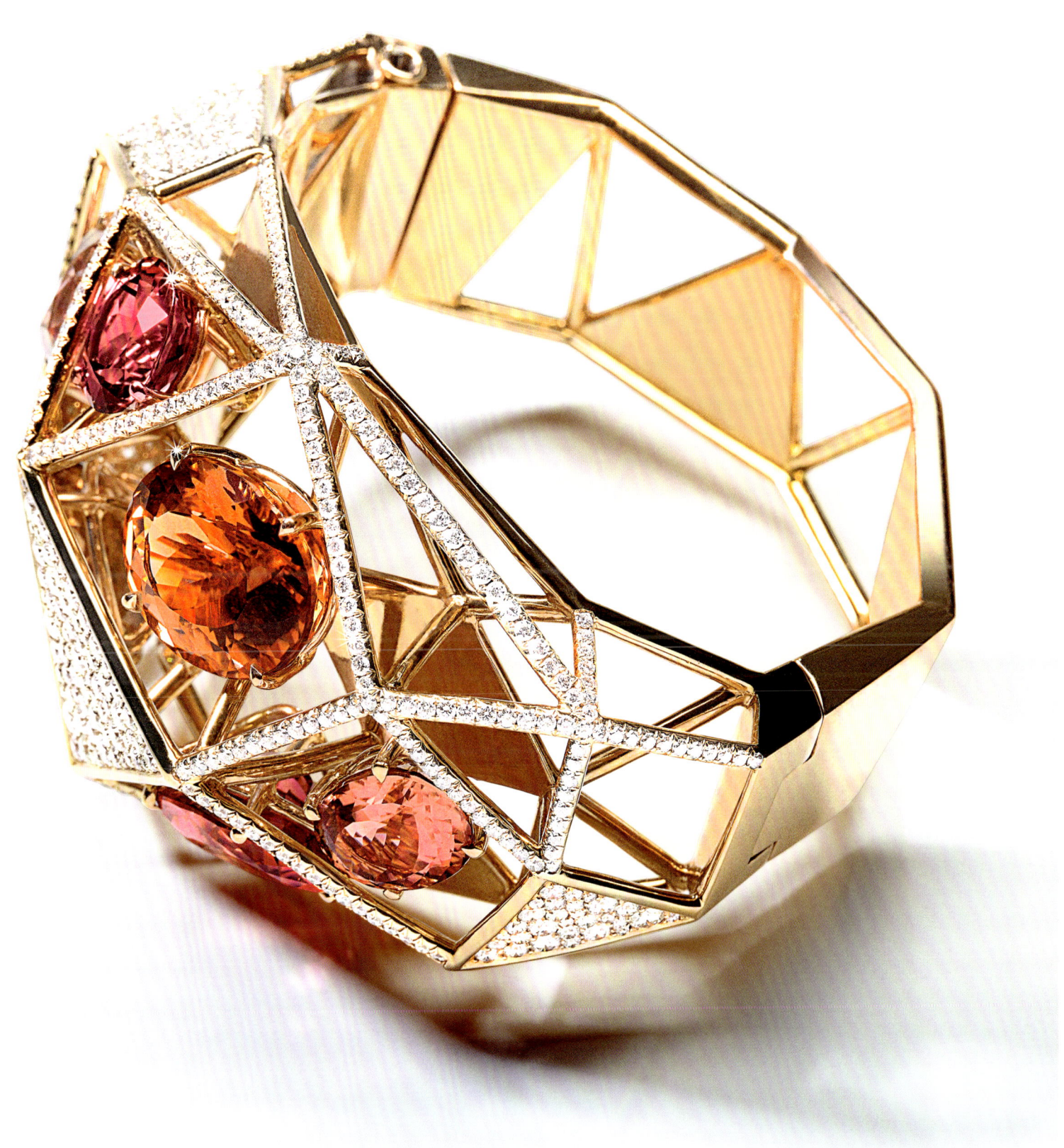

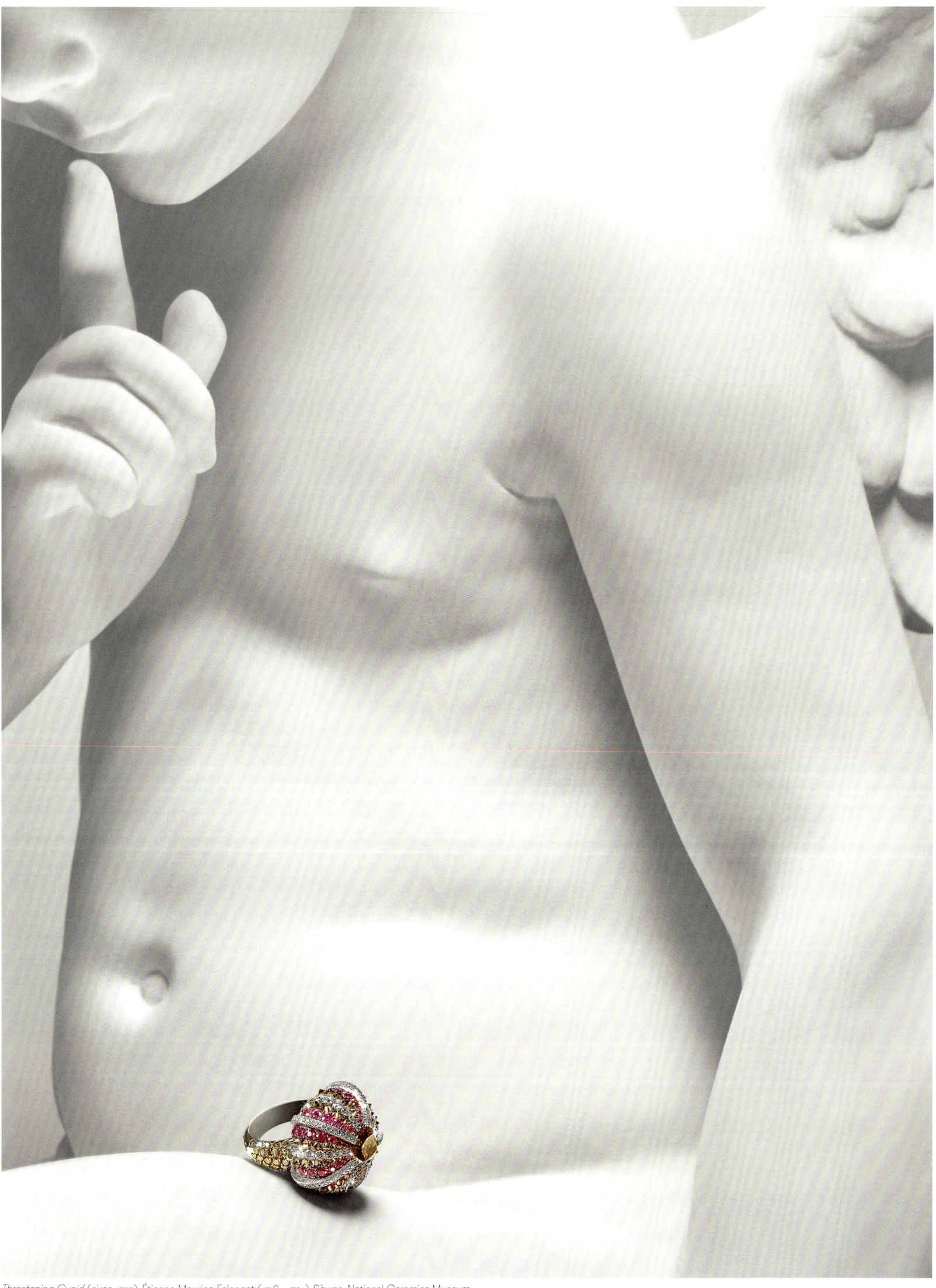

Threatening Cupid (circa 1757), Étienne Maurice Falconet (1716—1791), Sèvres, National Ceramics Museum.

SEA UR CHIN

In the last thirty years, the jewelry world has undergone a real revolution and Lorenz, with his exceptional talent, has been one of its key players. This revolution was brought about by the world of fashion entering the realm of jewelry, meaning customers could choose from larger, more whimsical, and more creative jewelry pieces, often with semiprecious stones in a wider variety of colors. My husband and I are passionate about the 19th century and buying jewelry from Lorenz takes me back to the experience of real luxury that one would have had in those days. This involved buying an object of superior quality, often one of a kind, that had been created as part of a dialog between client and designer. This unique experience is what Lorenz still offers. I'm very fortunate to have received several of his iconic and enduring, museum-worthy pieces as gifts from my husband. Of particular note are the *Gourmandise* bracelet, which has pride of place in a display cabinet at the French Musée des Arts décoratifs, and this *Sea Urchin* ring, which graces the cover of the first book about Lorenz's work.

Cécilia Hottinguer
Collector

I've known Lorenz for thirty years. We have a firm friendship that spans the generations as I am godfather to one of his sons, and one of my daughters had the joy of starting her career with him. In addition to being a great designer, Lorenz is an intelligent and inquisitive man. His work and his zest for life are inextricably linked. For example, we share the same passion for beautiful Japanese-inspired objects from the late 19th century. At that time, the decorative arts were marked by the union of Japanese minimalism and new technologies introduced by the Industrial Revolution, with new ways of melting metals and inventing alloys. This ingenuity characterizes Lorenz's art today. On the one hand, he offers the technical rigor of the engineer-entrepreneur and innovation in every respect. On the other, the unique and timeless talent of his hand. I love his creative freedom. He doesn't worry about designing things as they are supposed to be. He does as he pleases. Like this *Sea Urchin* ring, which could be a piece from the Italian Renaissance, with its impressive tactile and sensual side. It is a magnificent jewel, as perfect in its proportions as it is touching through the stories it tells.

Jean-Conrad Hottinguer
Banker and collector

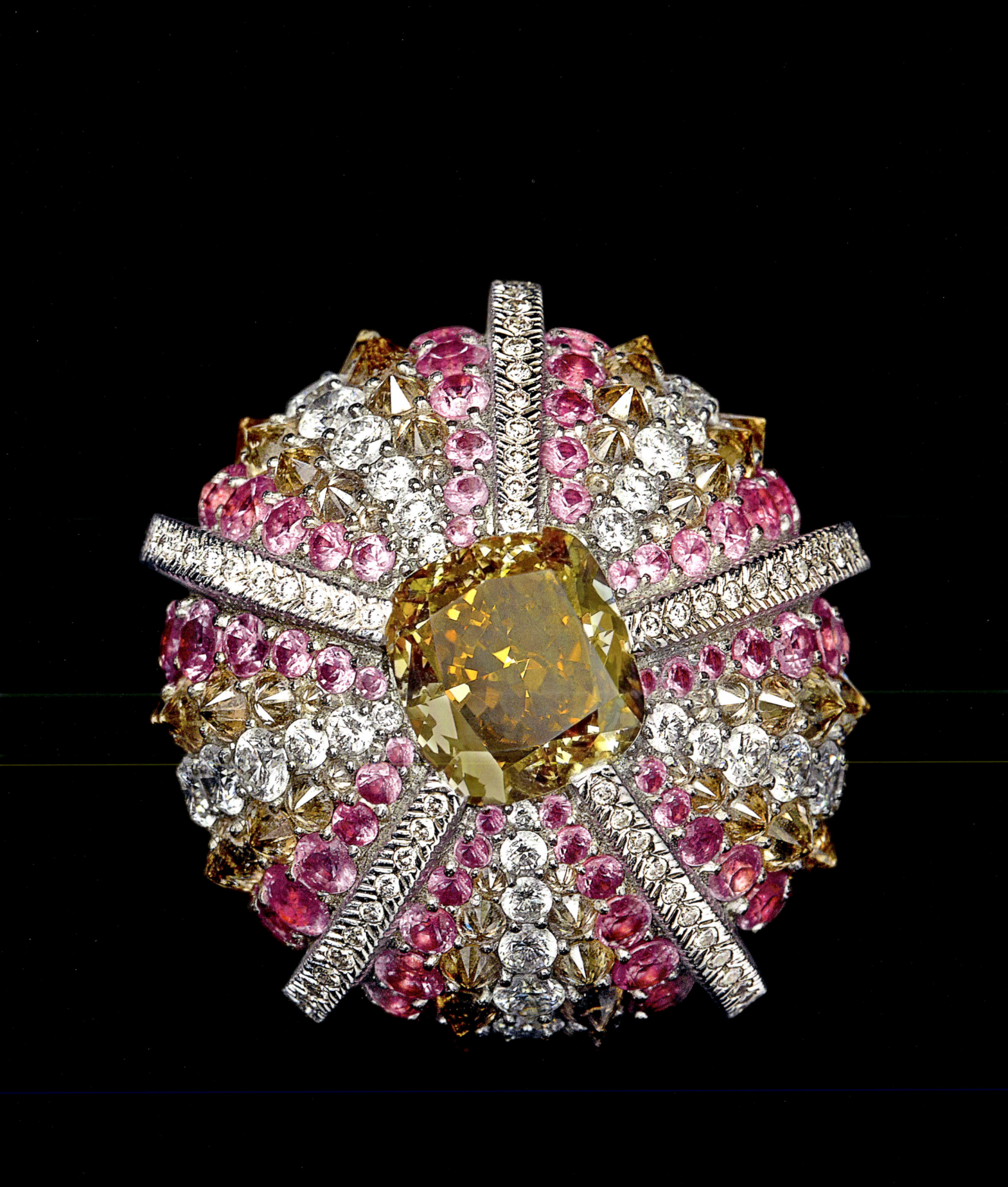

À LA FOLIE

I met Lorenz on the Basque coast. I knew him as a surfer first! I discovered the work of Lorenz the jeweler shortly afterwards, in his studio on the Rue Royale. There, I saw a great deal of rigor, complexity, and precision. You can sense the engineer in everything, fed by an insatiable curiosity. Everything he creates is just right. He creates tangible things from very well-structured intangible things and that's what generates emotion and pleasure. Not a fragile feeling or mere surprise, but stable and enduring emotion. Nothing is left to chance in his work. Everything is masterly. The *À la folie* ring is the perfect example of this. It's a very well-organized jumble! And that says a lot about Lorenz's personality, which is highly receptive to the world around him. He is very open-minded in our conversations about cooking. He truly loves what he tastes. He wants to understand. Our professions both have a highly technical element. We chefs are constantly questioning things, and our creations are etched into the memories of the people who eat them. Lorenz's creation leaves a permanent mark, through jewelry. But both of us try to give pleasure and explore as yet uncharted territory. And to deliver new stories, you need a great deal of mastery and know-how.

Alain Ducasse
Chef and entrepreneur

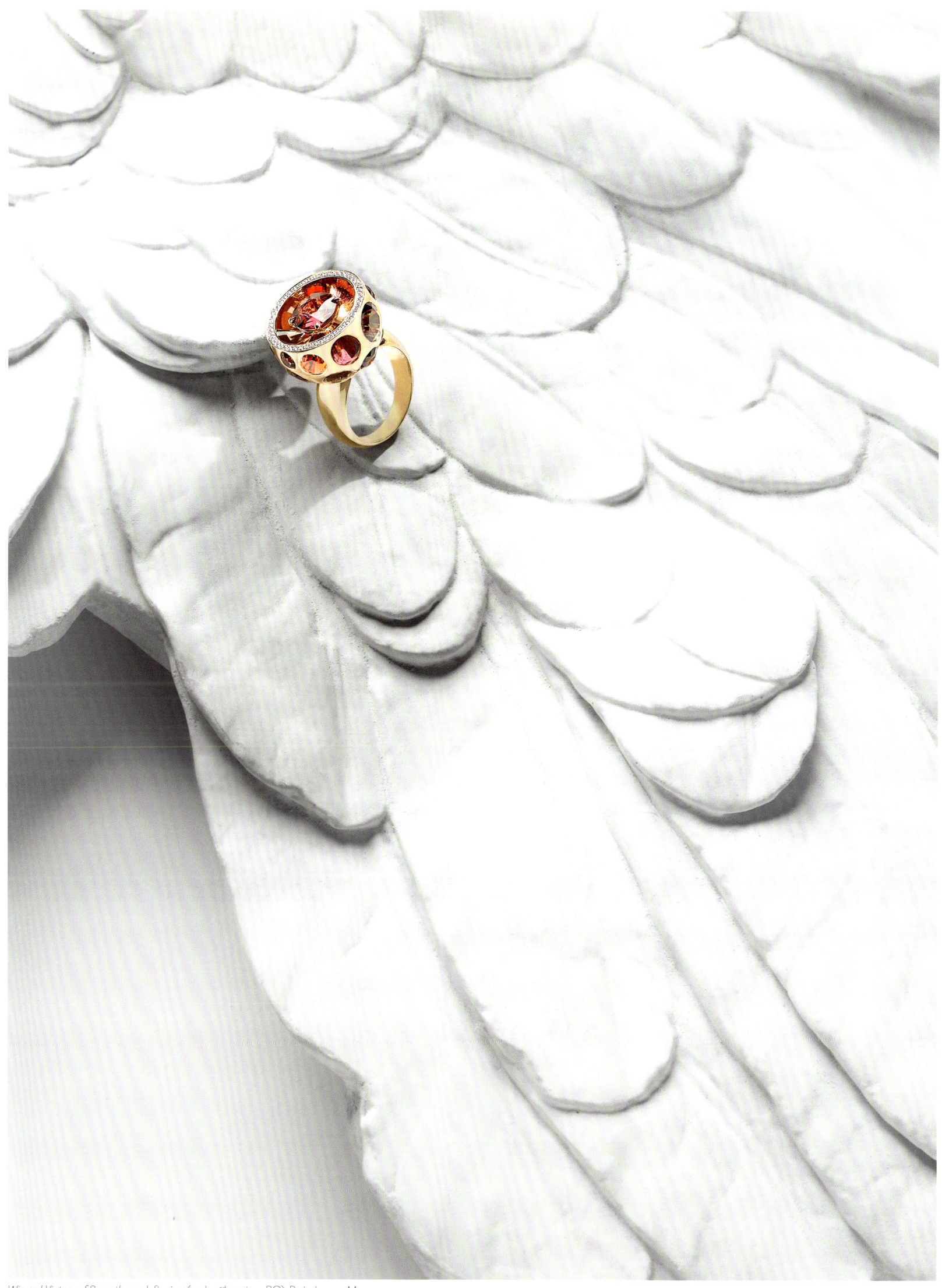

Winged Victory of Samothrace, left wing (early 2ⁿᵈ century BC), Paris, Louvre Museum.

À LA FOLIE
RING

This ring is a real extravaganza showcasing the undersides of the stones, whose colors intermingle and reflect off the polished gold of the cup.

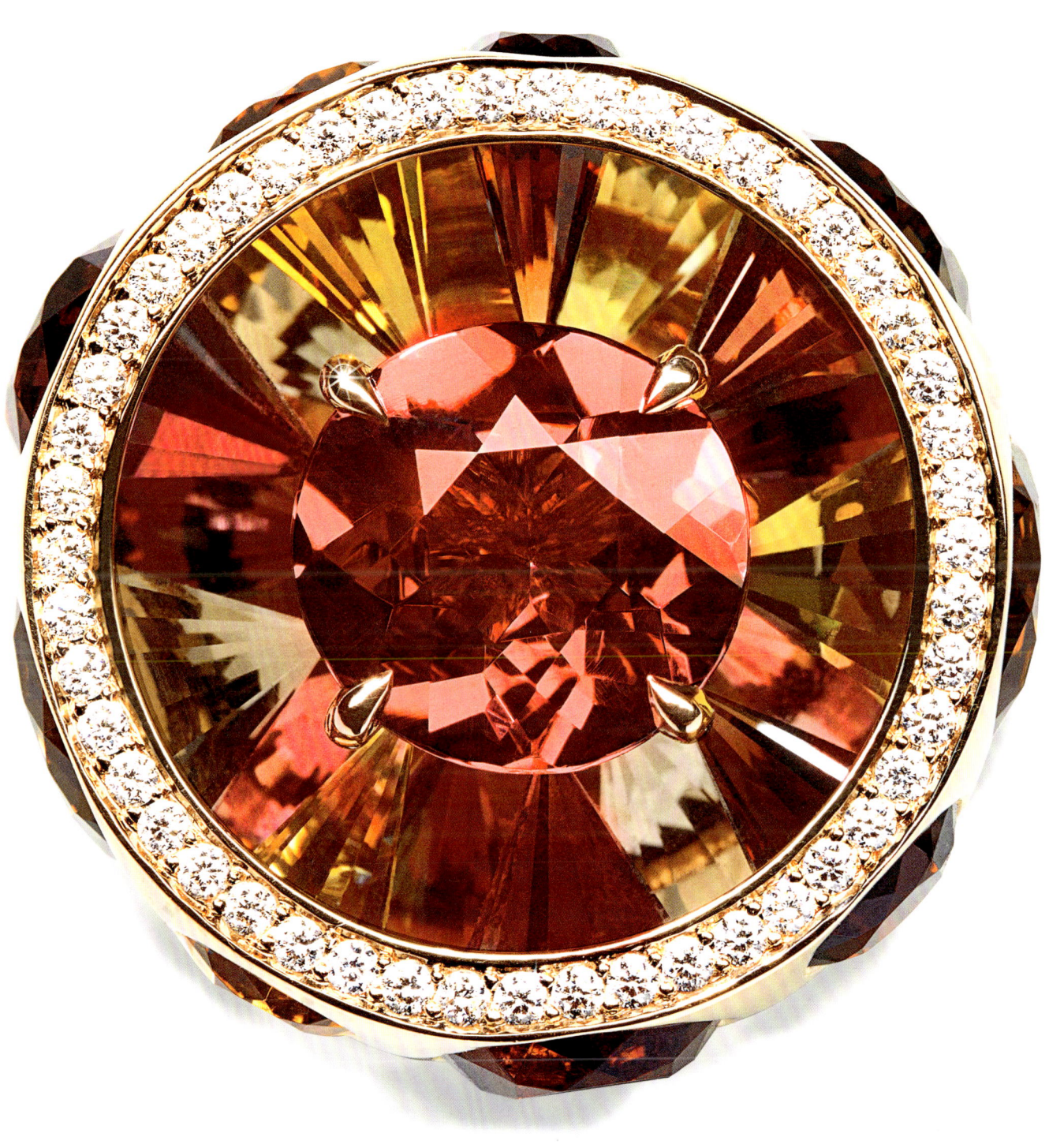

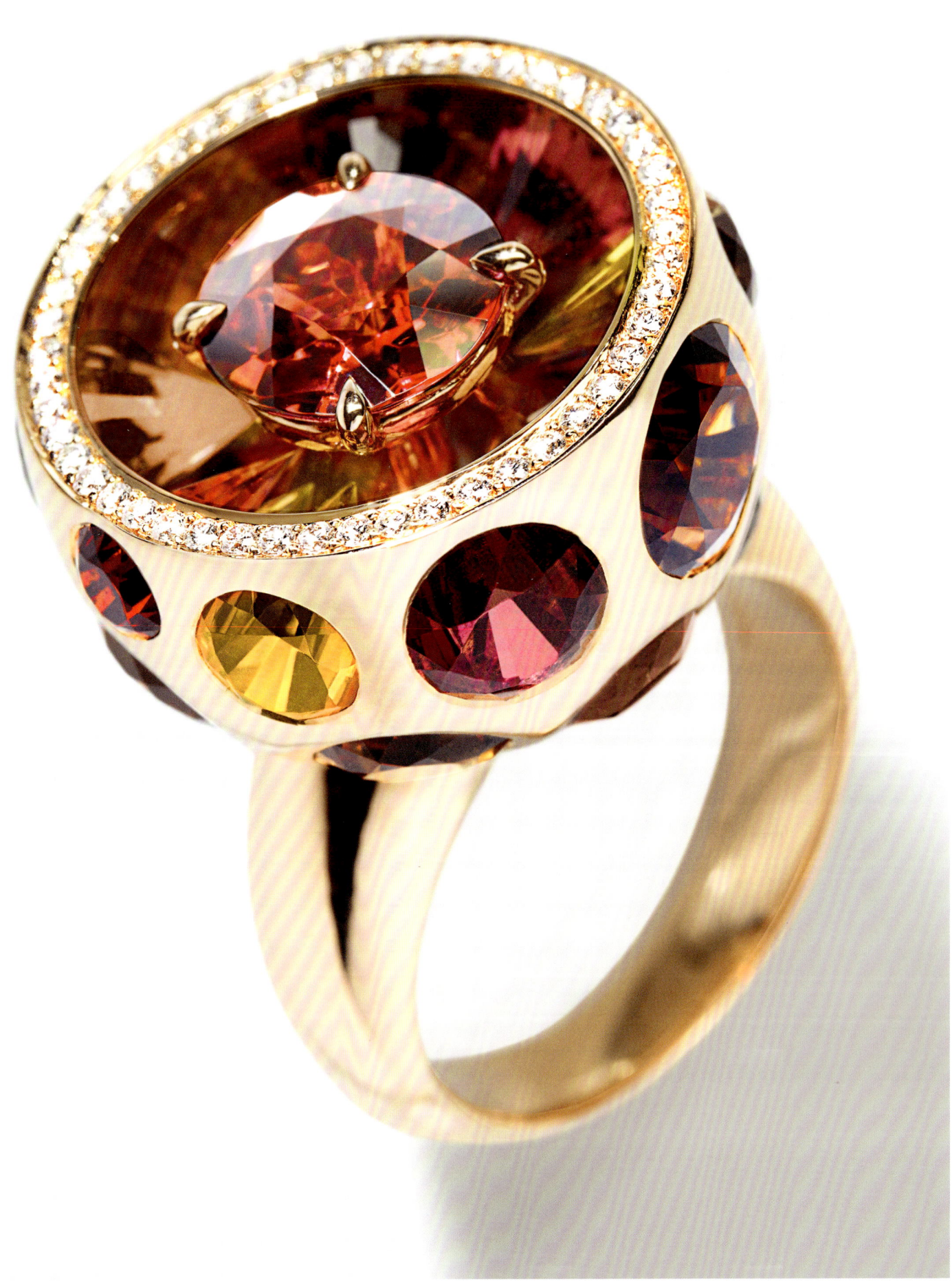

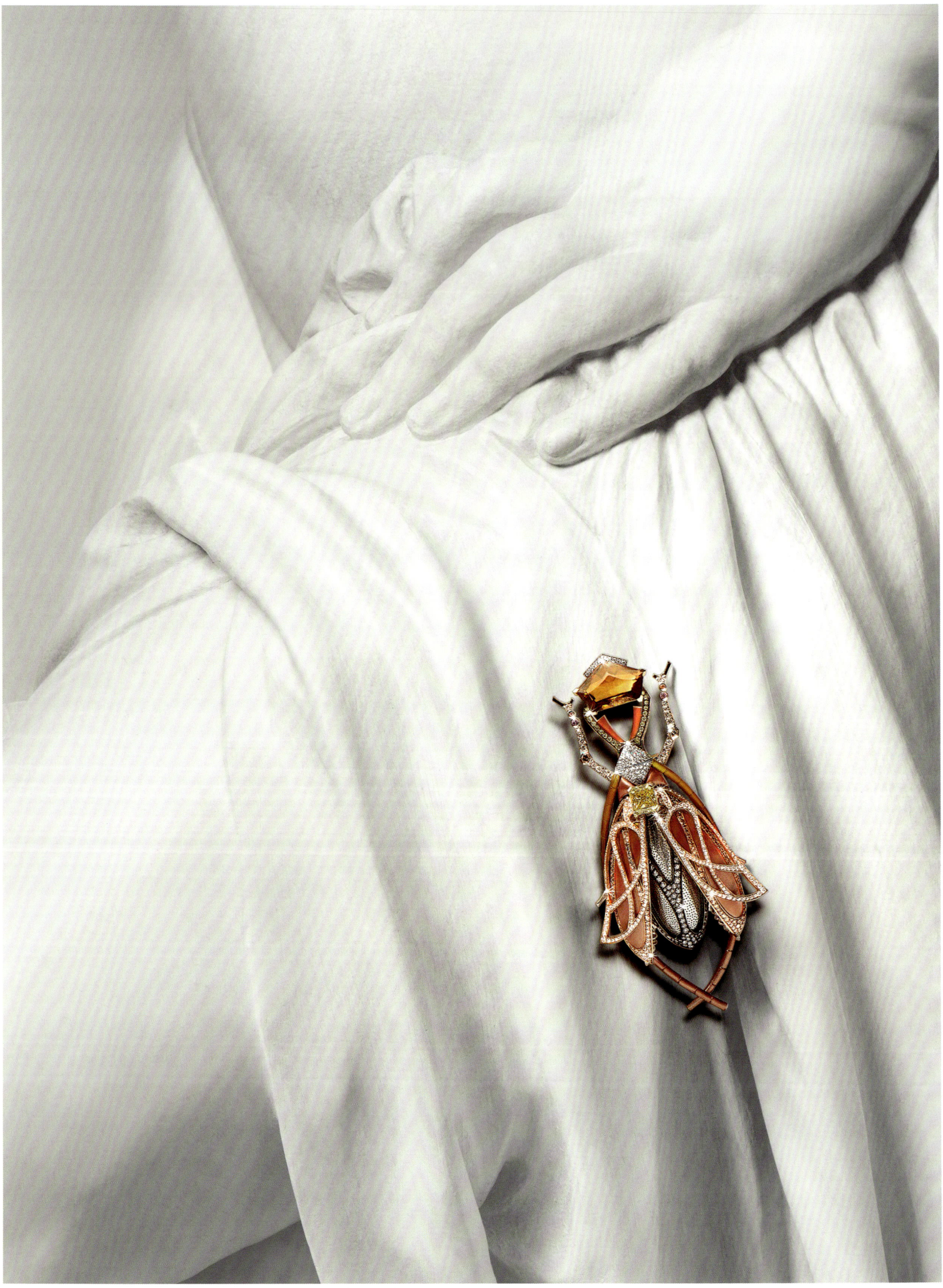

Venus at her bath, known as *The Bather* (1767), Christophe-Gabriel Allegrain (1710—1795), Paris, Louvre Museum.

SCA RAB

I met Lorenz in 1998 through a mutual friend, Jean-Pierre Brun. Back then, I was mostly making bespoke watches and wanted to develop the ready-to-wear side. To support the investment needed to create a manufacture, I launched a presale of a special edition of twenty watches. Lorenz contributed by buying one of them. The arts of watchmaking and jewelry-making are more different than it might seem—not least in terms of the materials used. Only natural materials and stones are used in jewelry, whereas watchmaking uses man-made alloys, particularly to provide resistance. Lorenz's originality as a jeweler lies in his training as an engineer and his interest in watchmaking can be seen in certain pieces, such as this Scarab brooch, which conceals a secret mechanism.

François-Paul Journe
Watchmaker

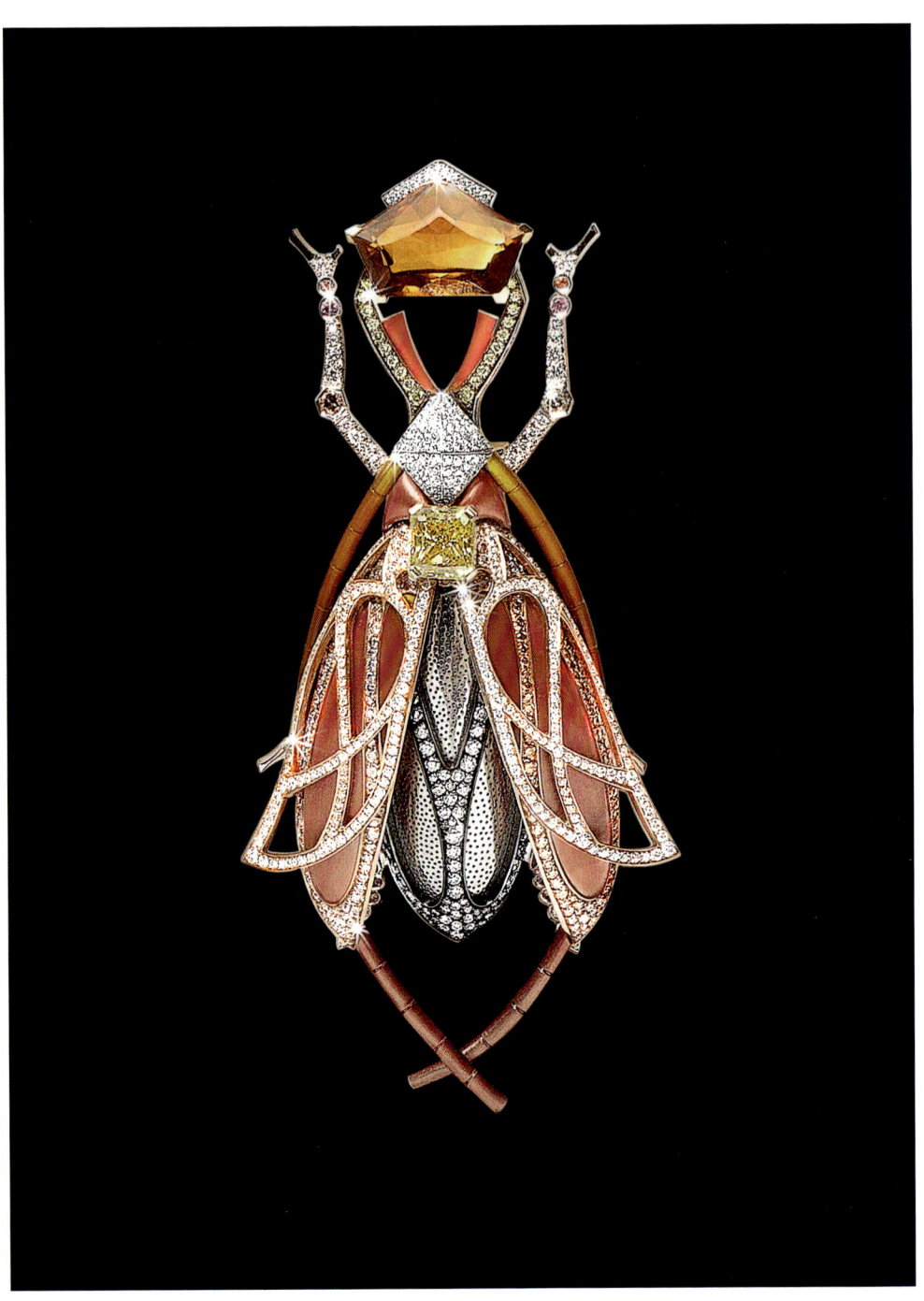

SCARAB
BROOCH

I love transcending the mysteries of nature
in my creations. I wanted a beetle with
a body that could hold a perfume to add
a new sense to jewelry: smell.

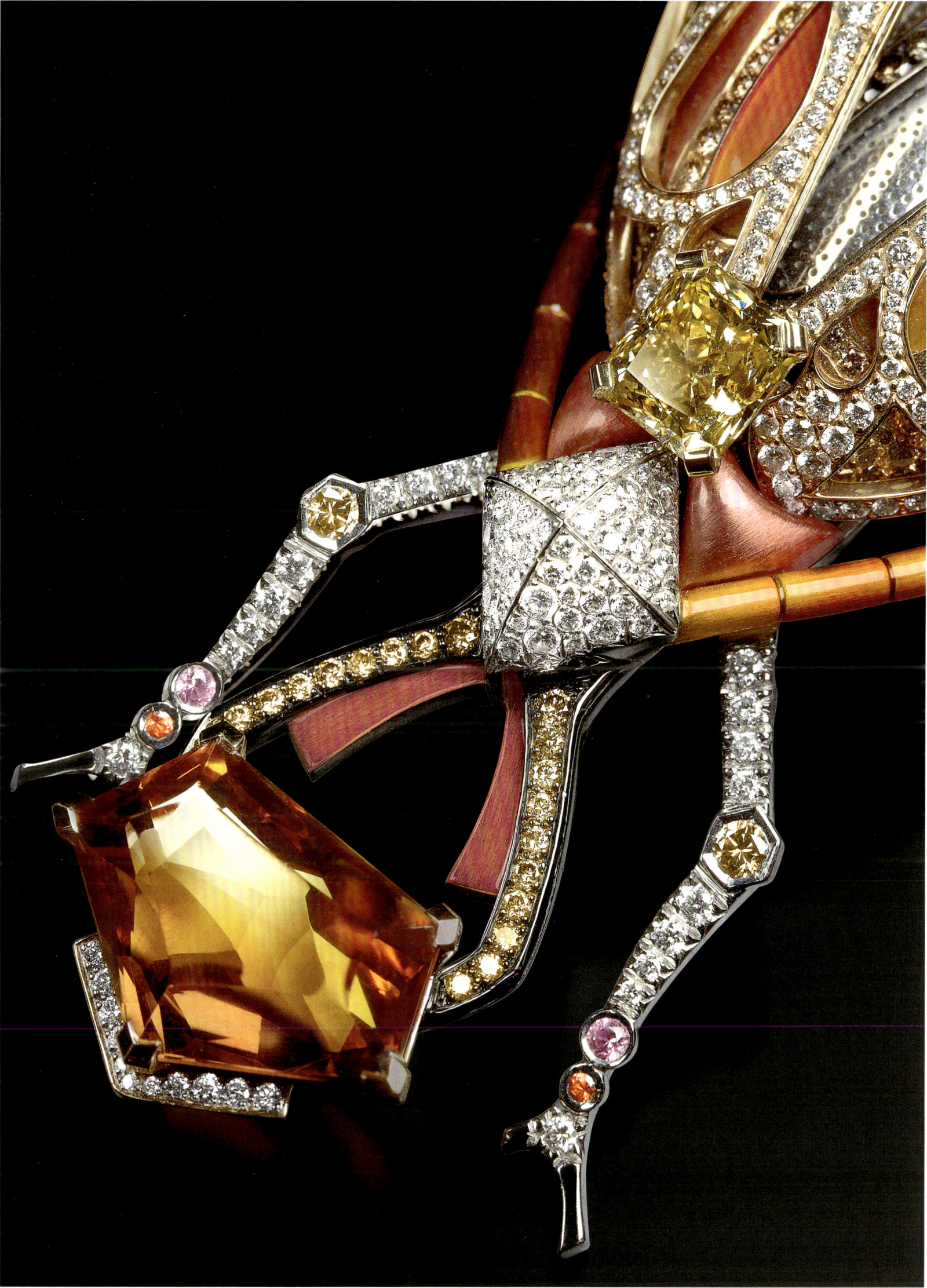

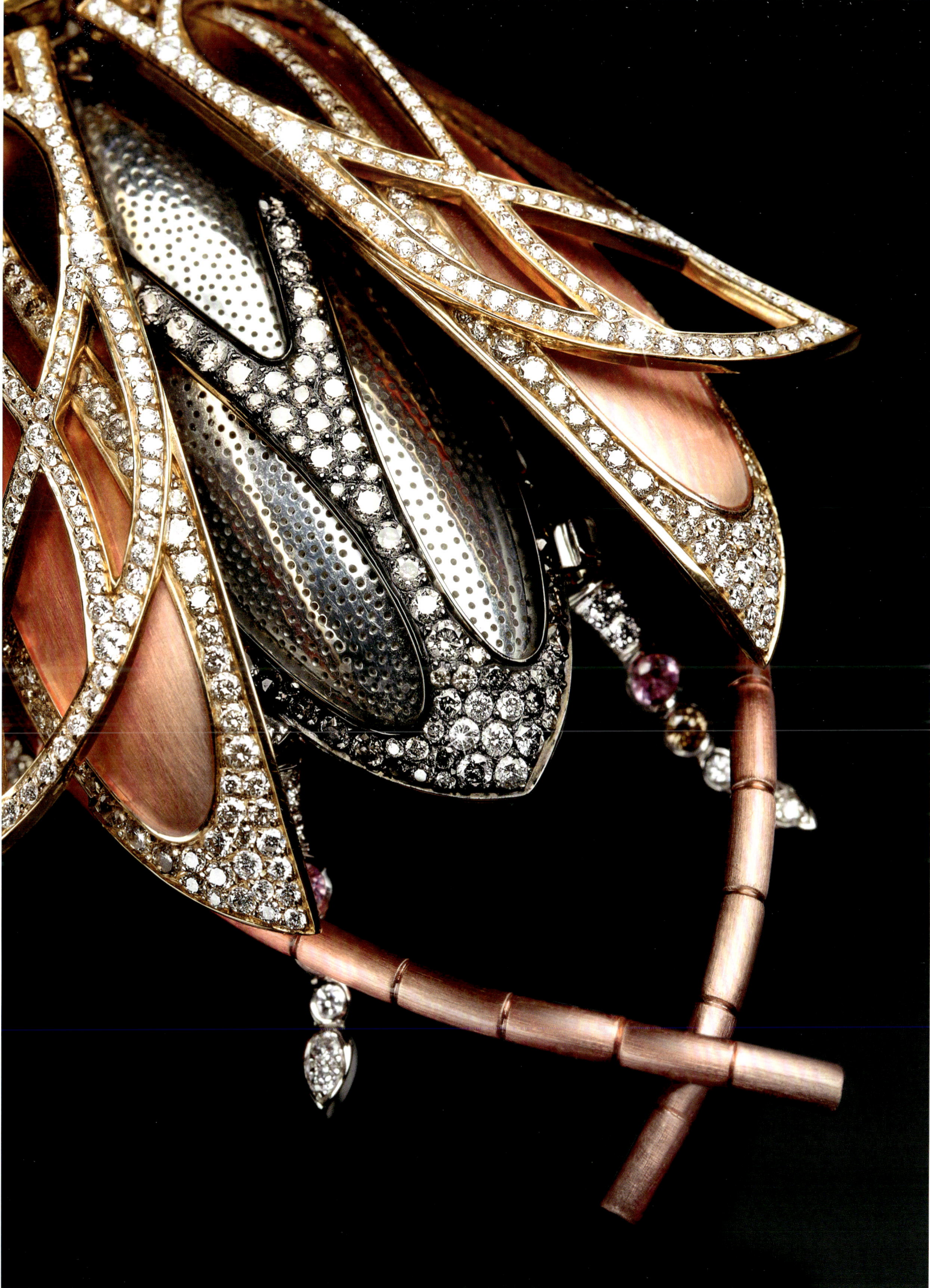

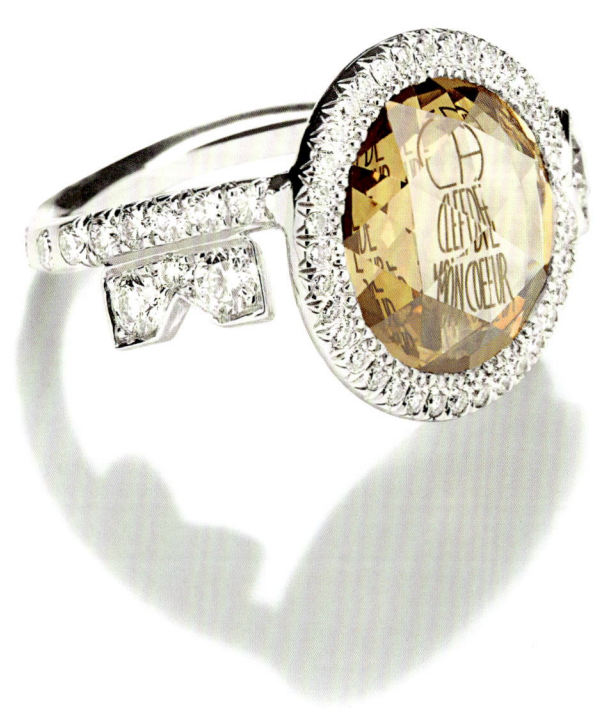

THE KEY TO MY HEART

I've known Lorenz for thirty years. His style—a cross between Germanic rigor and French creativity—is a perfect fit for me. He has designed jewelry for all the important events in my life, always with a great deal of sensitivity. So much so that my collection has become a kind of diary of my life. I'm very attached to it because Lorenz's jewelry reminds me of a host of happy times. This ring, for example, which has a diamond "tattooed" with a secret personal message, conveys Lorenz's talent for creating unique and very romantic pieces. He has the ability to invent marvelous and surprising things. No one makes jewelry quite like him.

Princess Astrid von Liechtenstein
Entrepreneur and collector

TATTOO RING THE KEY
TO MY HEART

I love it when innovation helps enhance beauty.
Sharing a message with a tattooed diamond
is a promise of happiness.

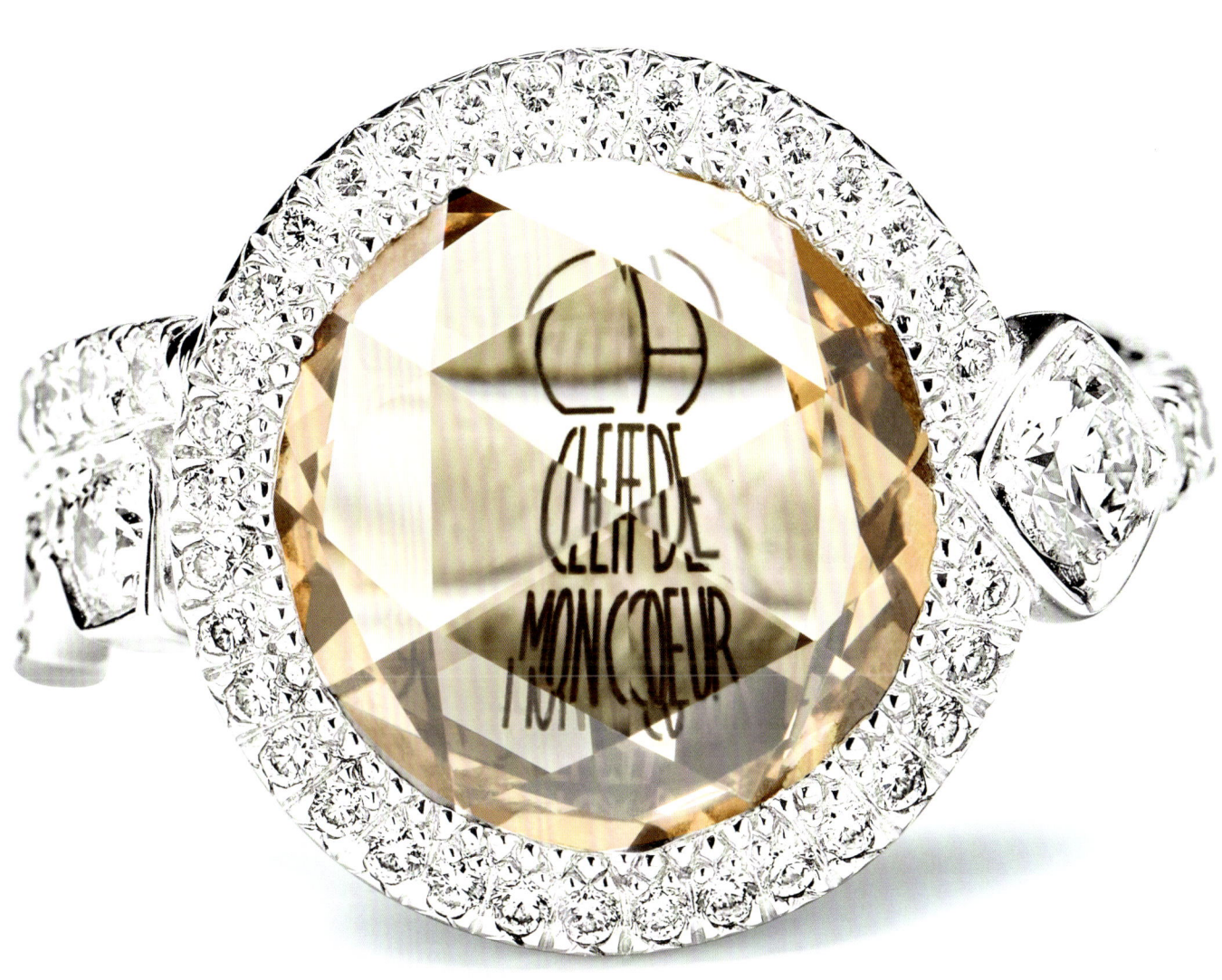

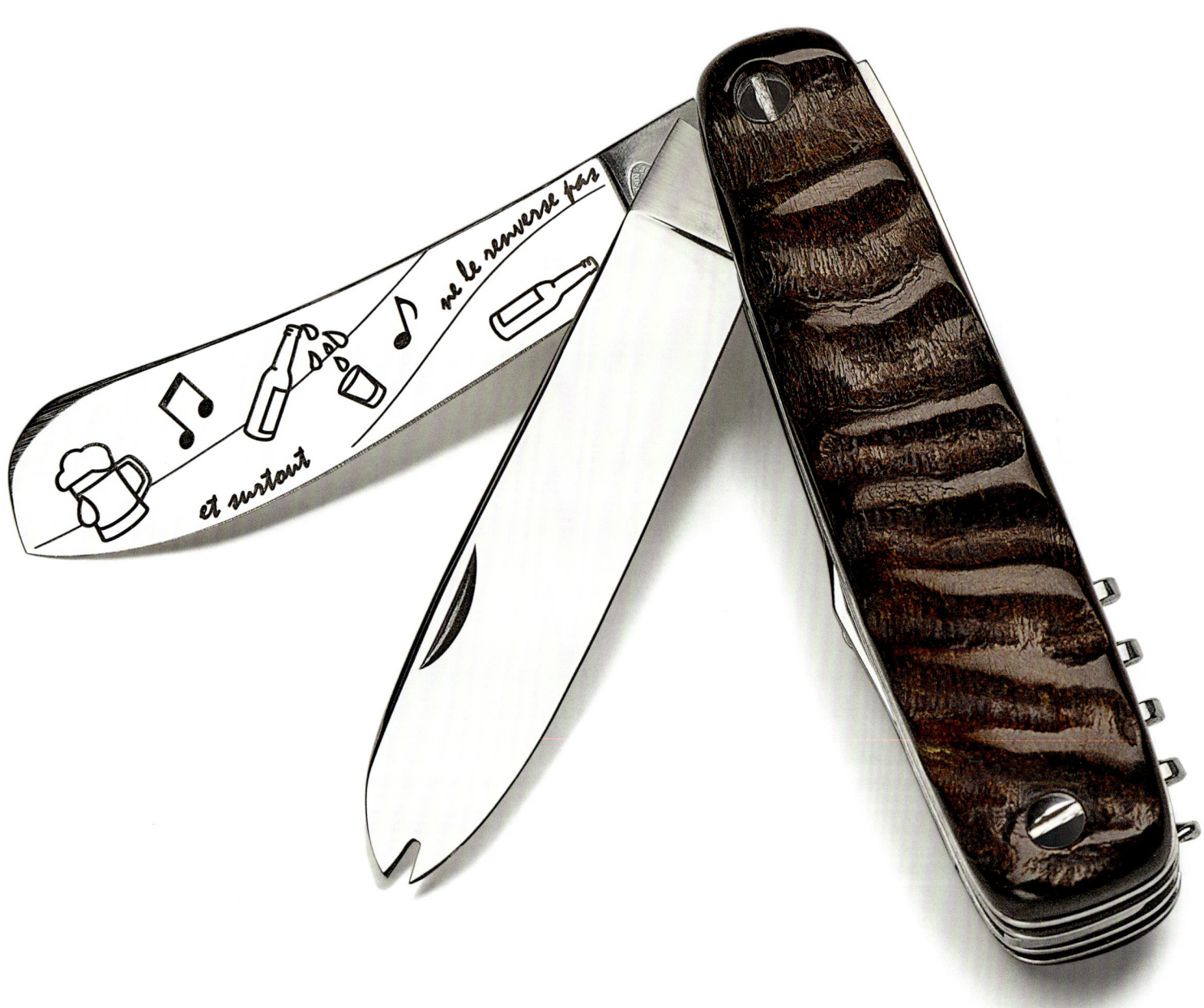

FRIEND
SHIP
KNIFE

Lorenz's genius lies in being able to see things others don't. He can understand and draw complex structures very quickly. In addition to this unique talent, he has a strong sense of beauty. In my view, it's the rare combination of these two qualities that makes Lorenz's work so unique. His art is highly innovative, it's both technical and sensitive. Lorenz doesn't see the people who wear his jewelry as clients—they are people he loves. He designs for them. I am incredibly lucky to be able to spend time with a creative genius. He is the only one working on Place Vendôme. Our partnership was built on my admiration of him. Slowly but surely, it turned into friendship and this knife tells our story. We have a great deal of trust in one another, and we share a love of life's simple pleasures—like a good meal and good company.

Cédric Aumonier
Entrepreneur, actor and philanthropist

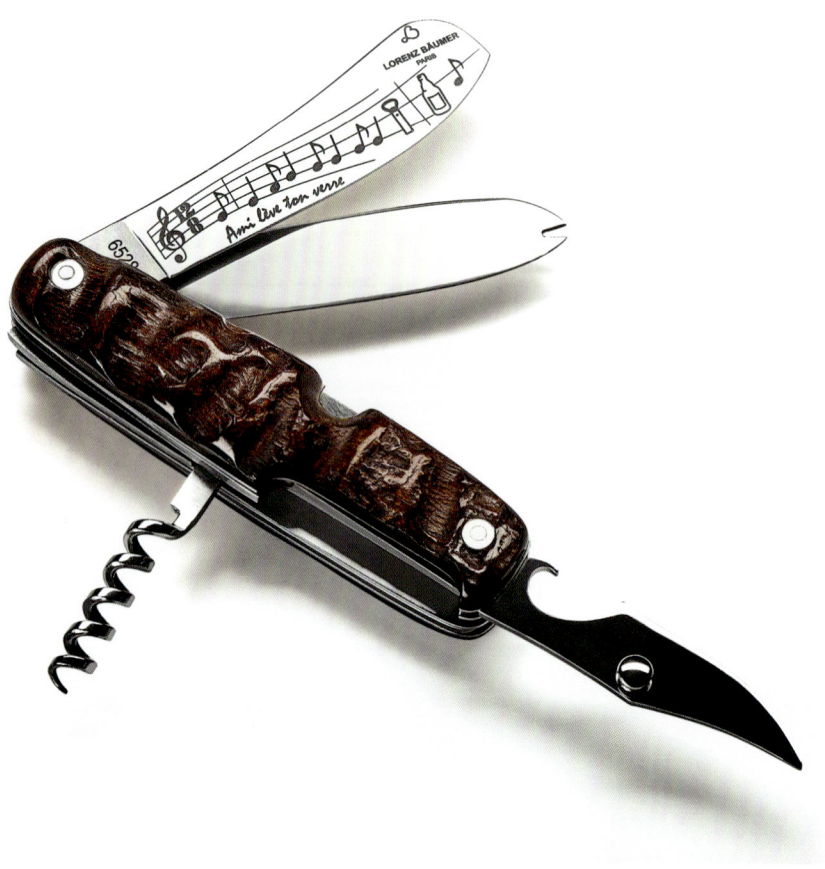

FRIENDSHIP
KNIFE

Accompanying the most precious moments
of our lives, this knife offers all the tools
we need to enjoy quality time with others.

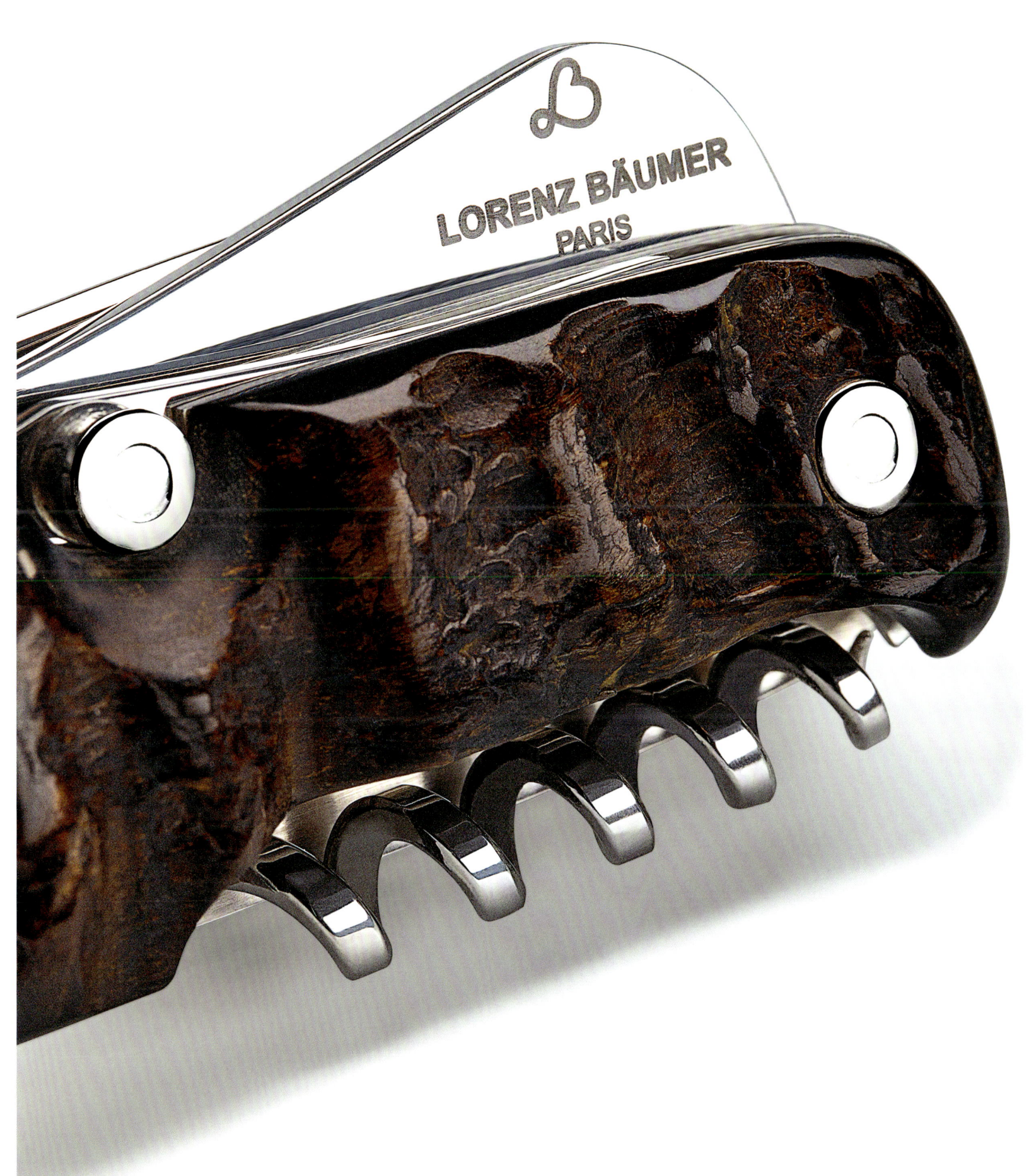

HED GE HO G

Lorenz isn't just a designer. He is also a great art lover who is discerning and knowledgeable, which stops him from imitating others. He knows a lot about the history of jewelry and his inspiration is linked to characteristics of style rather than technical or formal features. This is the case with humor, for example, which has become rare in jewelry. Lorenz puts a lot of wit into his designs. His animal rings, despite drawing on major historical periods, are his and his alone. The hedgehog on this ring is shy, calm, and sweet. From its proportions and its placement on the band, you can tell that it's the work of a sculptor as much as a jeweler. What characterizes Lorenz's work is that he never goes to extremes in terms of stones or dimensions. He makes no concessions to fashion. He is free. He has found the clientèle that fits his imagination and that's a great strength. That is why he is very difficult to copy. Lorenz is a *Mensch*, a decent and conscientious man. He is guided by his heart and a great deal of generosity. He doesn't allow himself to be confined to certain ways of doing things. He designs ingenious, witty, and fantastically feminine jewelry. That's what makes him absolutely unique.

Jean-Norbert Salit
Jewelry expert

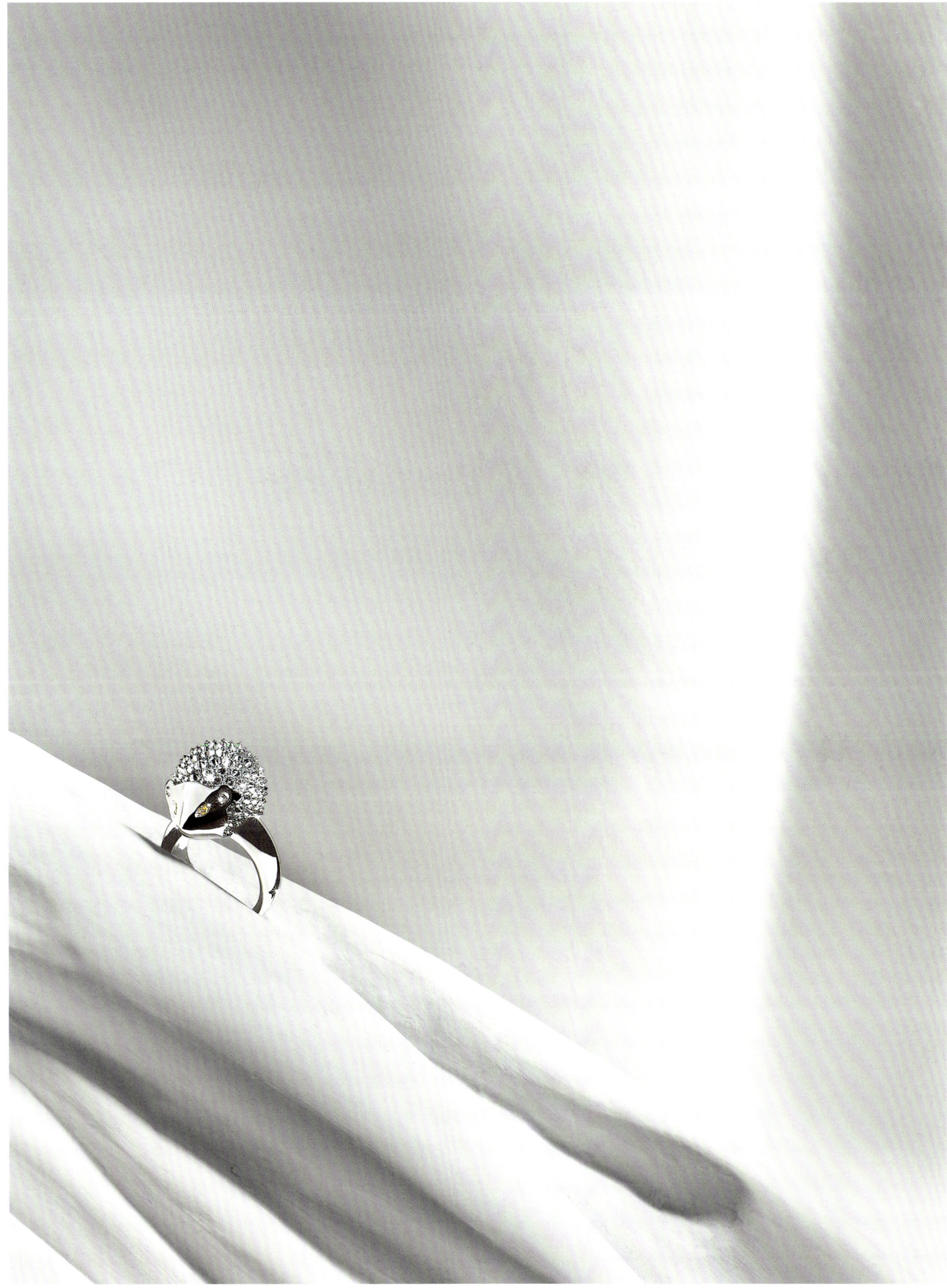

Venus of Arles (circa 360 BC), Paris, Louvre Museum.

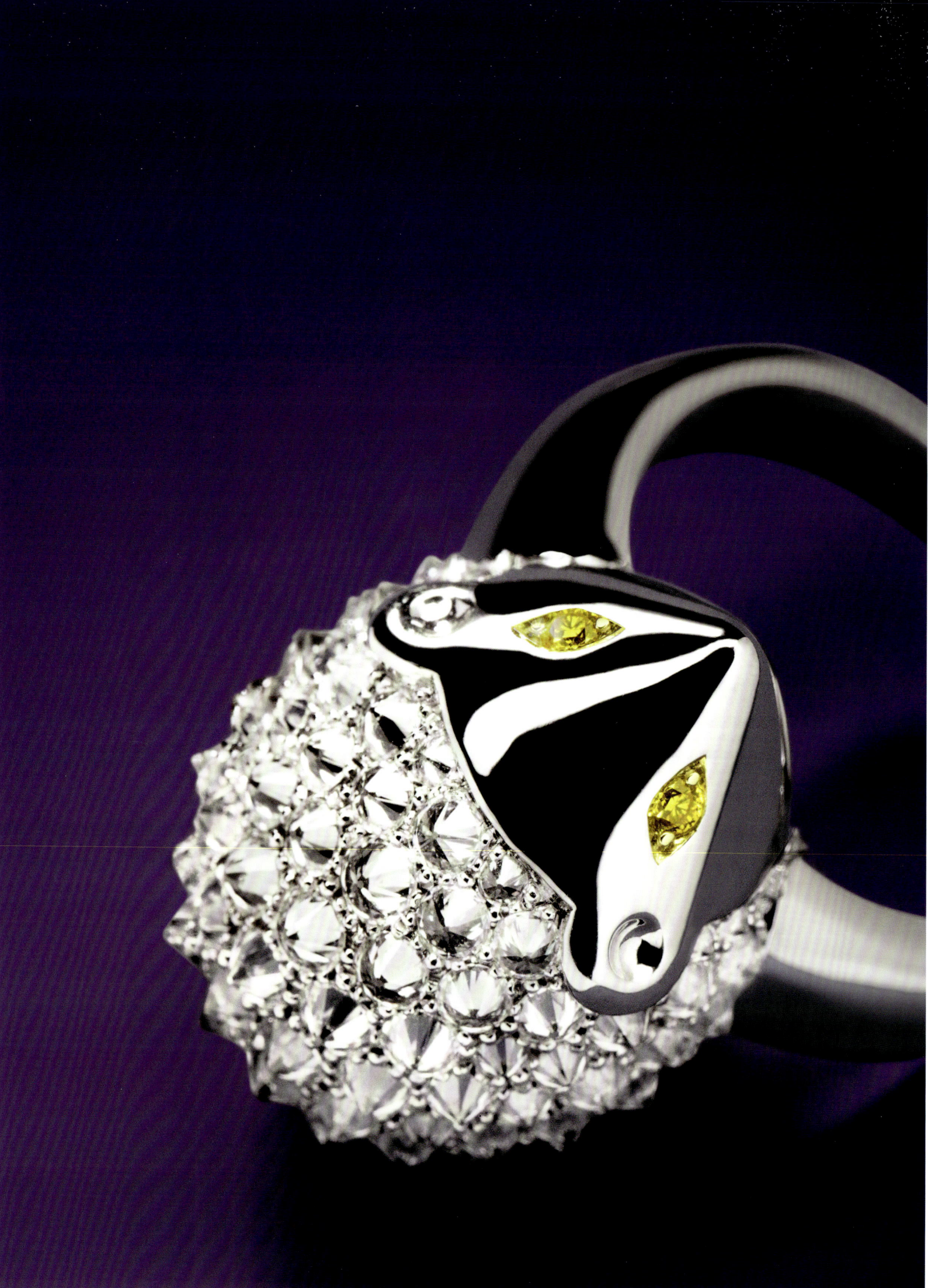

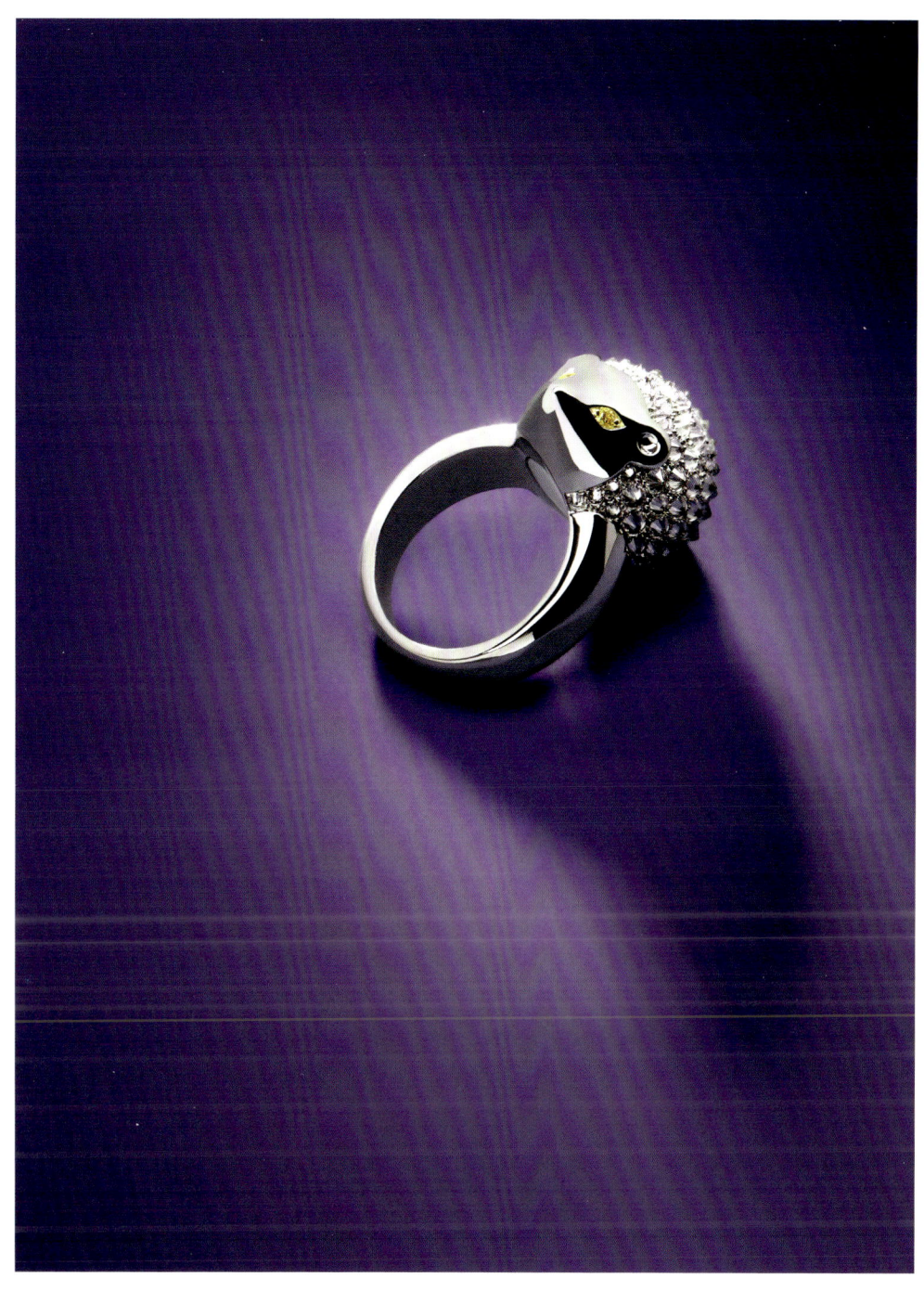

HEDGEHOG
RING

This sweet and spiky animal keeps
all its secrets on the inside, underneath
its reversed pavé-set diamonds.

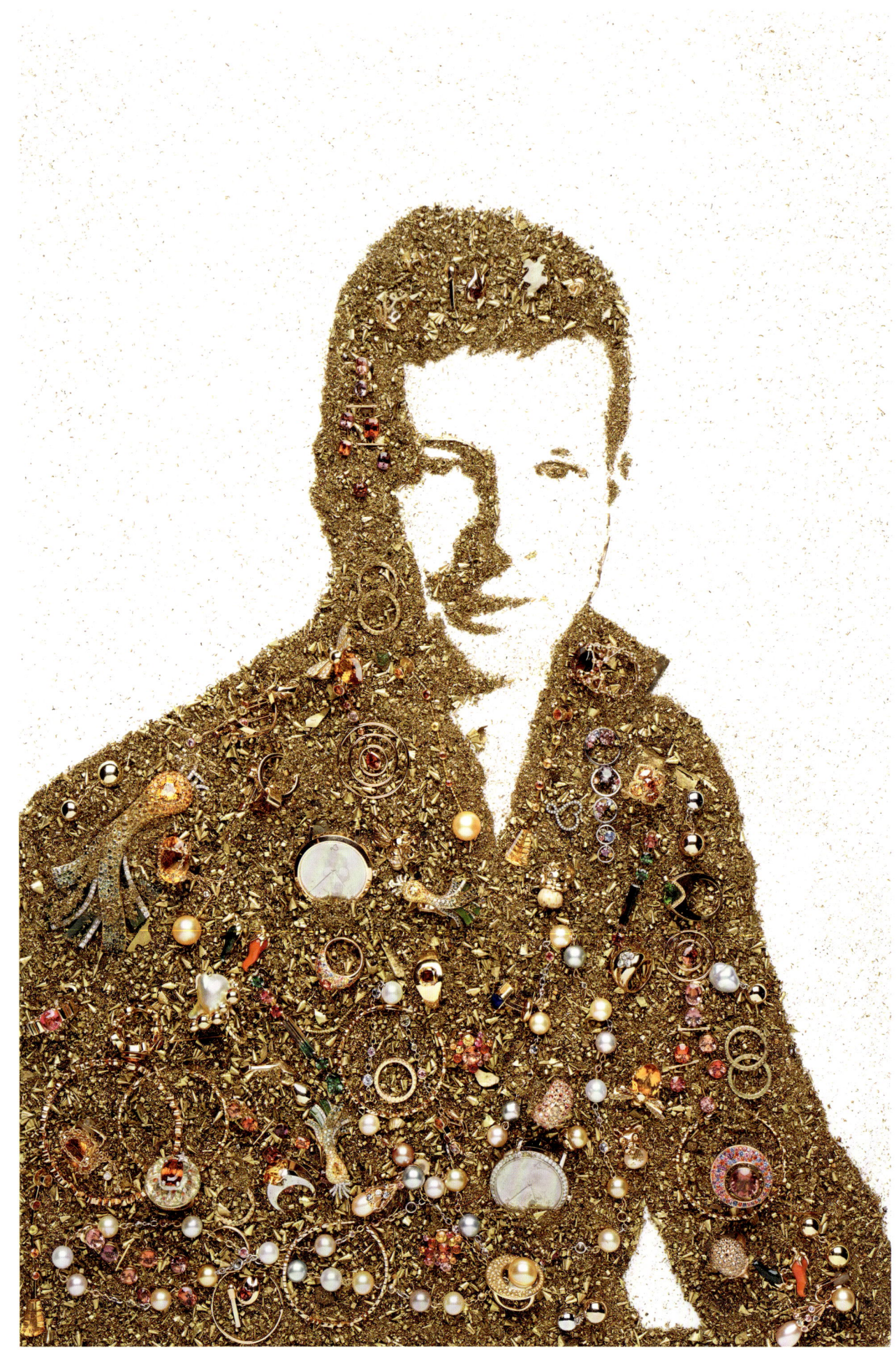

LORENZ BÄUMER BY VIK MUNIZ

LORENZ BÄUMER

Maker of dreams

Fine art is that in which
the hand, the head, and the
heart of man go together.

John Ruskin

BÄUMER. At eleven o'clock on the elegant façade of the Place Vendôme,
these six letters, written in a graceful font, stand above the entrance
to a unique address. On the other side of the store window, which
tells a different story with every season, one is immediately struck
by the spirit of the premises. Purple velvet, plush carpeting, photographs
of the Vendôme column, books, and curiosities set the stage for
the jewelry creations, showcased like sentimental items in a private
apartment. On the wall, the first sentence of a manifesto also sets
the tone: "I believe that jewelry has a soul rather than a price!"
There can be no doubt that this place belongs to the author of these
words, the very man who created it: Lorenz Bäumer.

Bespoke emotions

Admirers and connoisseurs know well that when they visit this
gifted jeweler, they are looking to do more than buy his creations.
They bring him their dreams and task him with giving them form.
After all, that is Lorenz Bäumer's real forte: transforming the evanescent
substance of desires into unique, sentimental and eternal designs.
Everyone is greeted attentively in his rooms on the Place Vendôme,
where they set out their wishes, their tastes, and their references.
Lorenz's task is to transcribe them and put them into color using his
brilliant lexicon of stones, pavé settings, and other secret mechanisms.
His designs are always born from understanding the other person,
who is seen more as a guest than a client. Authentic emotion emerges
from the fruitful dialog between the intimacy of a dream and the world
of an ever-shifting designer. And that is what gives jewelry its soul.
A soul so precious that the studio's excellent model makers, jewelers,
gemcutters, gemsetters, gem carvers, polishers, and engravers strive
to give it shape. He harnesses this generosity and passion—which
ensures his independence—to satisfy lovers of beautiful designs
in a way that is unparalleled in the world of contemporary jewelry.

A unique trajectory

While this distinctive feature does not tell the whole story,
it does speak volumes about Lorenz Bäumer's personality and
the unique thirty-year career that has shaped the modern-day face
of the House. On graduating from the école Centrale Paris at 22,
this young German—born to a German diplomat father and
a French mother—could have aspired to a high-flying career just about
anywhere in the world. Instead, he chose this moment to shut himself
in a bathroom with a piece of white opal and carve his first piece
of jewelry for his mother! Any disappointment or worry she may have
felt about her son's surprising decision was tempered by his reassurances
that if he had not achieved success after two years, he would return
to a more conventional career choice. His gamble paid off. His fashion
jewelry was wildly popular and, after just a few months, Chanel invited
him to design its first jewelry collections. His boundless creativity
and gift for design truly blossomed in this art form and its many
technical constraints. Lorenz Bäumer loves creating a dialog, whether
with artisans or with the past. On the one hand, his creative brain
thrives on references from every field and every era, compiling,
deconstructing, and reassembling them, inventing new shapes and
color ranges, and incorporating multiple homages to the designers
who came before him, while breaking with convention. On the other,
his left brain operates like an engineer, adapting groundbreaking
technologies and industrial processes to his intuition, pushing
back outdated boundaries, and opening up new fields of expression.
He immediately established himself as a one-of-a-kind creator
capable of solving the fundamental physics problems inherent
to jewelry-making without compromising on his creativity.
Orders began to flood in from Louis Vuitton, Guerlain, Cartier,
Hennessy, and more. Lorenz seized every subject with
insatiable curiosity while closely guarding his independence.

Art in the present

At the same time, he opened his first own-name boutique on the second floor of 23 Rue Royale, followed by 4 Place Vendôme. Many remember it well and agree that it was more than just a series of reception rooms—it was a personal museum. Here, as if it were his own home, Lorenz exhibited his collections, drawings, paintings, photographs, minerals, designer furniture, curiosities, and more. He received guests surrounded by his personal tastes, passions, and inspirations. He advised clients and produced bespoke creations, always motivated by the desire to move and delight. His inquisitive, overactive, and outward-looking personality became apparent, revealing his jewelry collections in a new light. An electrocardiogram of his eldest son Artus's heartbeat provided the design for the Heartbeat line. For Carl, his family's first names were intertwined to form bracelets. Like an alchemist of matter, Lorenz Bäumer has the ability to seize a moment and transform time into jewelry. Lorenz, a keen surfer since his youth in Tel Aviv, is a follower of Kairos, the minor Greek deity representing an opportunity to be seized—like the waves. Whether he draws inspiration from his knowledge of historical objects, from nature or from contemporary art, Lorenz creates in the present. His work is a remedy for nostalgia and embodies Picasso's principle that "In art there is no past or future. Art that does not inhabit the present can never be art."

A creative dialog

When shifting his focus from fashion jewelry to fine jewelry, Lorenz Bäumer did not abandon his convictions—quite the opposite. He brought an air of levity to a discipline that had come dangerously close to languishing in the display cases of museums and collectors. To achieve this, he became a master of coordination. From his new address next to the Ritz, he continued his creative dialog with the artisans whom he admired to continually push the boundaries of what is possible. Those whom he has dubbed "makers of beauty" include woodwork specialist Guillaume Féau, art dealer Louis de Bayser, metalworker Jean Delisle, designer Hubert Le Gall, photographer Jean-François Fortchantre, ceramicist Louisélio, frame-maker Christophe Nobile, engraver Louis Boursier, glass-maker Bernard Pictet, pastry chef François Perret, florist Julien Moulié, and upholsterer Alexandre Phelippeau. And although this list may seem inconsequential, Lorenz Bäumer's work can only truly be understood in the context of this continual dialog with people who have become masters in their respective forms of know-how and who constantly strive for excellence.

Boundless dreams

Just like his interests, Lorenz Bäumer's inspiration is polymorphic, varied, and multifaceted. It can be sentimental, like the pair of *Love Bird* hoops designed for his wife Géraldine to mark the birth of their daughter Alma, or it can be romantic, like the passionate knots of the *Pense à moi* ring. It can reach the pinnacle of glamor when it takes the shape of the *À la folie* ring, dripping with stones and colors. It can become futuristic when it follows the lead of digital art, giving rise to the *Damascus Rose* NFT (non-fungible token), or, on the contrary, become melancholy and nostalgic when reinterpreting one of art history's favorite themes—man and death—in the diamond-set skull of the *Vanitas* ring. It can be subversive by shaking up the conventions of jewelry techniques and creating new technical standards for using novel materials, like the *Meteorite* ring or the *Titanium Ocean Crush* earrings. Or, conversely, it can rewrite the construction of articulated pieces, as seen on the *Scarab* brooch and *Treasure Island*, the playful yet luxurious bracelet that conceals a secret. It may delight in mirroring the extraordinary malleability of nature, as seen in the sensual feel of the *Sea Urchin* ring, or mimic its touching timidity, like on the Hedgehog ring. It can try to trick our senses with jewelry that looks good enough to eat, like the *Gourmandise* ring. It can become intimate and talisman-like by compiling the first names of loved ones into the *Writing* bracelet, or by inventing a way to tattoo diamonds with a laser to engrave the hidden promises of *The key to my heart* ring. It can even take the mundane—yet oh-so crucial—form of a pocketknife celebrating friendship. It can go far beyond jewelry and become pictorial by creating a painting on the *Cubist Garden* ring, or architectural with the sculptural geometry of the *Black Magic Nébuleuse* bracelet. It can appear in the masterful hollows and solid forms of the *Mikado* architect bracelet, or almost vanish before the cause it champions, giving rise to the *Sumba* line, which honors Indonesian culture. And it can be used to celebrate a life and tenderly tell its story, with picture frames for children, or transform it into a symbolic message, like the sword of Xavier Darcos, Chancellor of the Académie Française.

Beauty on the horizon

As is plain to see, Lorenz Bäumer's inspiration knows no bounds. Still, it needs to be channeled and orchestrated by a person with an extraordinary ability to project and produce—and much more besides. Upon reflection, these thirty years of creation demonstrate clearly that Lorenz Bäumer is a free man first and foremost. At a time when industry-wide tendencies for storytelling and marketing are simplifying design methods, he continues to grow and expand. The more he creates, the surer his technique and style become, and paradoxically the more uncategorizable he becomes. However one thing that does remain is his constant quest for beauty. Not beauty for beauty's sake but because, as Stendhal said, beauty is the promise of happiness.

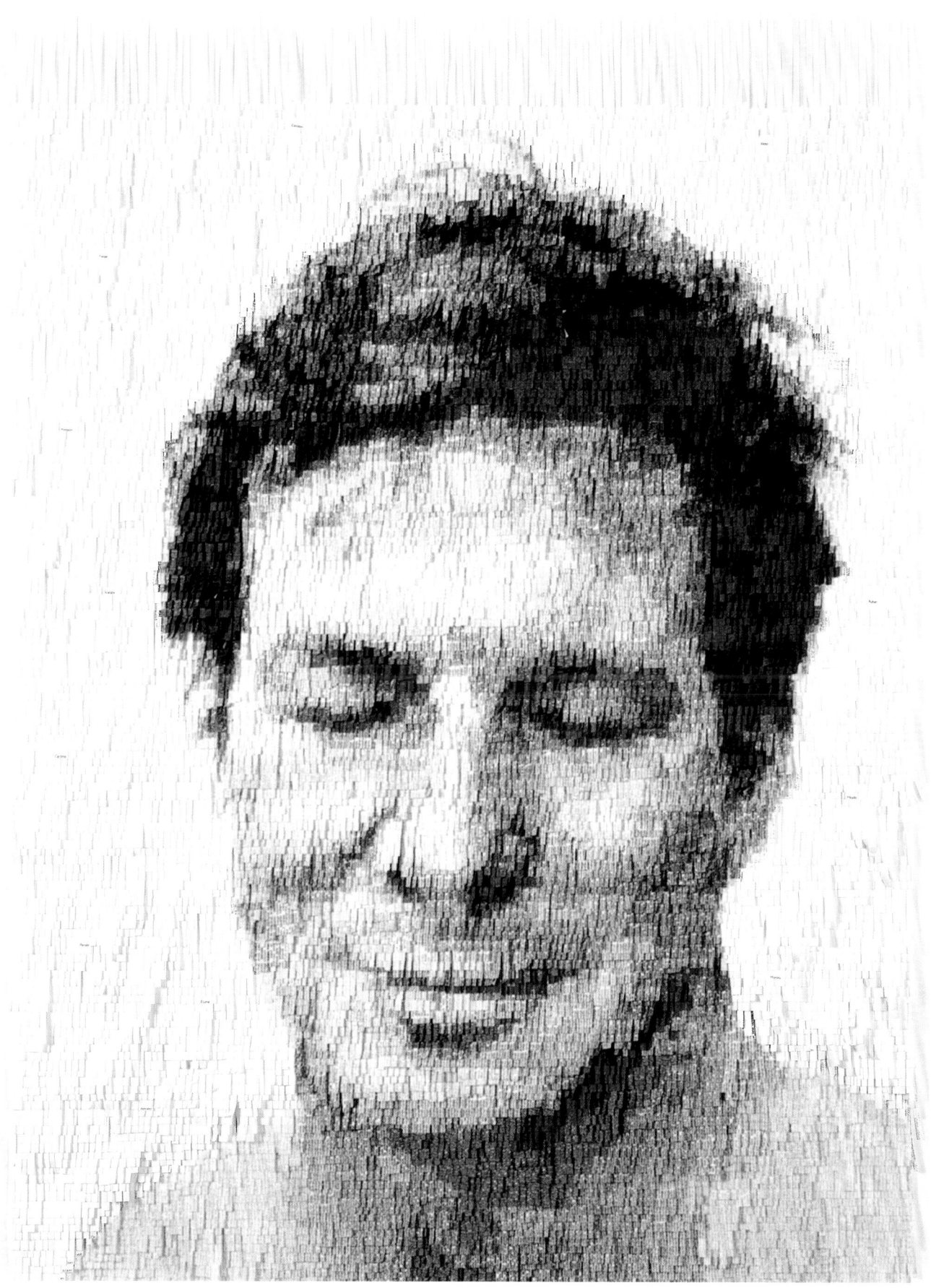

LORENZ BÄUMER BY NATHALIE BOUTTÉ

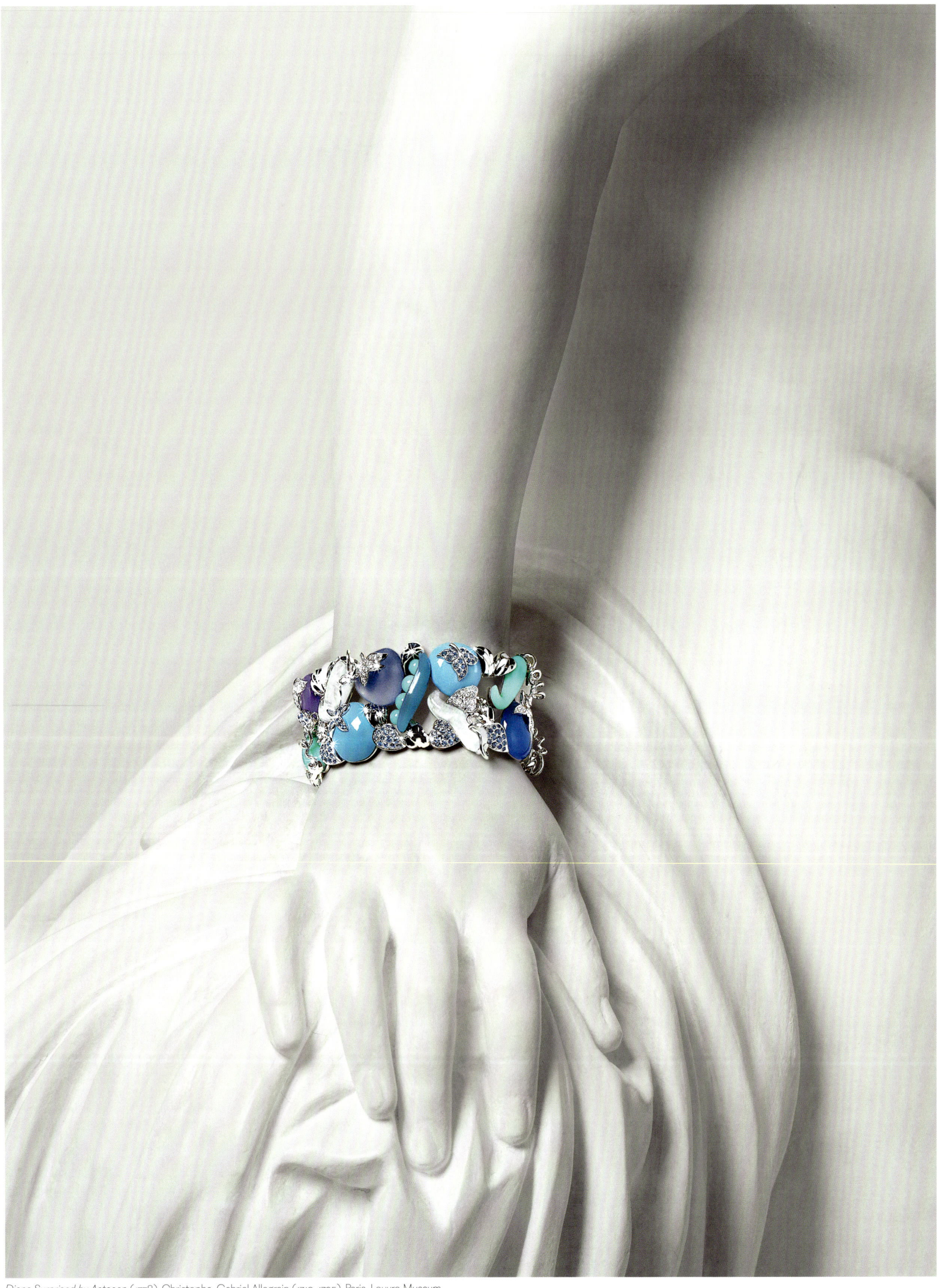

Diana Surprised by Actaeon (1778), Christophe-Gabriel Allegrain (1710-1795), Paris, Louvre Museum.

GOUR MAN DISE WINTER

I met Lorenz Bäumer for the first time through a group of "jewelry-crazy" professionals. They introduced Lorenz to me as "the most promising designer on the Paris market." At the time he was designing the new jewelry collection for Chanel, following in the footsteps of Paul Iribe. He showed promise and I had complete faith in the taste and knowledge of these jewelry lovers. One of them, who has since passed away, was a former jeweler and merchant who had made jewelry for Jean Schlumberger. Another was in charge of one of the most well-known jewelry-making workshops on the Paris market. I was lucky enough to be invited to lunch with them sometimes on Fridays at a brasserie opposite the Hôtel Drouot. As we all loved antique and modern jewelry, our conversations about the jewelry collections at the Musée des Arts décoratifs were very fruitful. They all supported the Galerie des Bijoux project, to which Lorenz Bäumer generously donated the *Gourmandise Winter* bracelet in 2004, the year in which the gallery officially opened. To our eyes, this bracelet incorporated all the ingenuity, humor, and appeal of Lorenz's art. His interest in both precious and semiprecious stones, some of which, such as rhodochrosite, are rarely used in jewelry, was a breath of fresh air for this unique art form.

Évelyne Possémé
Honorary head curator of the
Musée des Arts décoratifs, Paris

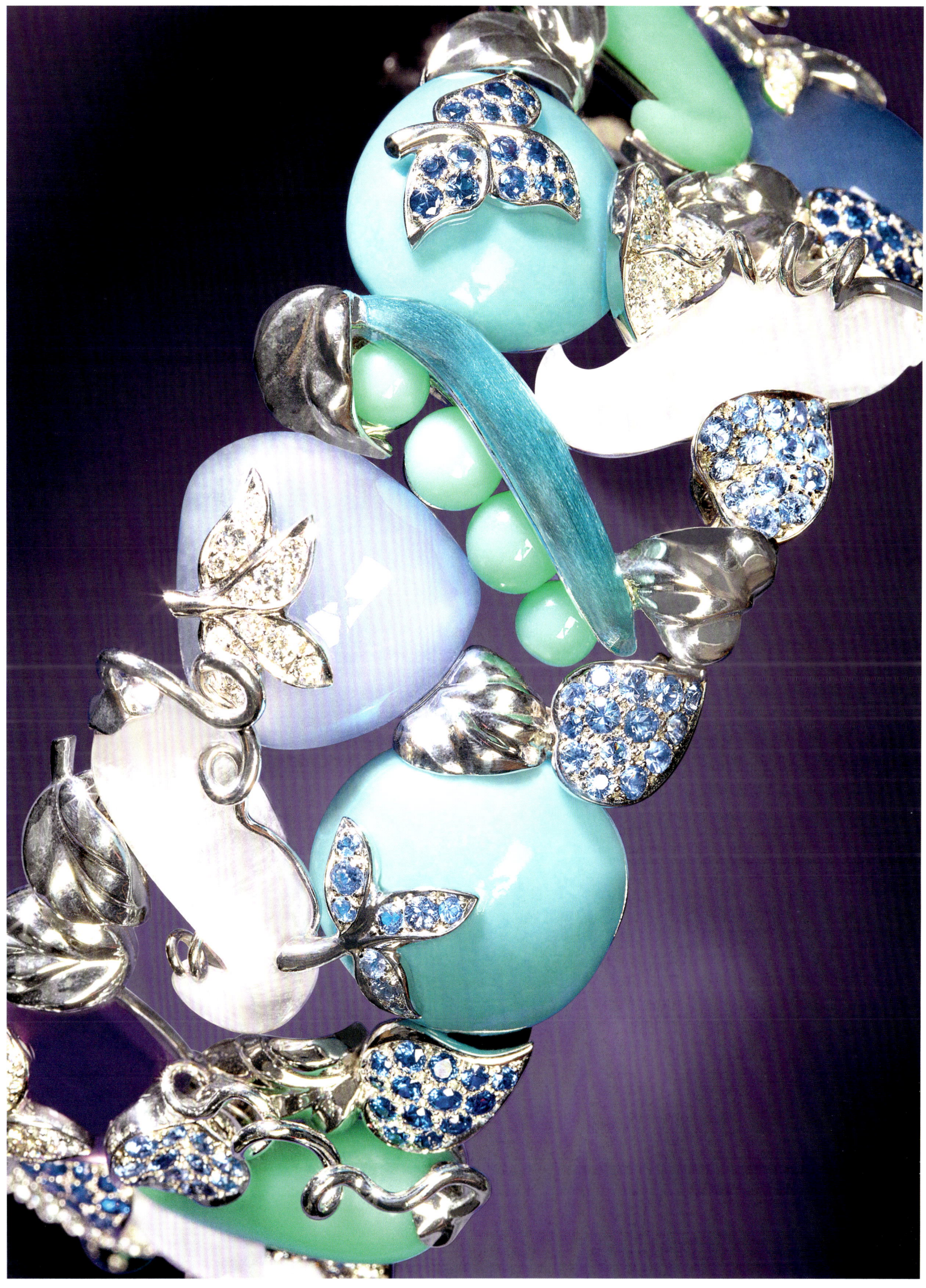

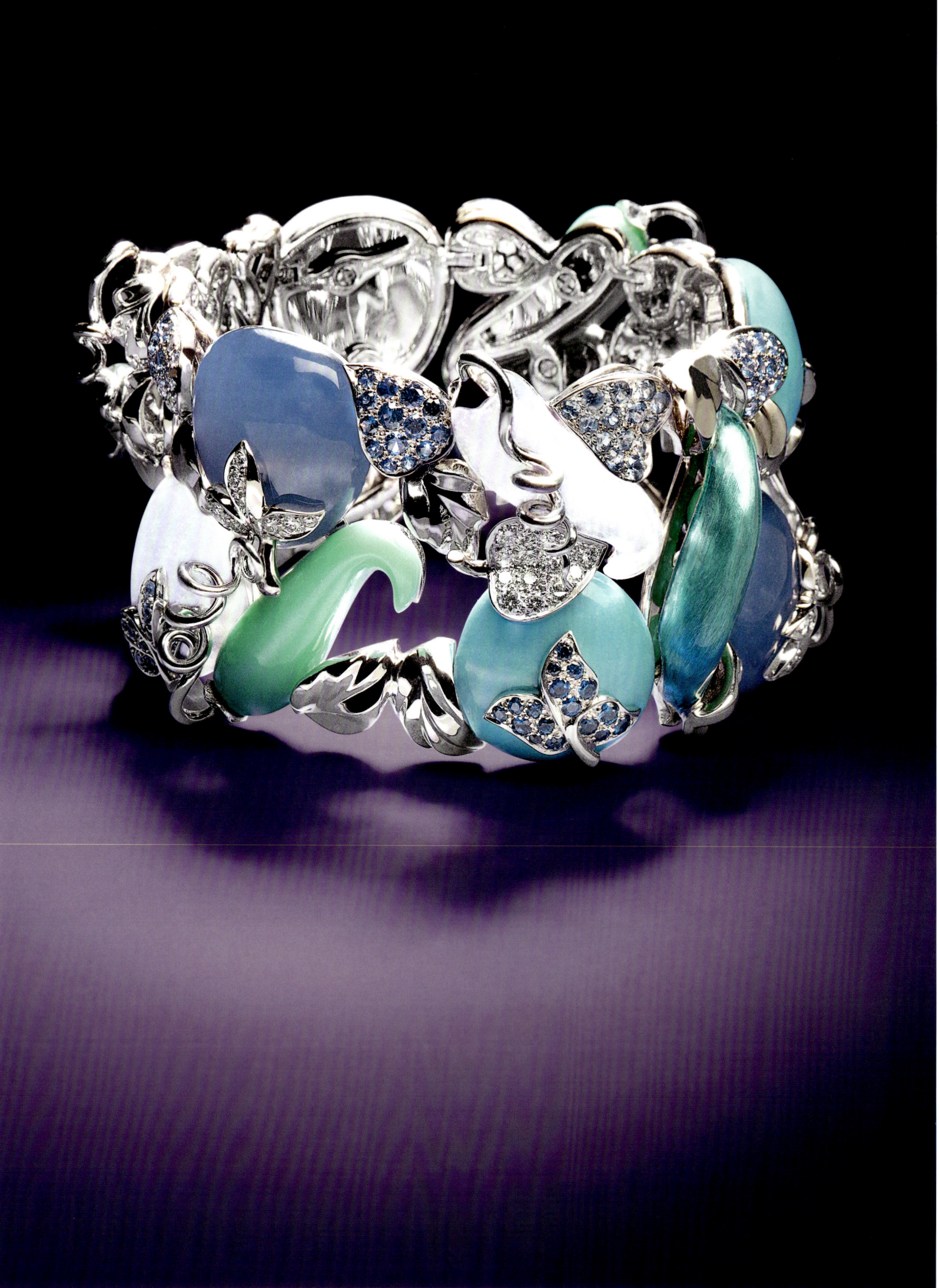

GOURMANDISE
WINTER
BRACELET

This bracelet, which is on display at the Musée des Arts décoratifs, is a homage to indulgence. The precious and semiprecious stones are combined with ornamental stones to form a feast for the eyes.

META
MOR
PH
OSE

When I discovered Lorenz Bäumer's work, I was immediately struck by its breadth. His pieces aren't just jewelry; they are whole worlds that connect his knowledge, his inquisitiveness, and his passions. His creativity is almost unrivaled in the world of jewelry but, as exuberant as they are, his creations are always extremely refined and elegant. Lorenz is an extremely intellectual designer who conveys a lot of stories and meaning through his jewelry. As an artist, he is in a state of perpetual transformation, just like these earrings which, with their sapphires, spinels, diamonds, and magnificent pink tourmalines, express the metamorphosis of a butterfly. They inspire a sense of always being able to bounce back and keep faith in your undertakings.

Alexandre Murat
Entrepreneur and author

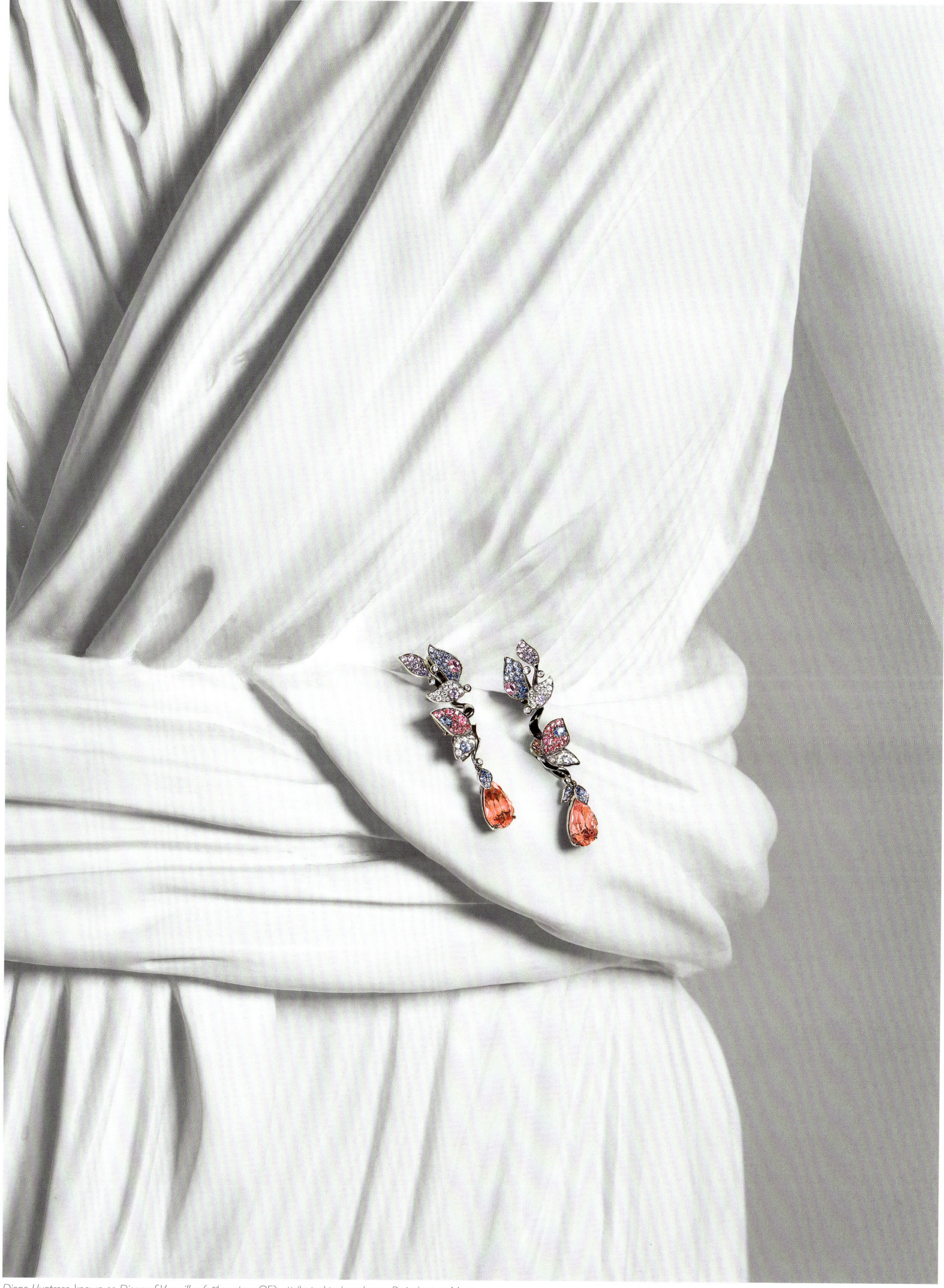

Diana Huntress, known as *Diana of Versailles* (2nd century CE), attributed to Leochares, Paris, Louvre Museum.

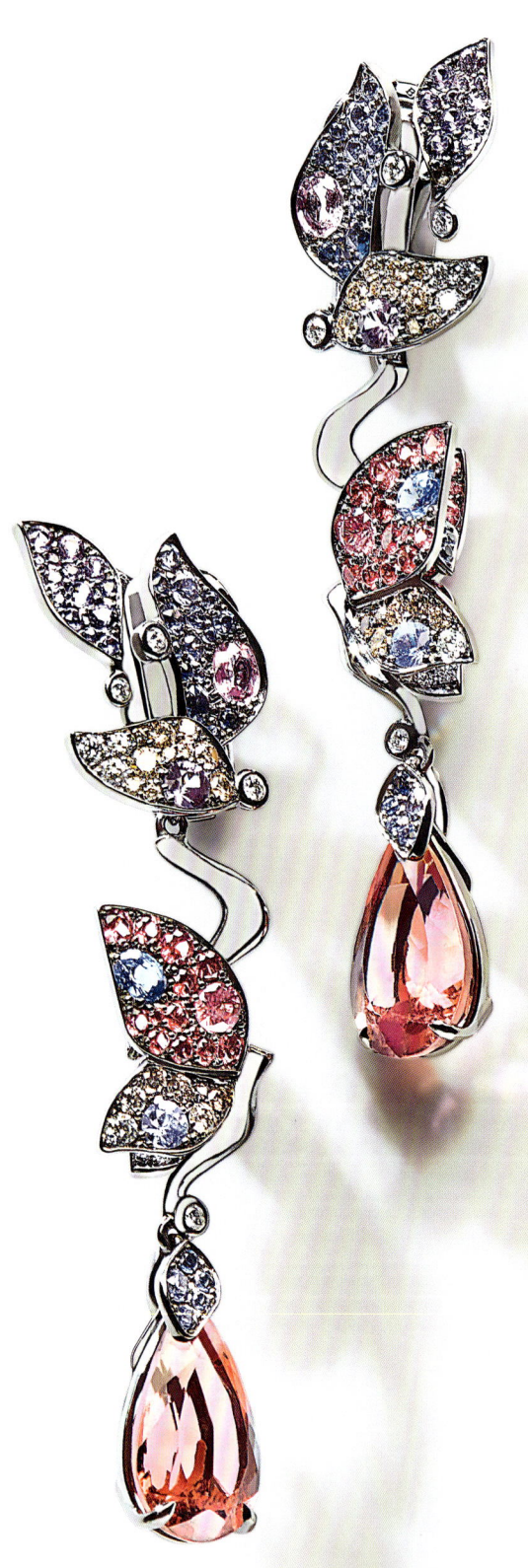

METAMORPHOSE
EARRINGS

These earrings are both leaves and a butterfly—
flora and fauna. They speak of how we all have
the ability to reinvent ourselves.

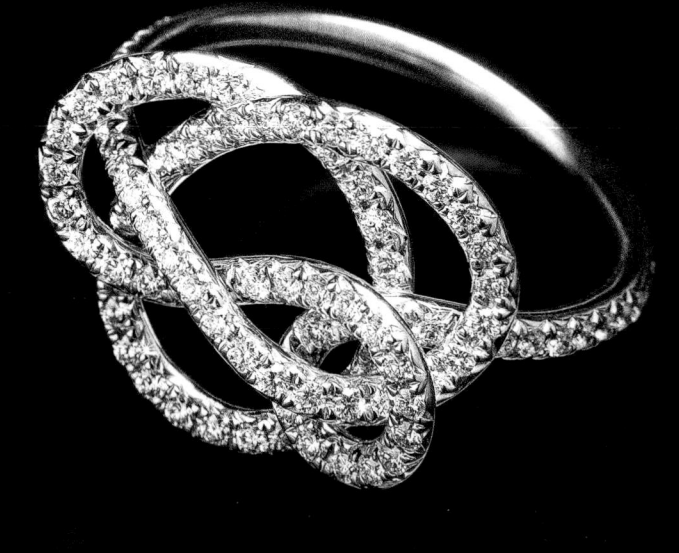

PEN
SE
À
MOI

I discovered Lorenz's extraordinary world when looking for a gift for my wife. I was immediately struck by his creativity, talent, and imagination. His jewelry is much more than objects for adorning a hand or a neck. His pieces are real works of art. They could absolutely be made bigger and turned into sculptures, and they would still have the same harmony, balance, and power. I can just picture a six-foot-tall version of the explosion on his *Supernova* ring! It would also work beautifully with the skull from the *Good Girl / Bad Girl* collection or the pretty knots from the *Pense à moi* ring. Lorenz's work, as beautiful as it is, goes beyond jewelry—which isn't surprising as he is an inquisitive man. For the last fifteen years or so, our friendship has been built on a shared taste for certain periods of art history.

Thierry Lhermitte
Actor, screenwriter and producer

PENSE À MOI
DIAMONDS
RING

My grandmother taught me how to tie knots
in napkins to remember everything. "Think of me,
I'm thinking of you"—here this bond is forged
in gold and diamonds.

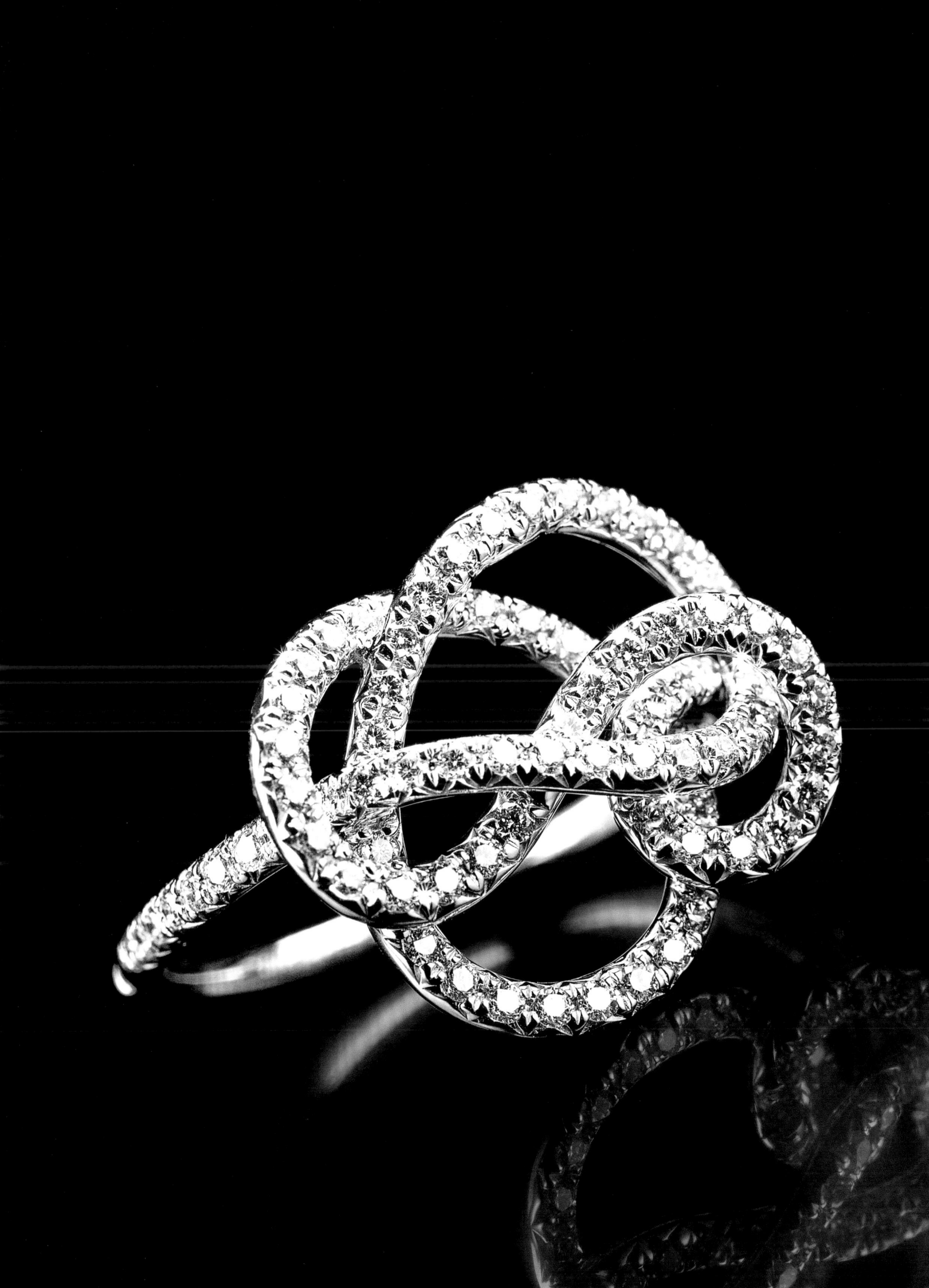

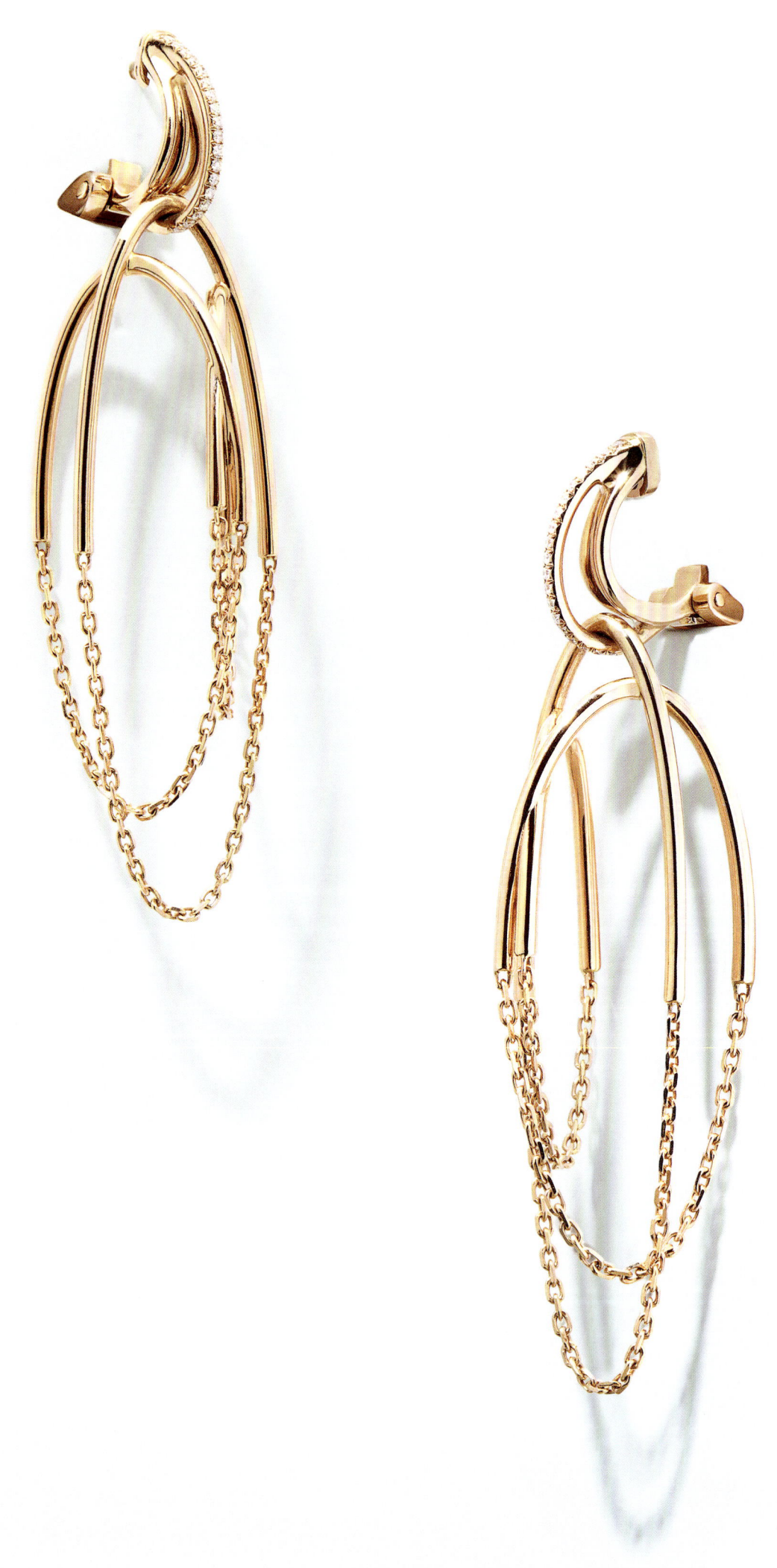

M OR A SE AMO UR

I vividly remember the first time I saw a ring made by Lorenz worn by a friend. The setting was so light that the diamond seemed to have been placed nonchalantly on her hand. This deceptive fragility had a hidden message: love can't be held down with prongs! Because Lorenz's jewelry speaks to us. Lorenz shakes up conventions, makes bold pairings, and plays with contrast. His work is eclectic, Gothic, Romantic... It glides, swarms, leaps, twirls, soars, trills, hides and awaits discovery, it astonishes and enchants! In Lorenz, the vanity of beauty should be considered as a homage to the beauty of nature. His jewelry is an ode to life. Like this pair of earrings with spinning rings that tell us that love can be enlaced but never restrained! Lorenz is a two-headed creature. One head is in the stars, the other is in the depths of the earth where crystals are formed. Artist and engineer coexist in him as in Renaissance thinker.

Hubert Le Gall
Artist and scenographer

MORSE AMOUR
EARRINGS

I love messages of love and particularly
Morse code, which can be used to share
a visible yet invisible declaration.

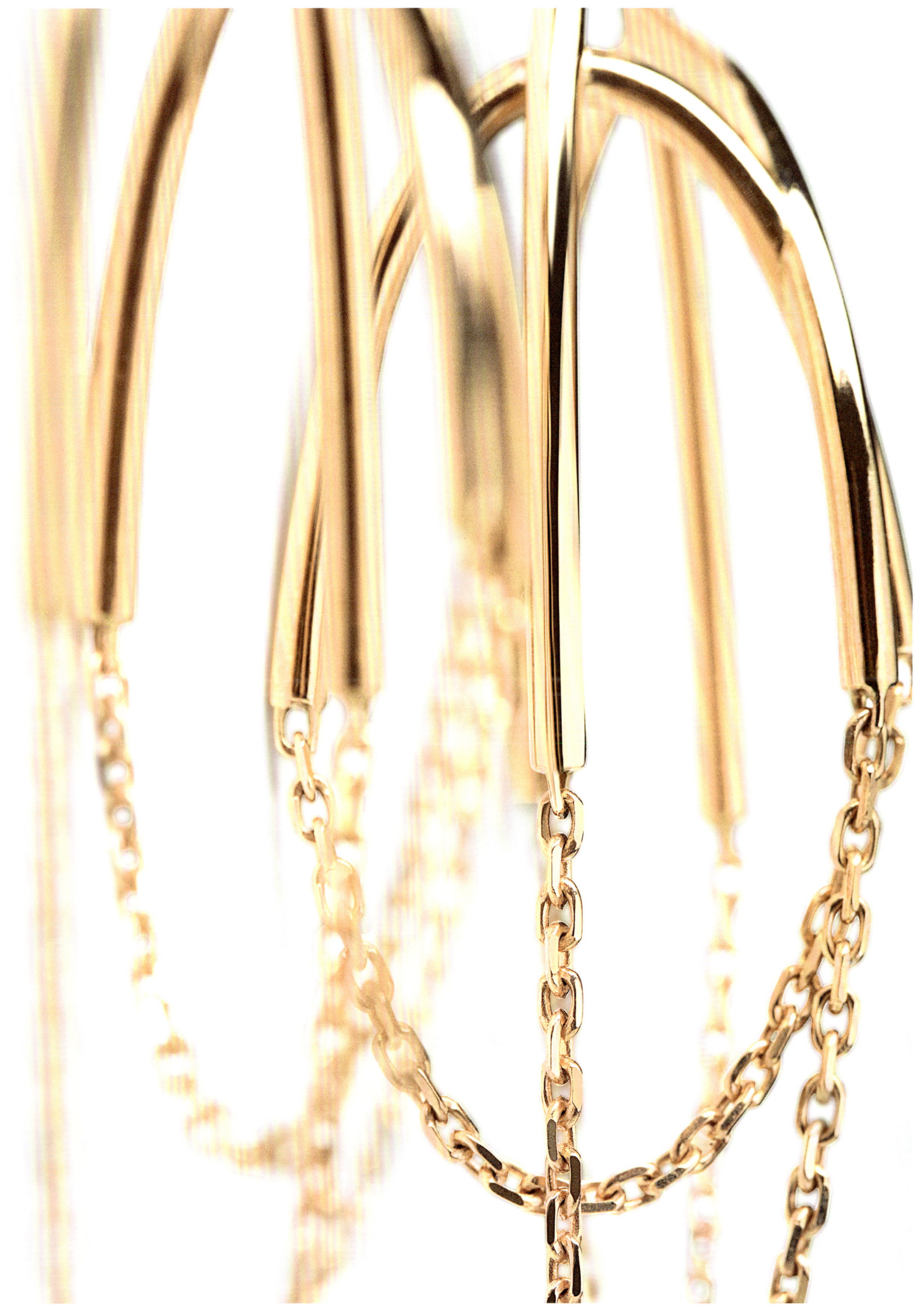

À LA FOLIE BLOS SOM

I've known Lorenz for over thirty years and our friendship is coupled with immense respect. Even though our personalities and practices are completely different, we have always had a lot of informal conversations and shared interests, particularly regarding man's relationship to nature. We try to create in a very special "chaos" that lies between the material world and the realm of ideas, in the thin interface that separates the raw material from the cultivated aesthetic. Our artistic practice involves designing objects capable of inspiring the same wonder we feel when contemplating certain natural creations. Lorenz always has the same passion and energy for his work. He has never let himself be confined to a certain way of doing things. He has remained free and generous, as this ring perfectly demonstrates. It's an explosion of colors. It expresses a kind of randomness, as if the stones were placed freely, and an almost childlike, joyful nonchalance, despite the fact that it is an extremely technical piece to produce.

Vik Muniz

Artist

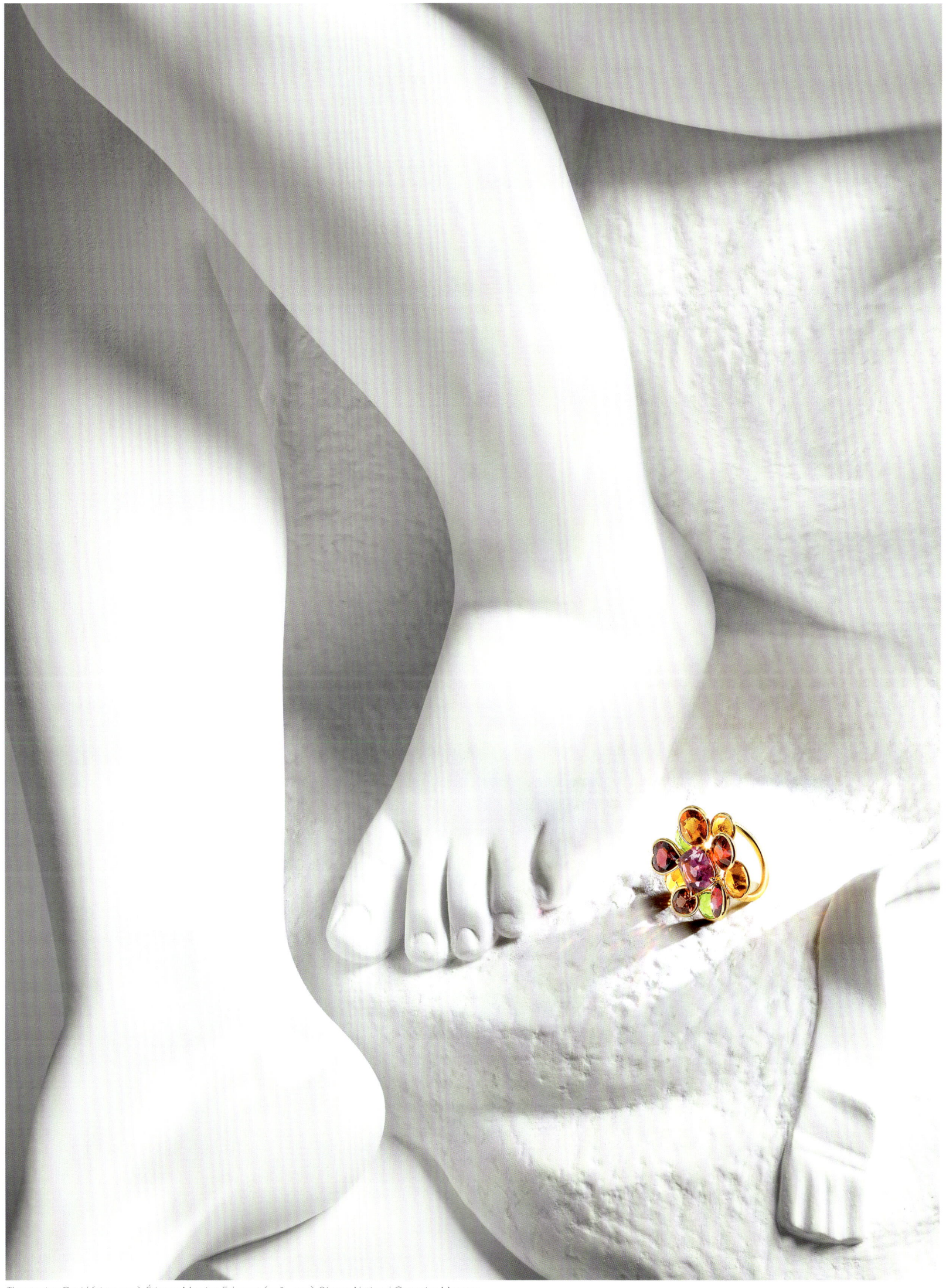

Threatening Cupid (circa 1757), Étienne Maurice Falconet (1716—1791), Sèvres, National Ceramics Museum.

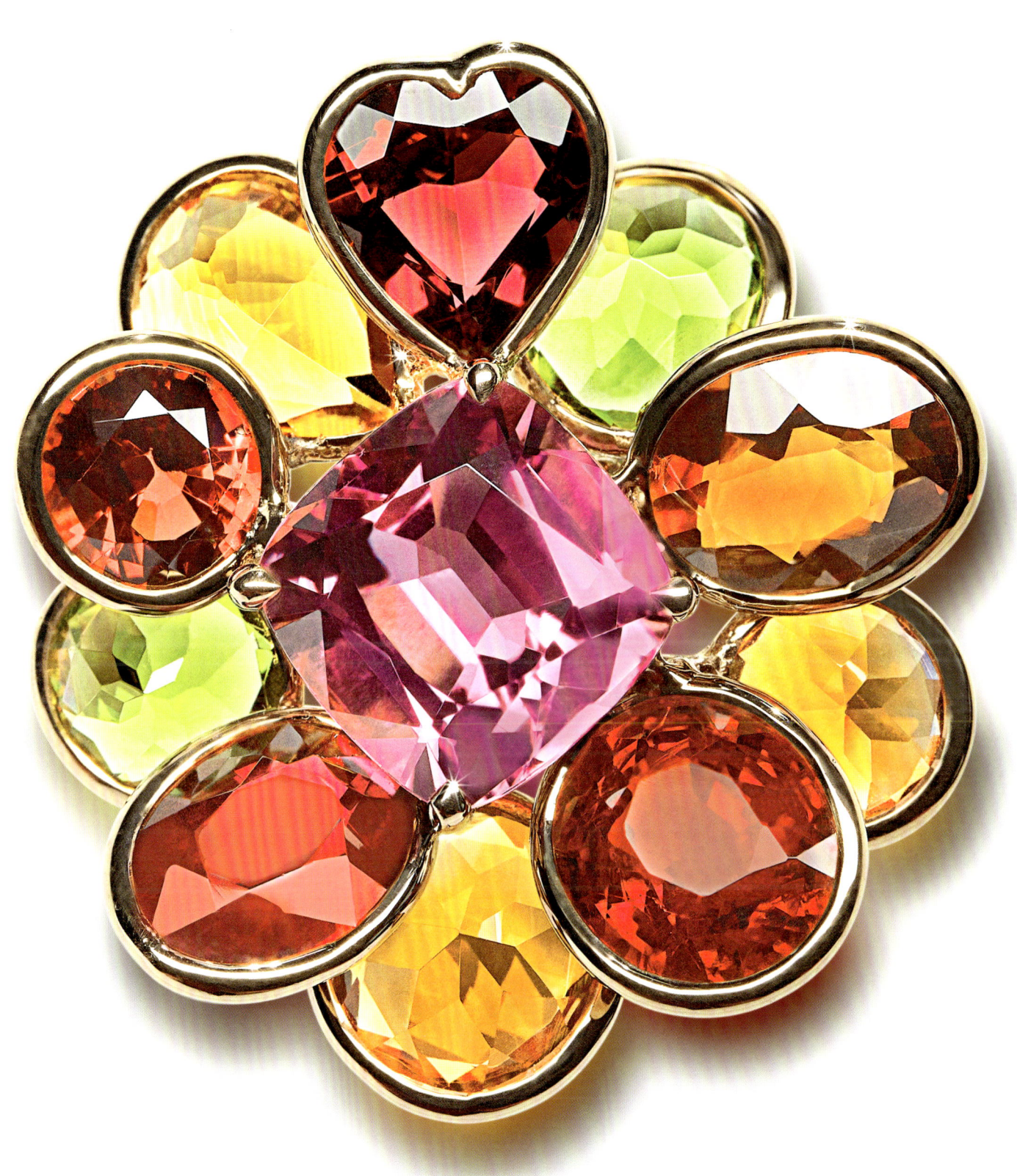

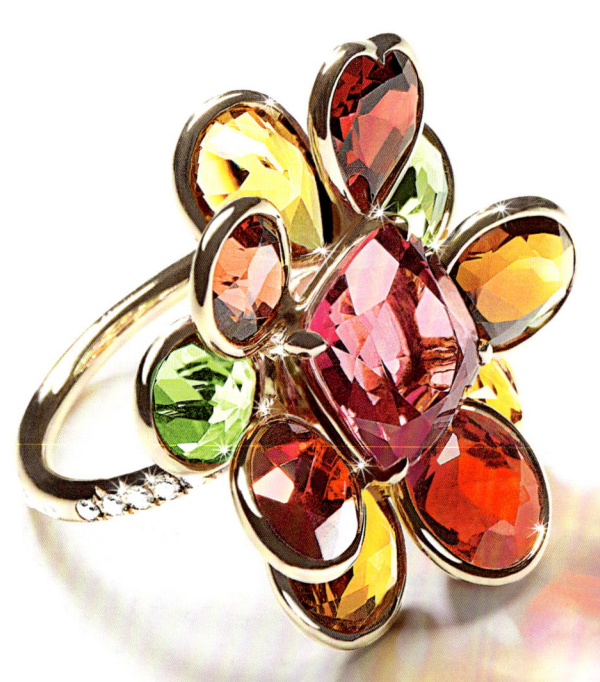

À LA FOLIE
BLOSSOM RING

A faceted heart with a loose assortment
of stones... This ring reads like a rebus meaning
"I'm madly in love with you."

VANITAS DAGUER REOTYPE

I met Lorenz Bäumer when he took over the artistic direction of Chanel jewelry. We made his first collections. He came to the profession with a novel outlook. He is very talented, and he could express his talent emphatically because he started at a time when the jewelry ecosystem was changing. We sold the family workshop in 2000 but we have stayed very close. We have some passions in common, including watchmaking. Lorenz has designed some very beautiful watches, like this one. He always does things in his own way. His ideas are very original—like how he used a daguerreotype of his own skull to illustrate the dial and the passage of time.

Jean-Pierre Brun
Jewelry maker

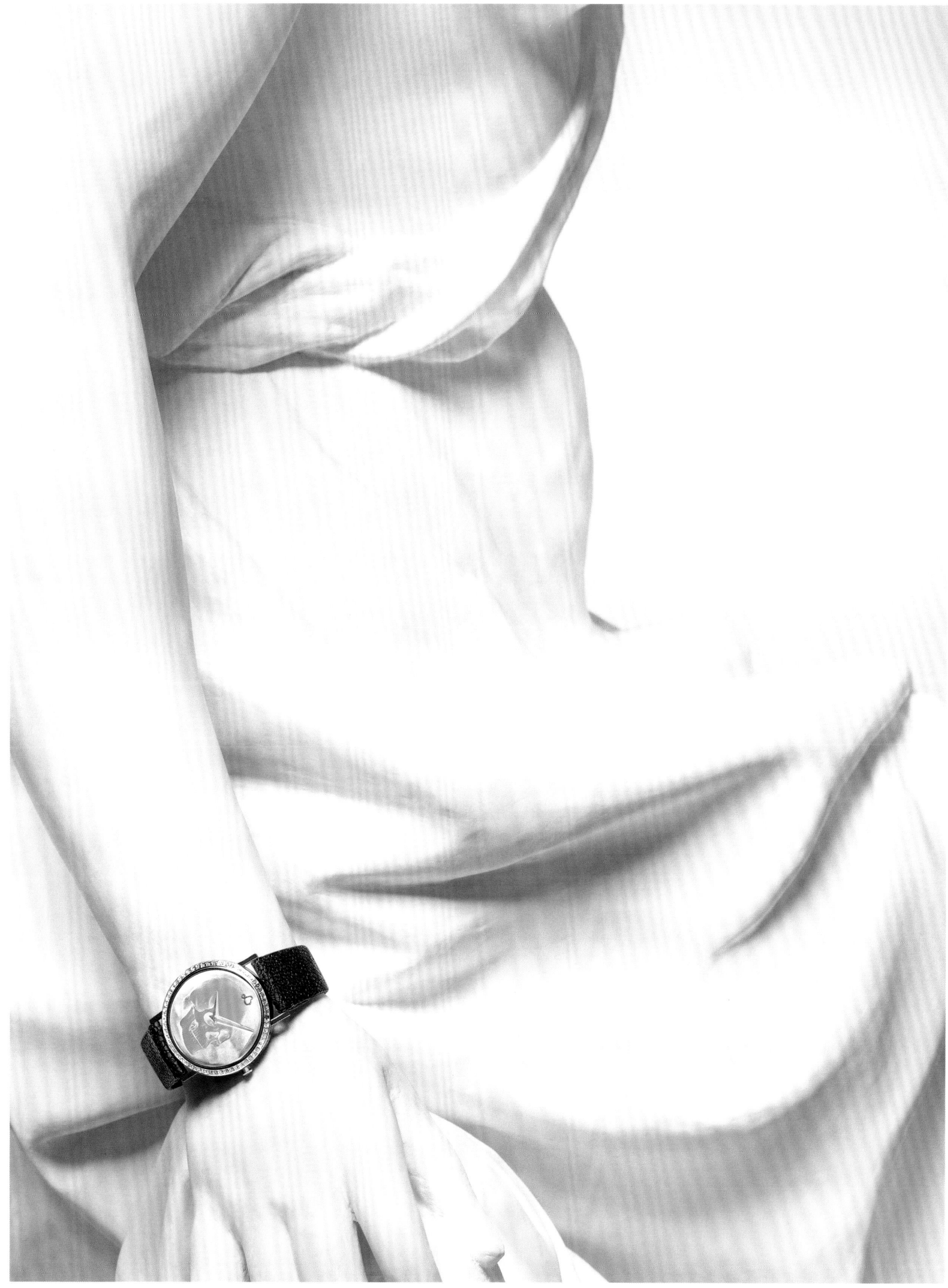

Hamadryad or *Nymph of the Woods* (1710), Antoine Coysevox (1640—1720), Paris, Louvre Museum.

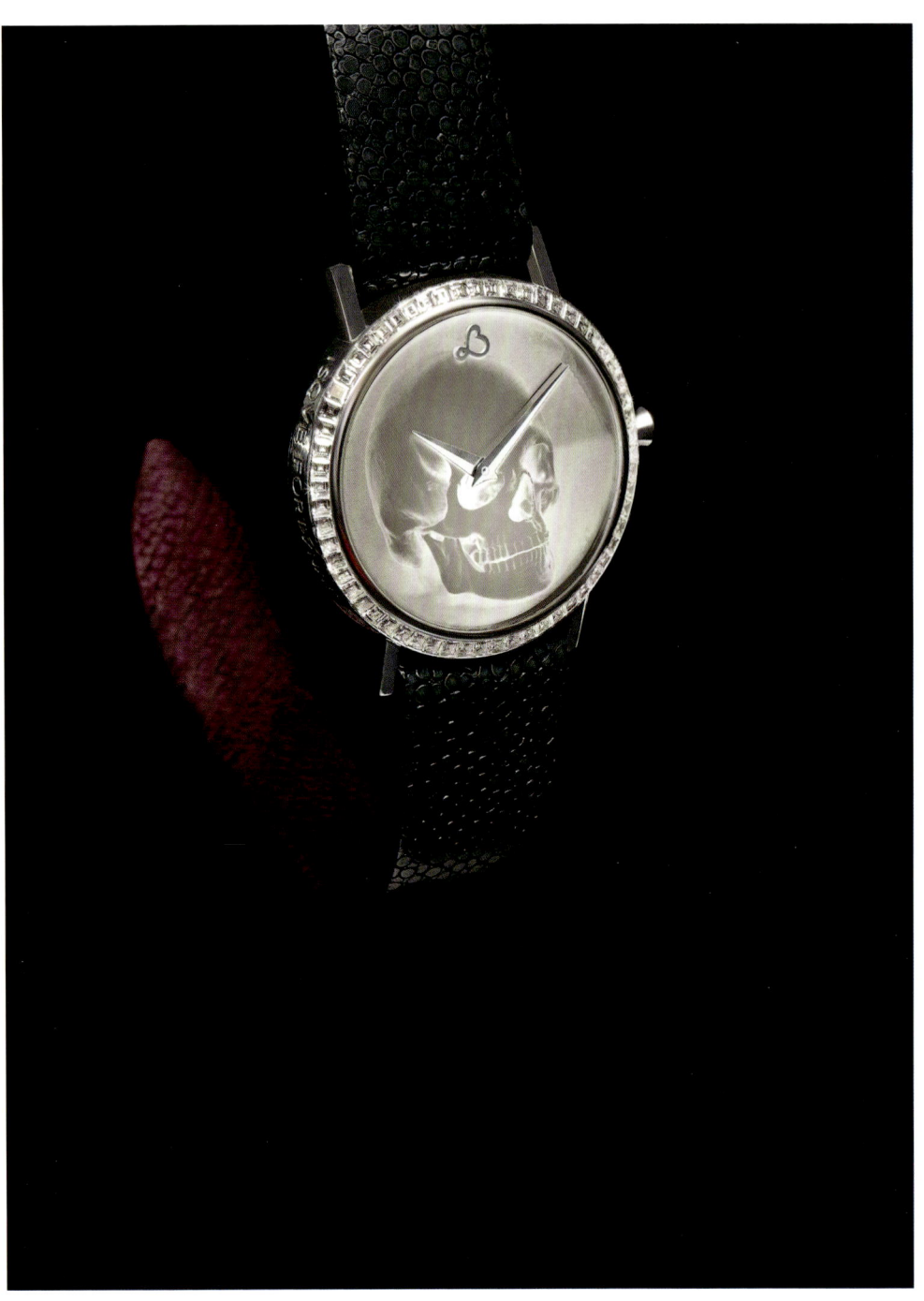

VANITAS DAGUERREOTYPE
WATCH

"Vanitas vanitatum et omnia vanitas" (vanity of vanities,
all [is] vanity). The dial of this watch features
a picture of my skull created using the daguerreotype
technique invented in 1839. I wrote my motto
on the edge: *"Chacun est l'artisan de son destin"*
(Every man is the architect of his own fortune).

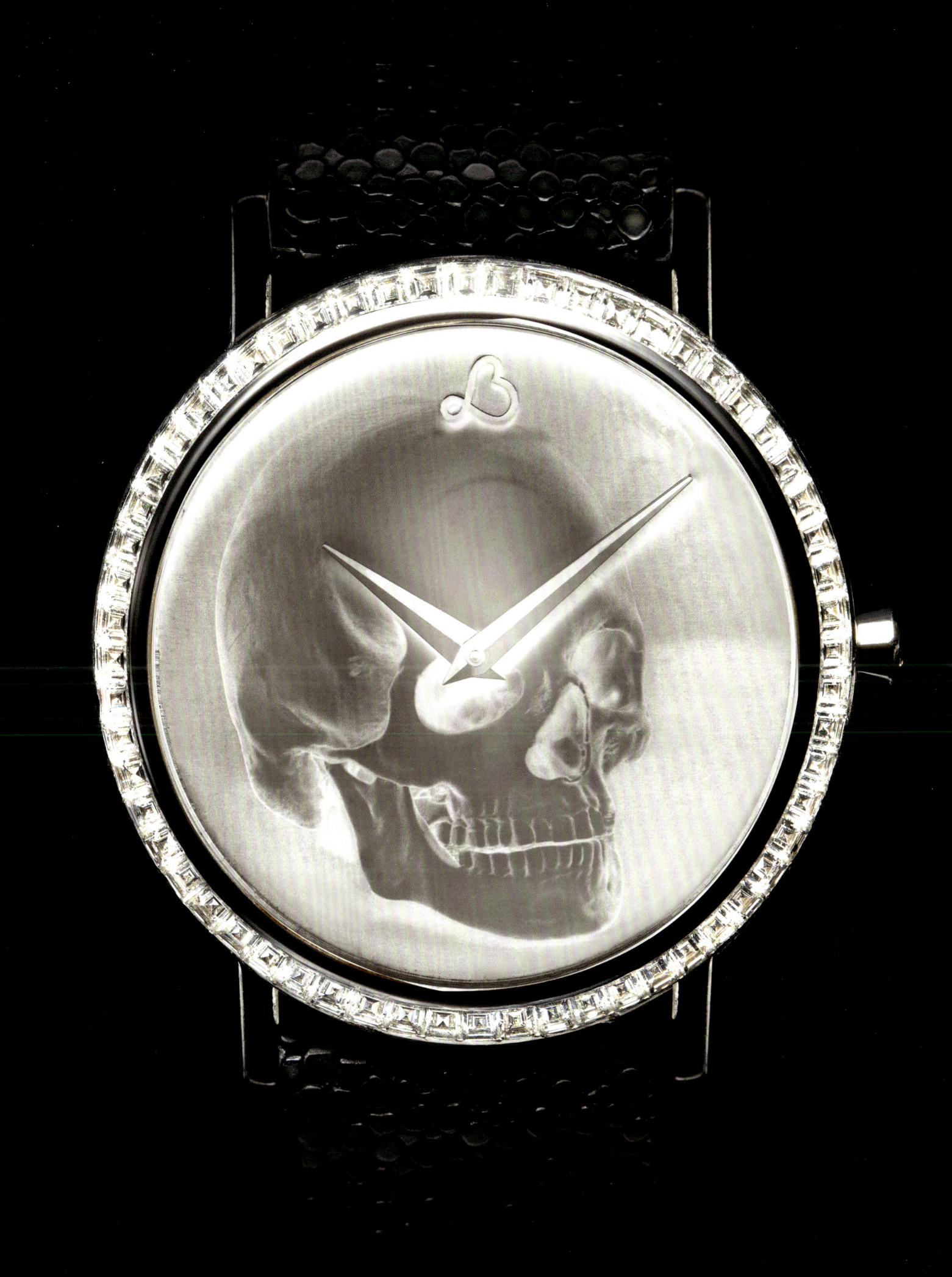

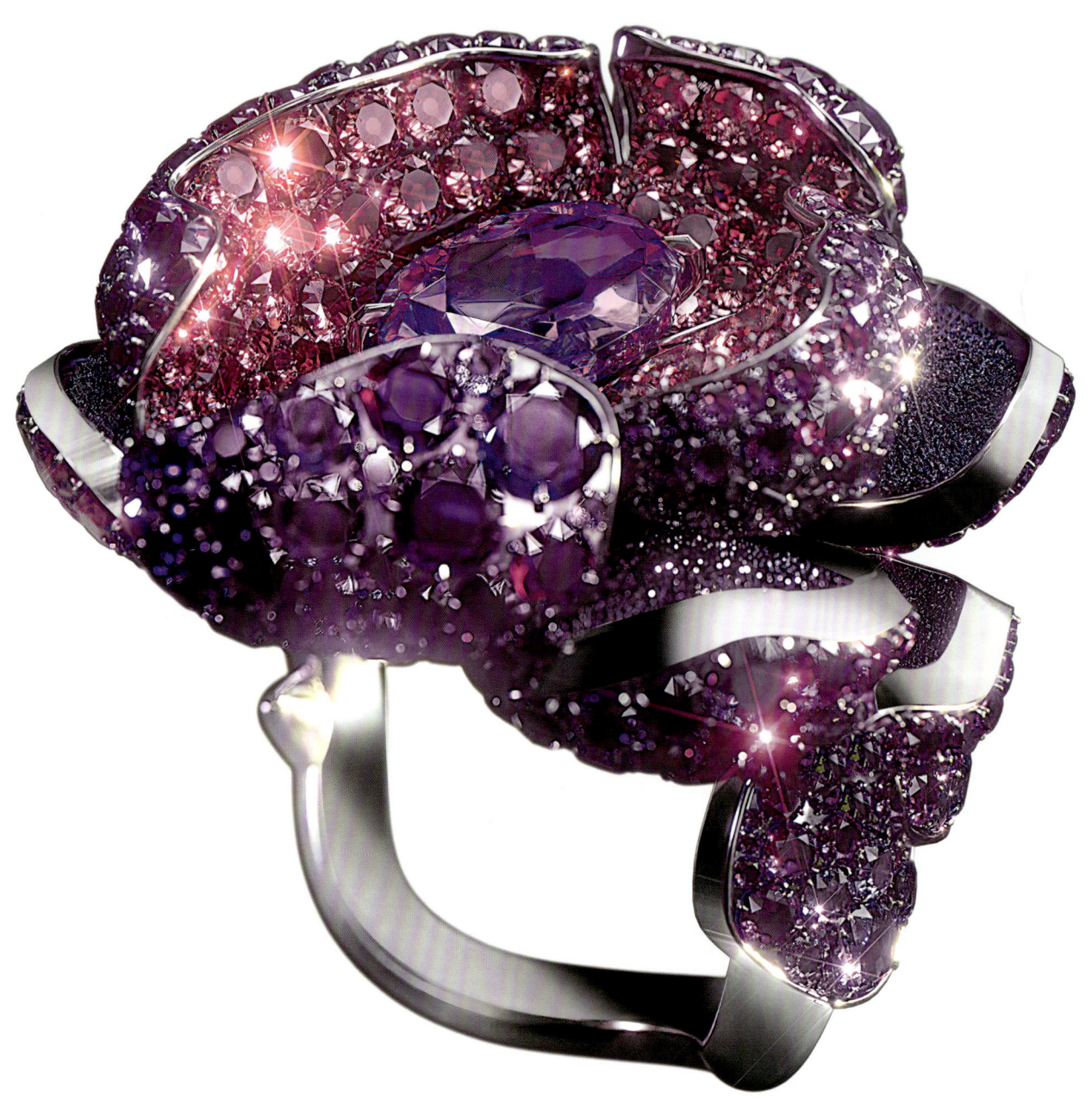

VIRTUAL IMAGE OF DAMASCUS ROSE NFT

DAMAS CUS ROSE

Of all the highly talented French jewelers, Lorenz is without a doubt the most interested in creativity and innovation where rings are concerned. His choice of an NFT continues to show this today. It was a chance to combine tradition and modernity while providing a reminder of the astonishing and ancient history of this exquisite jewelry piece. To punish Prometheus, who had given humans fire and the arts (technology) without his permission, Zeus had sworn by one of the rivers of the Underworld, the terrifying Styx—a vow that cannot be broken—that he would never free Prometheus from his rock. But one day, Heracles, in one of the twelve labors that he had to perform for the "glory of Hera," as his name dictated (*Herakleios* in Greek), came across the poor Prometheus in chains. Heracles was supposed to bring Hera three golden apples from the Garden of the Hesperides. However, they happened to be guarded by one of Prometheus's brothers, Atlas the Titan. Prometheus told Heracles how to get hold of the apples and, by way of thanks, Heracles killed the eagle that was devouring Prometheus's liver and freed him from his chains. Zeus could have been angered, but he was so proud of the feats of his son Heracles that he didn't want to disavow him. So as not to go back on his promise, the king of the gods accepted Prometheus release provided that he always wore a little fragment of his rock mounted on one of the rings from his chain, so that he would well and truly be in chains for the rest of his life! It is said that this agreement with the heavens is the origin of the ring given to a lady to ask for her hand in marriage, as a sign of eternal attachment...

Luc Ferry
Philosopher

DAMASCUS ROSE NFT RING

The Damas Rose NFT (Non-fungible token) is half real, half digital—like a bridge spanning past and future.

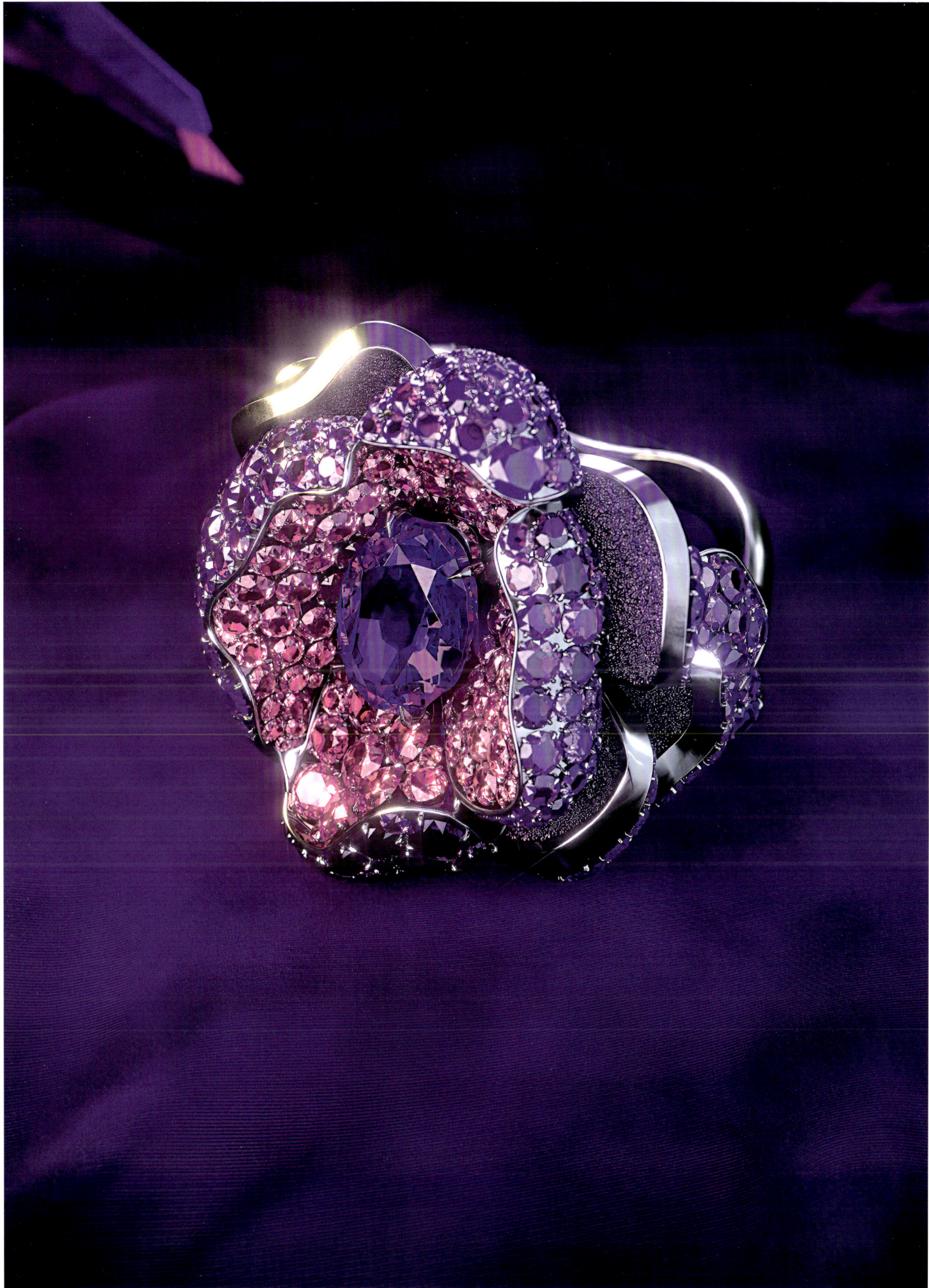

DIA
MON
DS
FO
AM

This tiara was designed to mark a very important moment in my private life. Lorenz was able to express these feelings with a great deal of sensitivity by taking inspiration from an element—water—to which I am deeply attached. Through its dissymmetric shape and the way in which the light sparkles across its many shapes of diamonds, he succeeded in recreating the lightness of a wave and its foam—its magic. I am very touched by the quality of the know-how and the extreme meticulousness that were needed to make such a piece of jewelry. It is a fabulous creation entirely worthy of a wedding, which is such an extraordinary day in a woman's life.

**H.S.H. Princess
Charlène of Monaco**

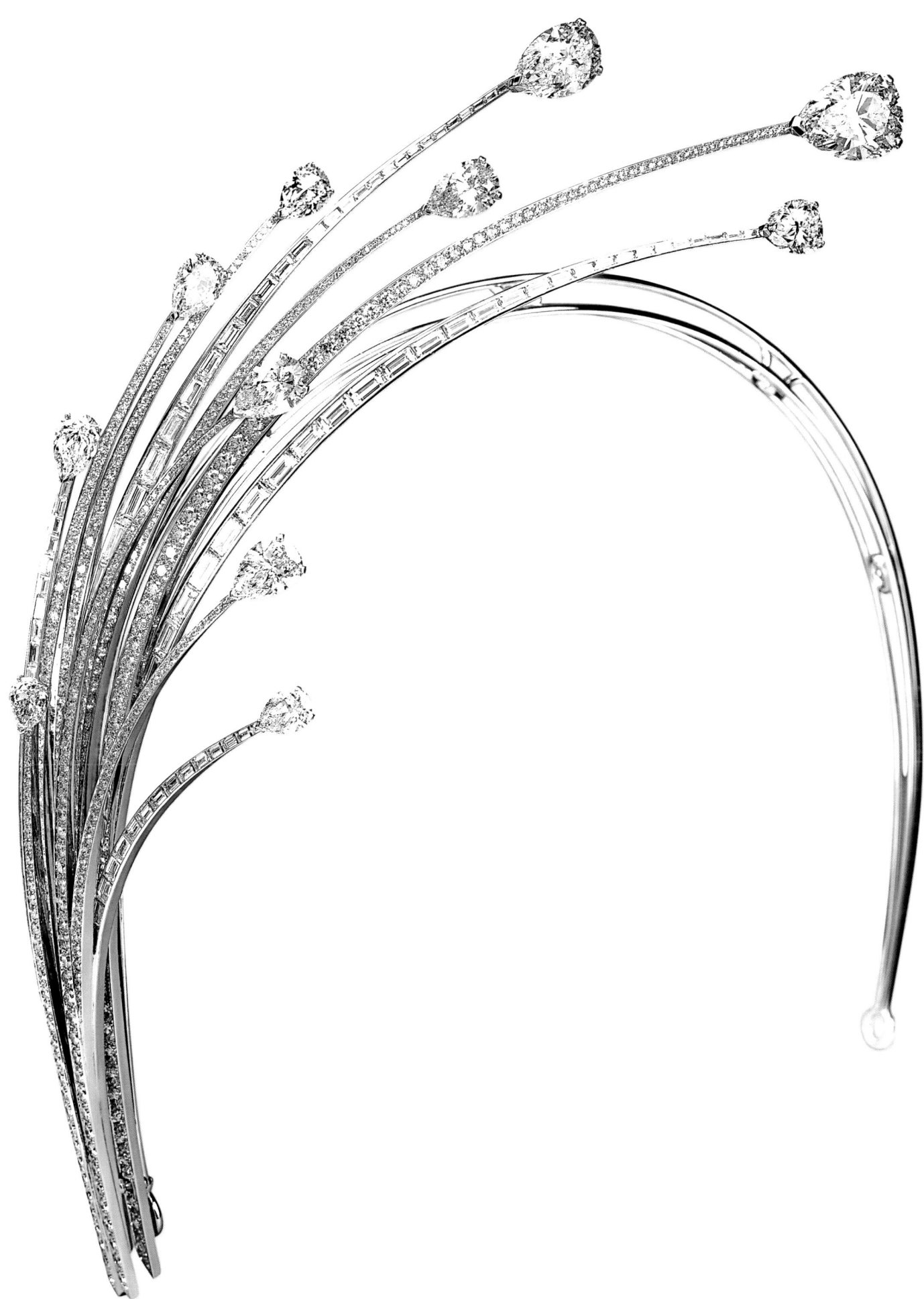

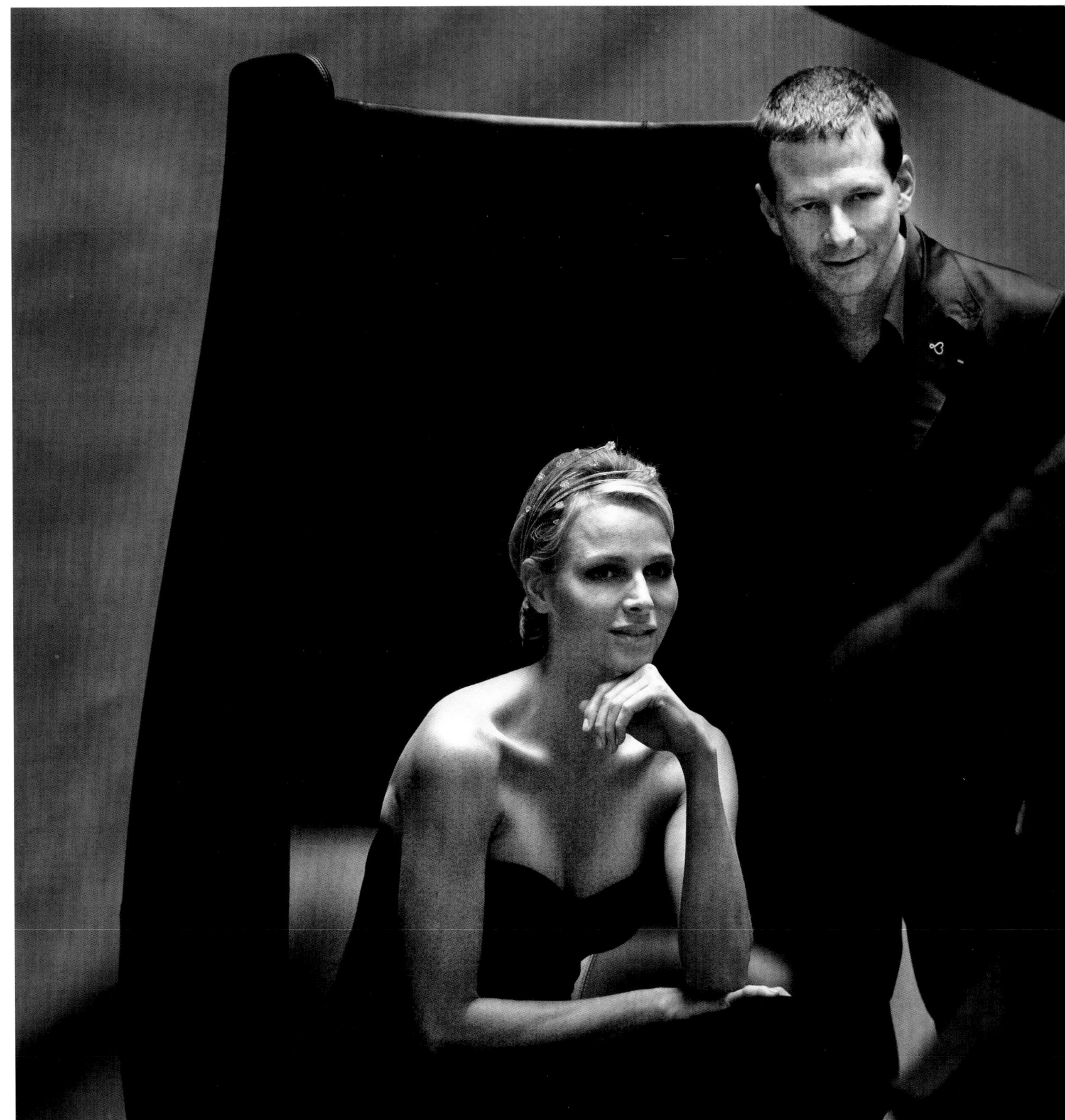

H.S.H. Princess Charlène de Monaco, Lorenz Bäumer and, from the back, Karl Lagerfeld.

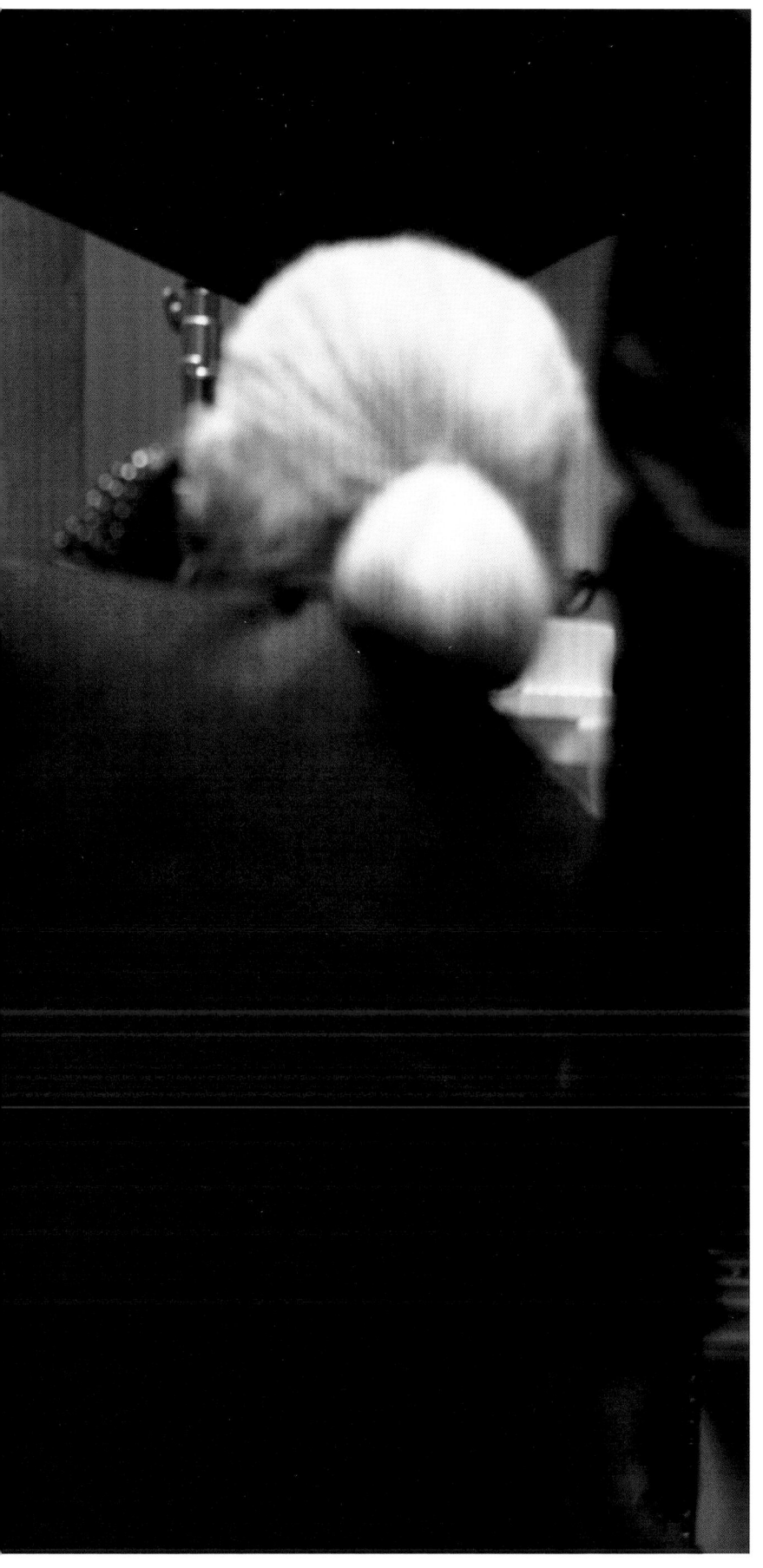

DIAMONDS FOAM TIARA

My calling came from a desire to turn every woman into a princess with my creations. This tiara is a homage to the sea and all the passions that we share with Their Serene Highnesses Prince and Princess Albert of Monaco.

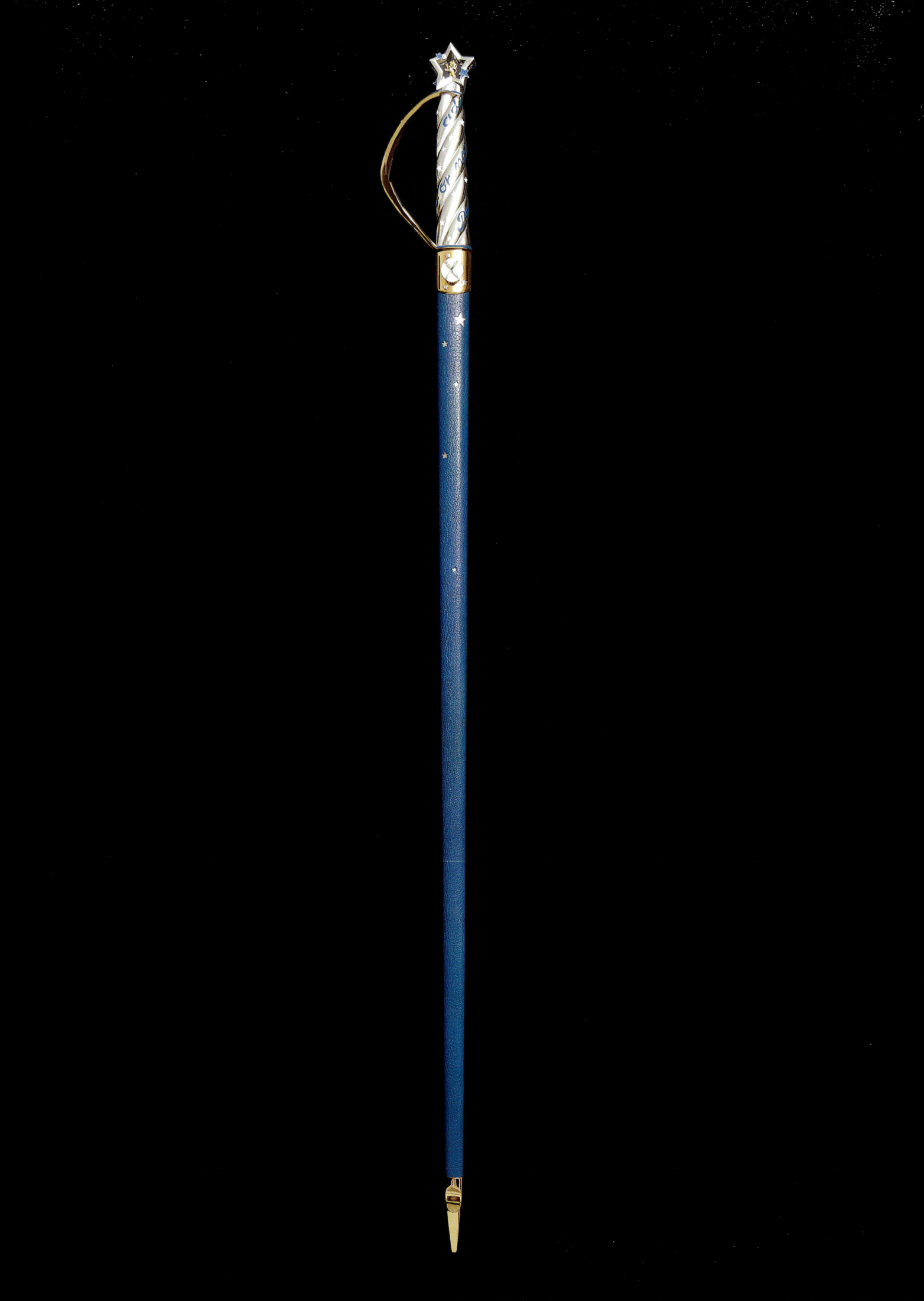

ACA
DEMI
CIAN'S
SWORD

When I commissioned my Académie Française sword from Lorenz, I hoped that the object would be more than an exercise in balance; that its refinement, airiness, and purity would be based on symbolism, the desire to decipher a being, so that a narrative could be expressed through a perfect object. I thought that Lorenz would be ideal for this as his jewelry pieces are both aesthetic and narrative. That is what has always struck me about his work. So the two of us set about a kind of self-inquiry to create this sword, with which I am delighted and will keep for the rest of my life. This object marked my admission to the council and will tell something of my story to my descendants.

Xavier Darcos
Member of the Académie Française
and Chancellor of the Institut de France

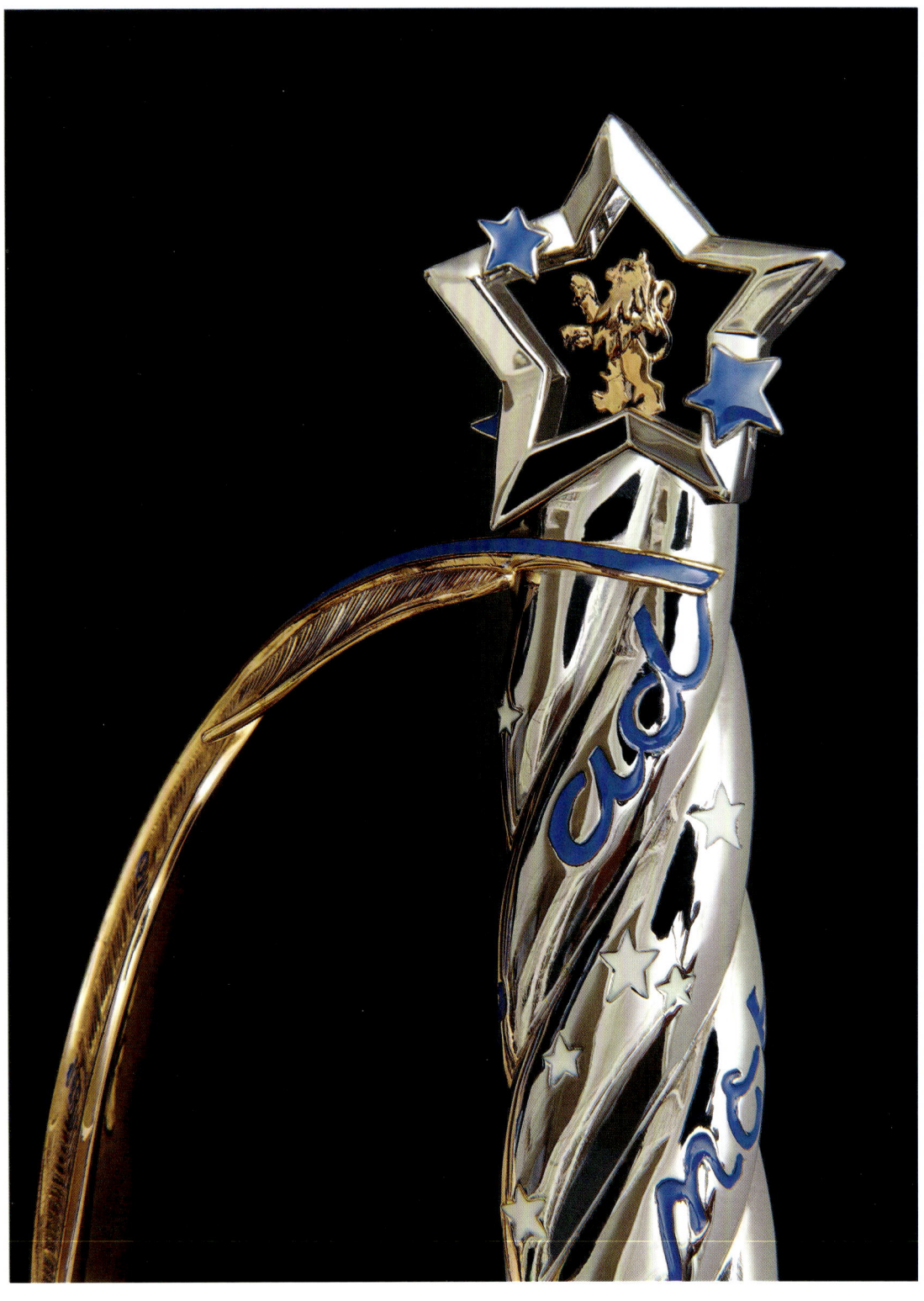

ACADEMICIAN'S SWORD

The Académie Française sword tells of the brilliance of the great minds known as "immortals." This creation crystallizes their genius and careers.

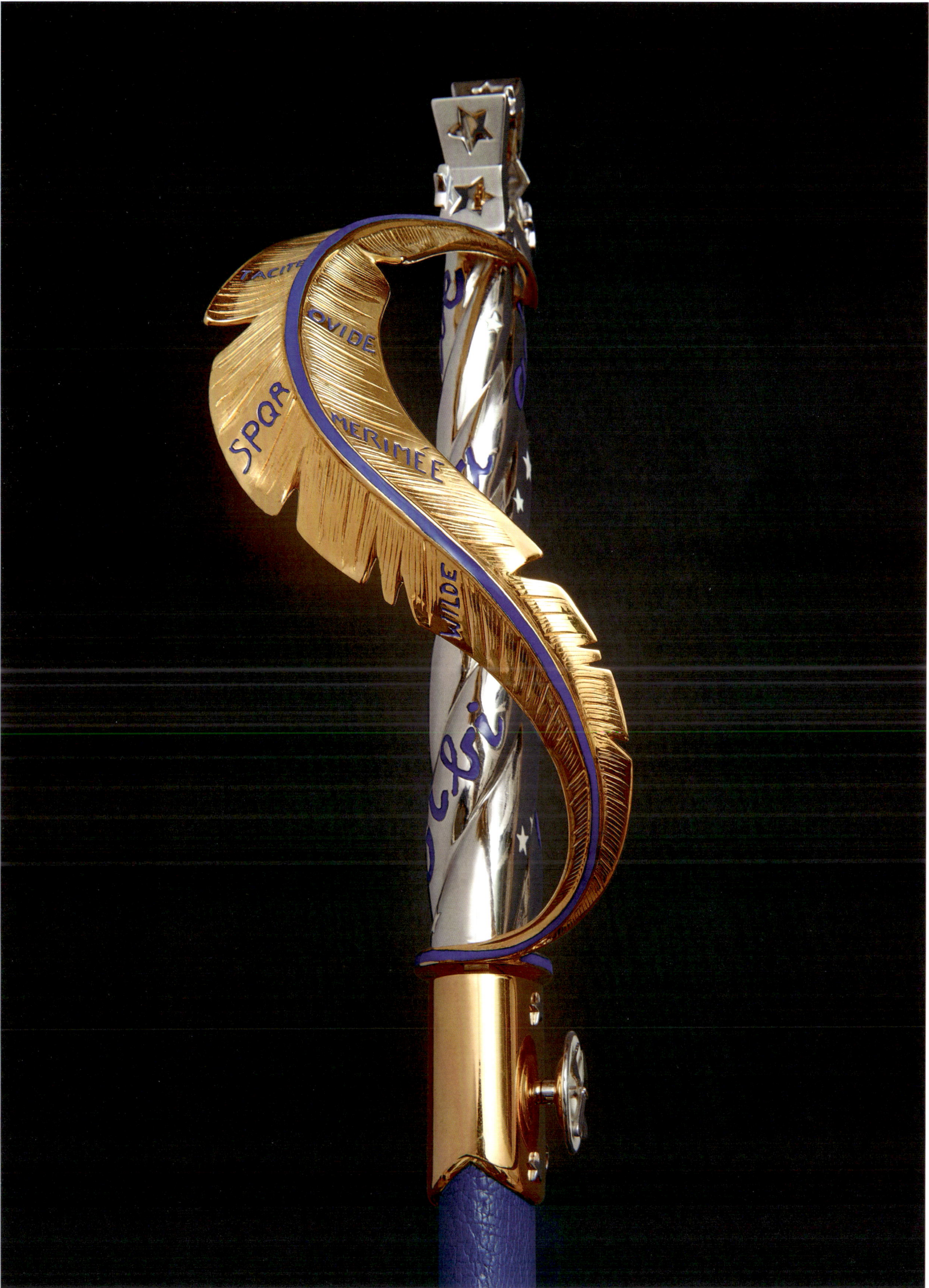

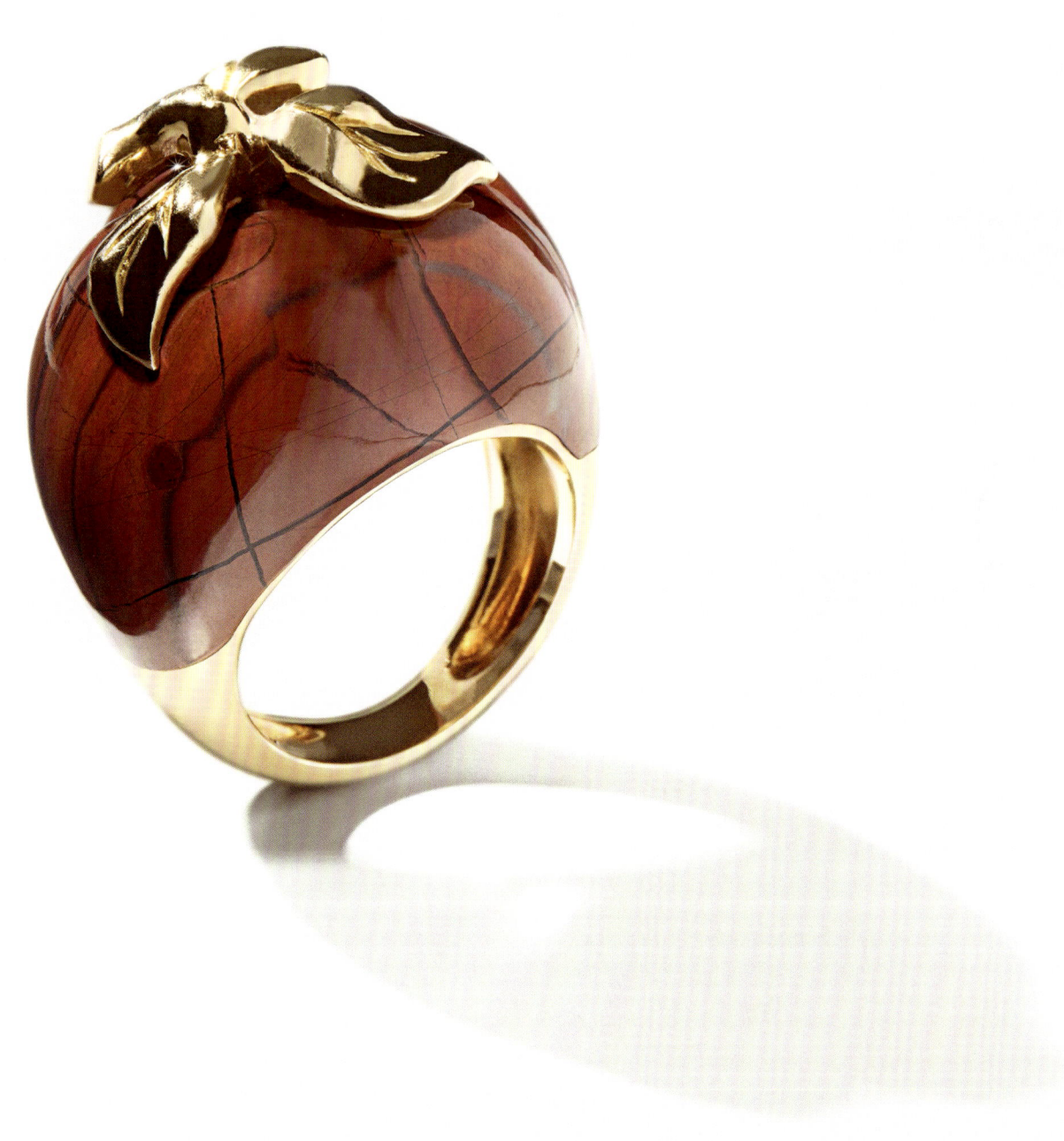

GOUR
MAN
DISE

I met Lorenz when he was shooting a series of short films presenting areas of know-how he admired. He had come to film me at the Ritz and I found his project interesting. Since then, Lorenz and I have been friends. Both of us are fueled by our passions. We dedicate our lives to them in order to give people pleasure. Whereas my creations are short-lived, Lorenz aspires to a kind of eternity with his jewelry. But the end goal is the same. Both of us seek to generate emotions and stories through the memory of a shared moment or by passing on an object. That childlike delight, that appetite for magic, is expressed in shapes and colors, such as in this magnificent *Gourmandise* ring that I could almost bite into!

François Perret
Best Restaurant Pastry Chef
in the World 2019 and
Pastry Chef at the Ritz Paris

SURF
ER

I discovered Lorenz's work on a friend's finger. She was wearing a magnificent ring that I just loved. Since then, I have become his most loyal client and we've enjoyed over thirty years of enriching friendship built on mutual respect and admiration. I am his most enthusiastic supporter. He is a creative genius and a very sensitive man. Nowadays, there are very few people who have his level of involvement in the jewelry they design for others. He understands his clients' tastes, passions, and emotions precisely and he has the ability to dream up unique pieces for them. These frames, which he made for my children to reflect their passions, perfectly illustrate what I mean. They are some of my favorite creations by Lorenz. The one horseback riding one was for my daughter. The pirate was for one of my sons, and the rock star for my other son. They are true works of art. For my mother's eightieth birthday, he also designed a necklace made up of little "link-objects" illustrating how her twelve grandchildren think of her. Lorenz doesn't only make jewelry; his work makes people happy.

Sloan Barnett
Collector

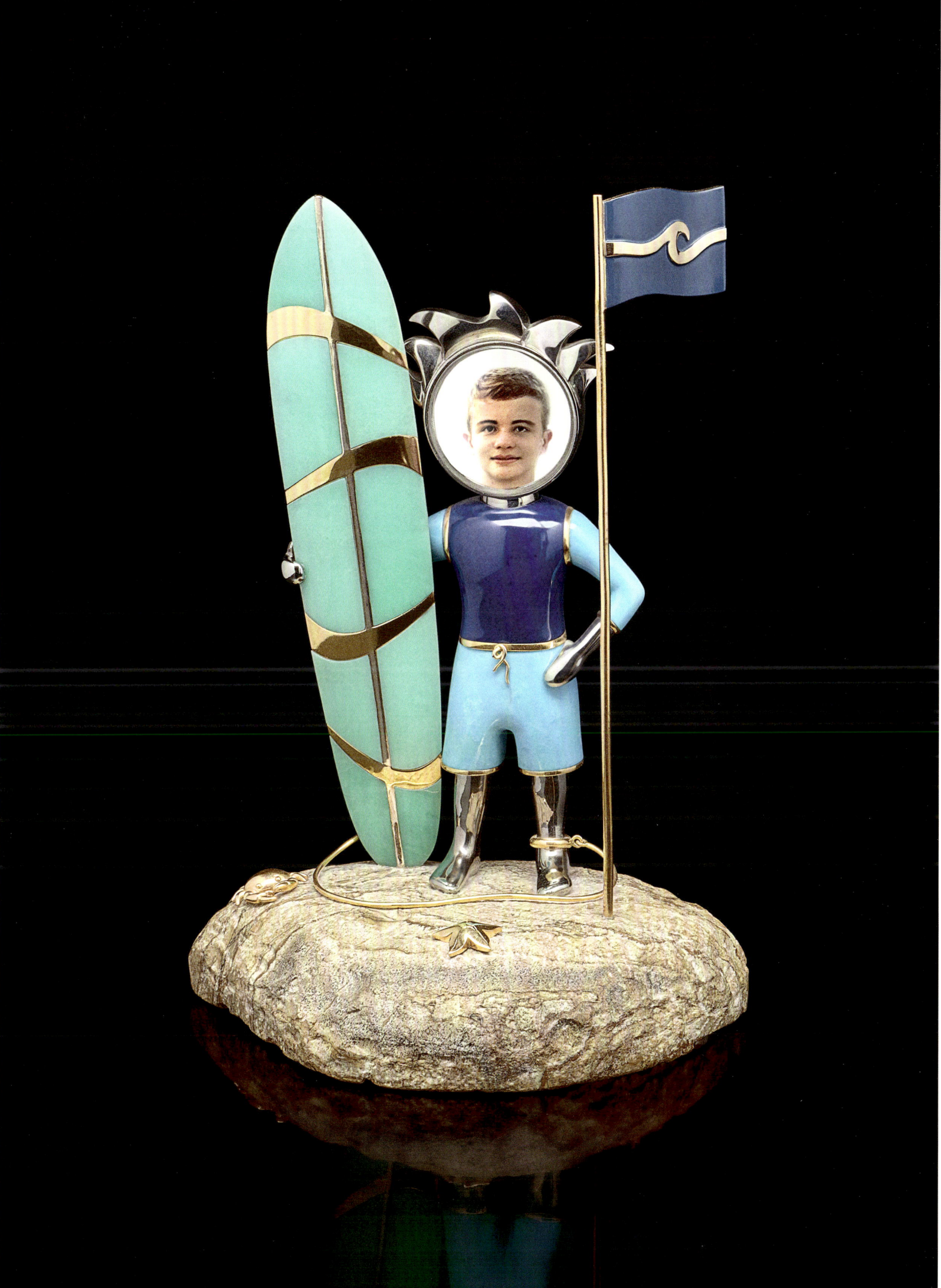

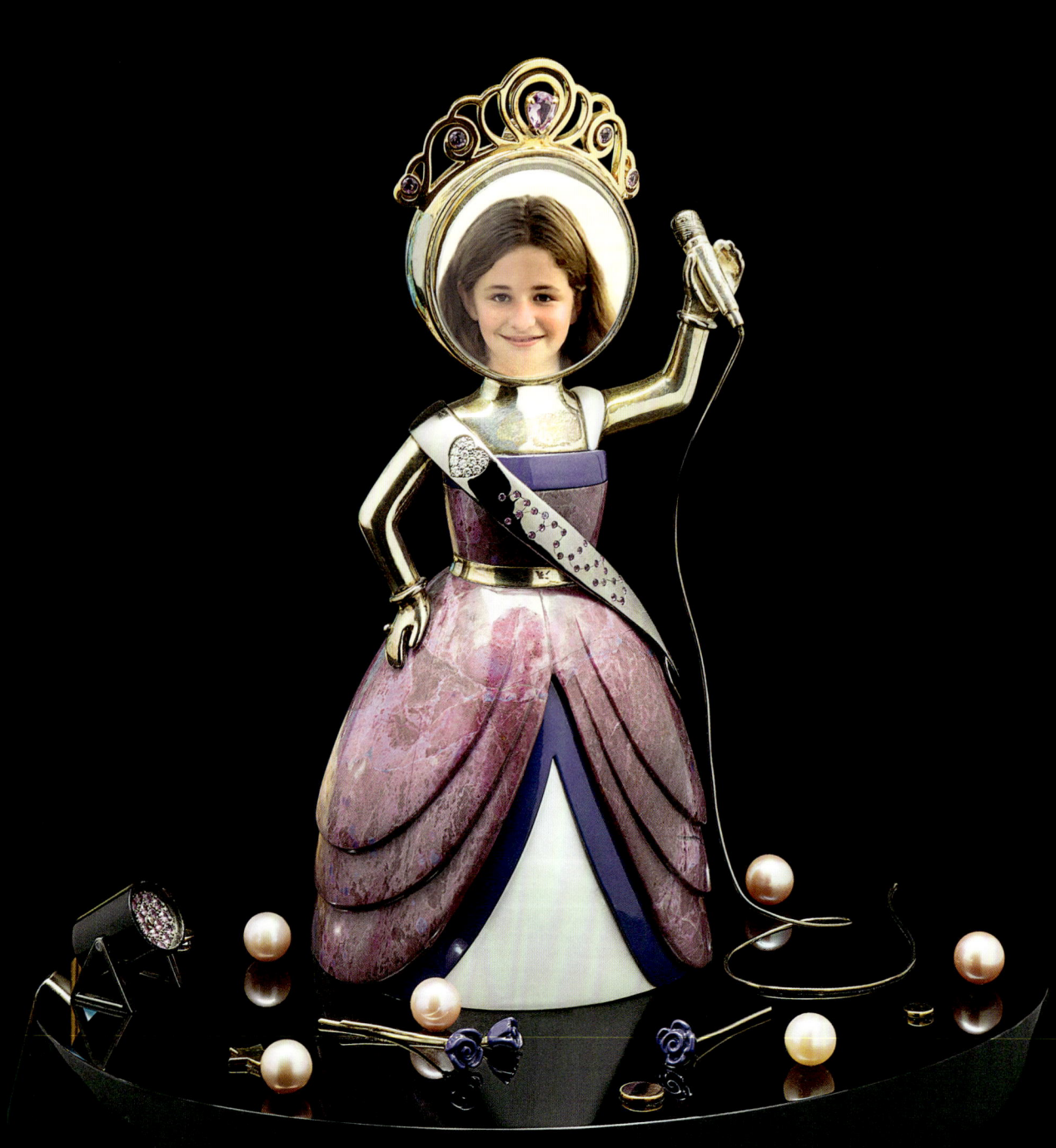

PRIN
CESS

SURFER
AND PRINCESS
FRAMES

The surfer and princess frames show
the ever-changing faces of our children
and their favorite costumes. They allow us
to hold on to the passing of time just a little...

TREE
OF
LIFE

Lorenz and his brother were wonderful children and I'm very proud of the people they have become, each in their own way. Lorenz's creative orientation initially came as a surprise to me as he had shone at École Centrale Paris at the age of 22. I'd noticed he had a gift for drawing—I remember, for instance, seeing him sketch a fountain in Rome—and he loved to paint porcelain with me. But when he left École Centrale Paris, even though he had worked so hard to get there, he made his decision. He went out and bought some little tools and spent all summer making me a very pretty ring with a white opal stone. I had some reservations about his choice because Lorenz had the leadership and organizational skills to have a great career as an engineer, but he reassured me by giving himself two years to succeed. And if it didn't work out, he would resume his studies. He started by making some beautiful novelty jewelry pieces—little animals, floral motifs, and trees like this one. A tree of life that has as many leaves as there are members of our family. My friends and I, who didn't have the means to treat ourselves to fine jewelry, simply adored them. Since then, he has continued to follow his dreams and it makes me very happy. He has managed to maintain his independence and his consideration and generosity towards others.

Marie-José Bäumer
Muse

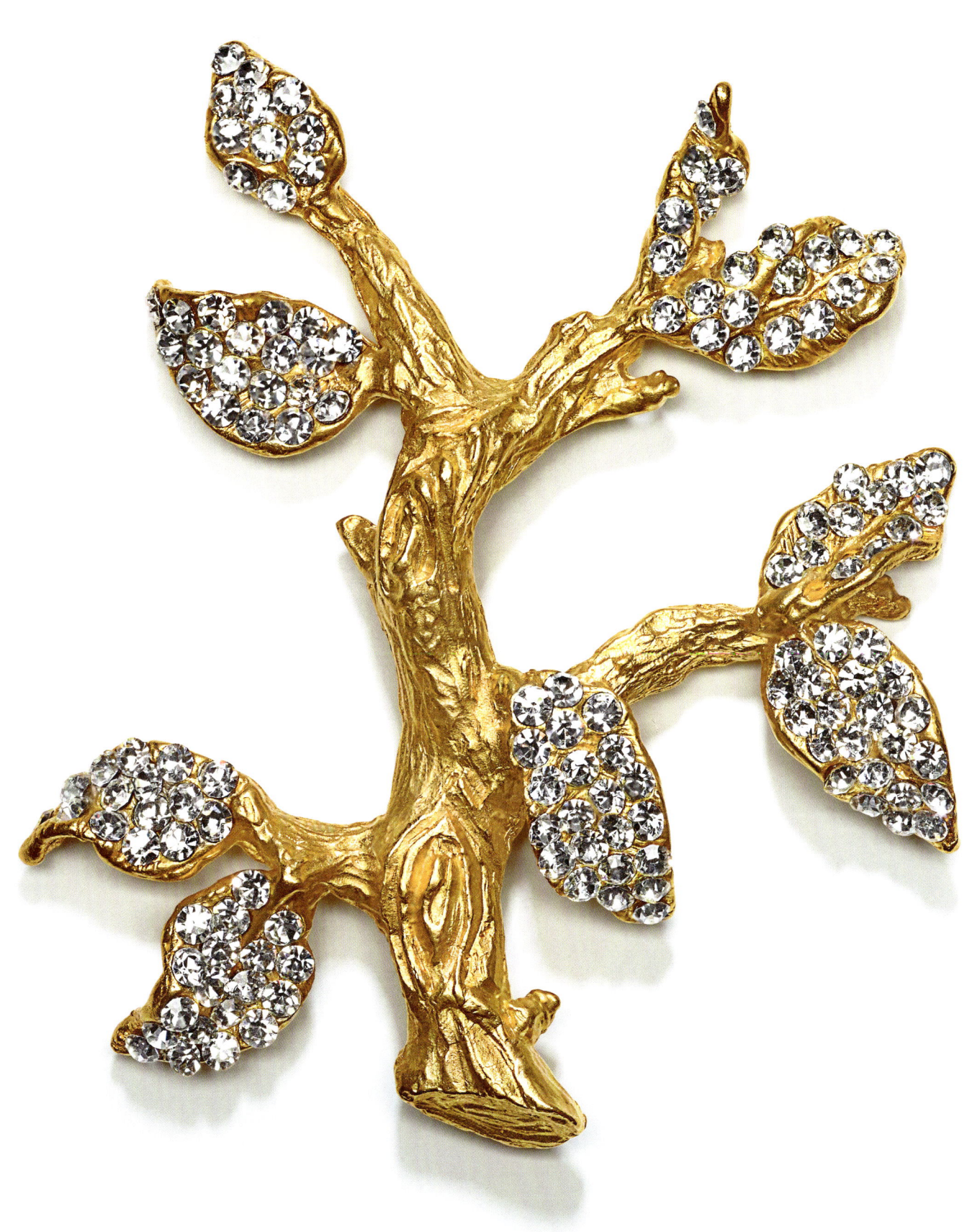

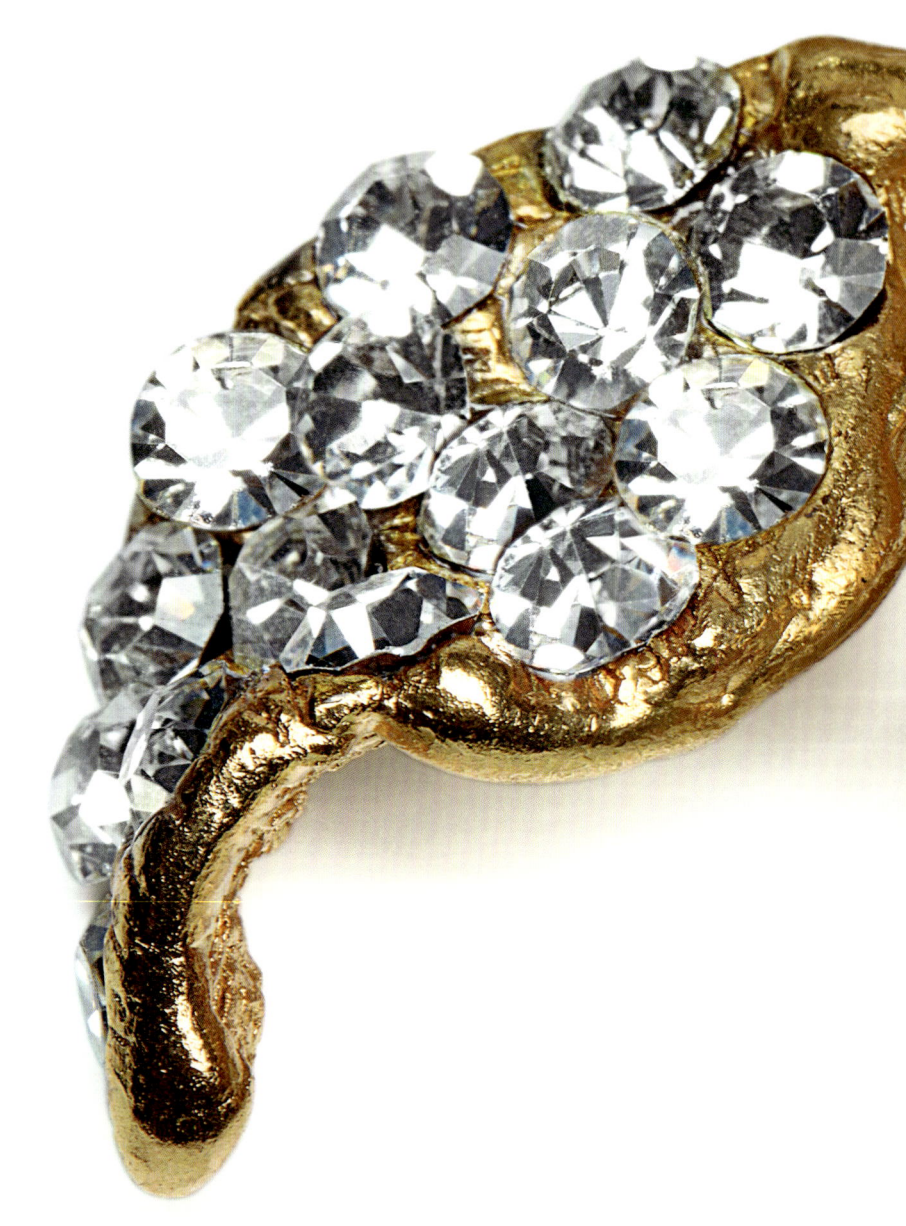

TREE OF LIFE
COSTUME
JEWELRY BROOCH

One of my first designs was a costume
jewelry piece. It symbolizes both family
and the tree that we grow to bring
all the future creations into fruition.

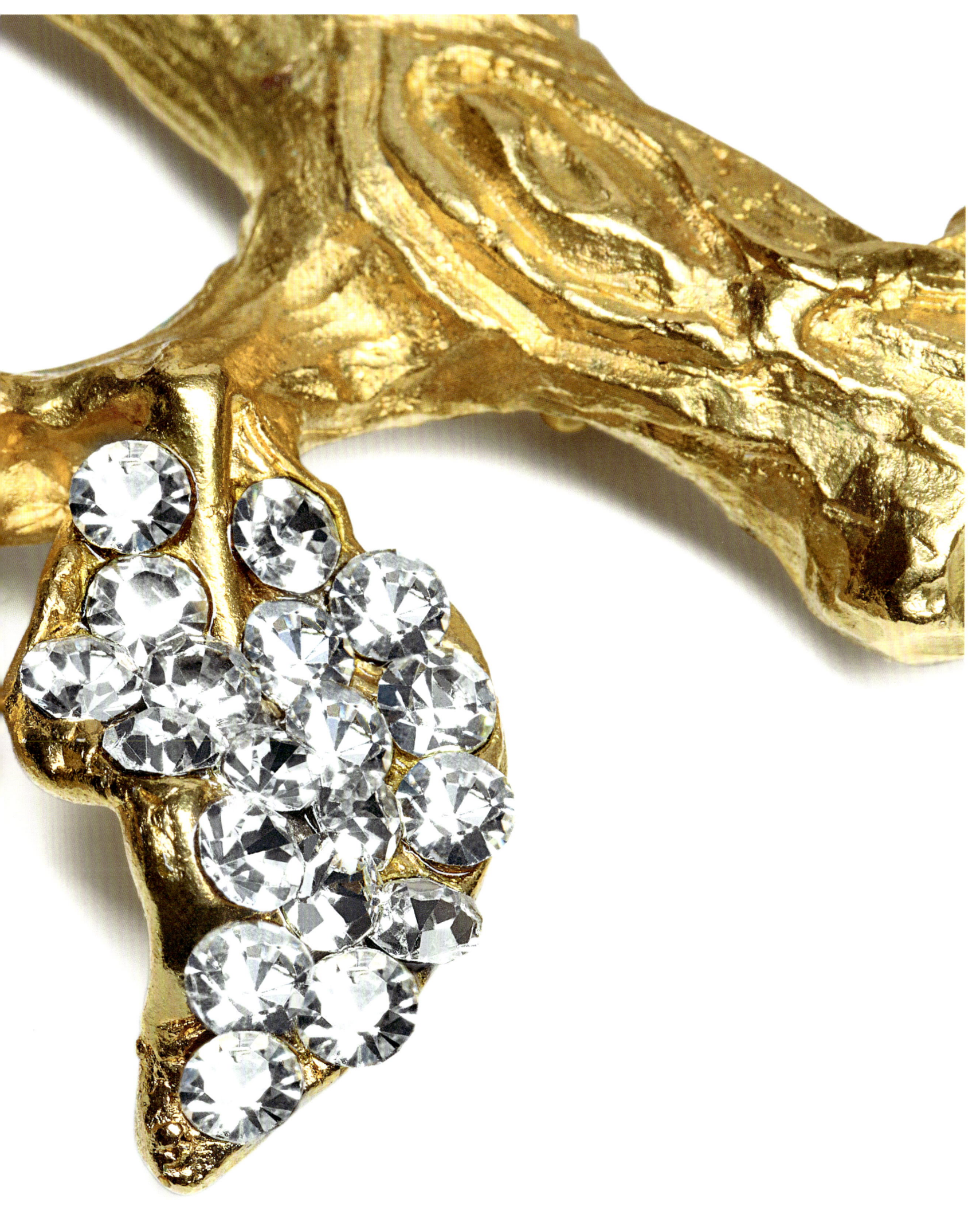

BÄUMER
DESIGN

For Lorenz Bäumer, designing objects is a natural extension of his high jewelry work. For thirty years, he has been called on by the greatest houses (Chanel, Louis Vuitton, Guerlain, Cartier, and Hennessy) to lend his quirky and irreverent perspective to their collections and to design objects that are full of surprises. In each project, Lorenz Bäumer tries to push the boundaries of what is possible, to create a space that is conducive to dialog with the incomparably skilled artisans. It is this pursuit of taking things further that yields unique creations that are as remarkable in the excellence of their execution as in the emotions that they arouse.

LOUIS VUITTON

SOUL OF THE JOURNEY

Yves Carcelle and I met Lorenz when we asked him to design jewelry for Louis Vuitton. He is a unique designer who has that rare ability to be amused by constraints and to elevate them. He can determine the basic structure of a collection very quickly, which then allows him to give free rein to his ingenuity. For Louis Vuitton, his first instincts were the right ones. He managed to translate the House's world into jewelry using elements of ironwork, canvas motifs, and groundbreaking techniques such as laser cutting, and diamonds cut into the shape of the flower monograms from the Louis Vuitton canvas. Some of these jewelry pieces were to become iconic. Lorenz is an inventor in the noblest sense of the word: he links the great tradition of art to our times. This necklace from the *Âme du voyage* collection, inspired by a twirling flamenco dress, demonstrates this perfectly.

Pietro Beccari
CEO of Louis Vuitton

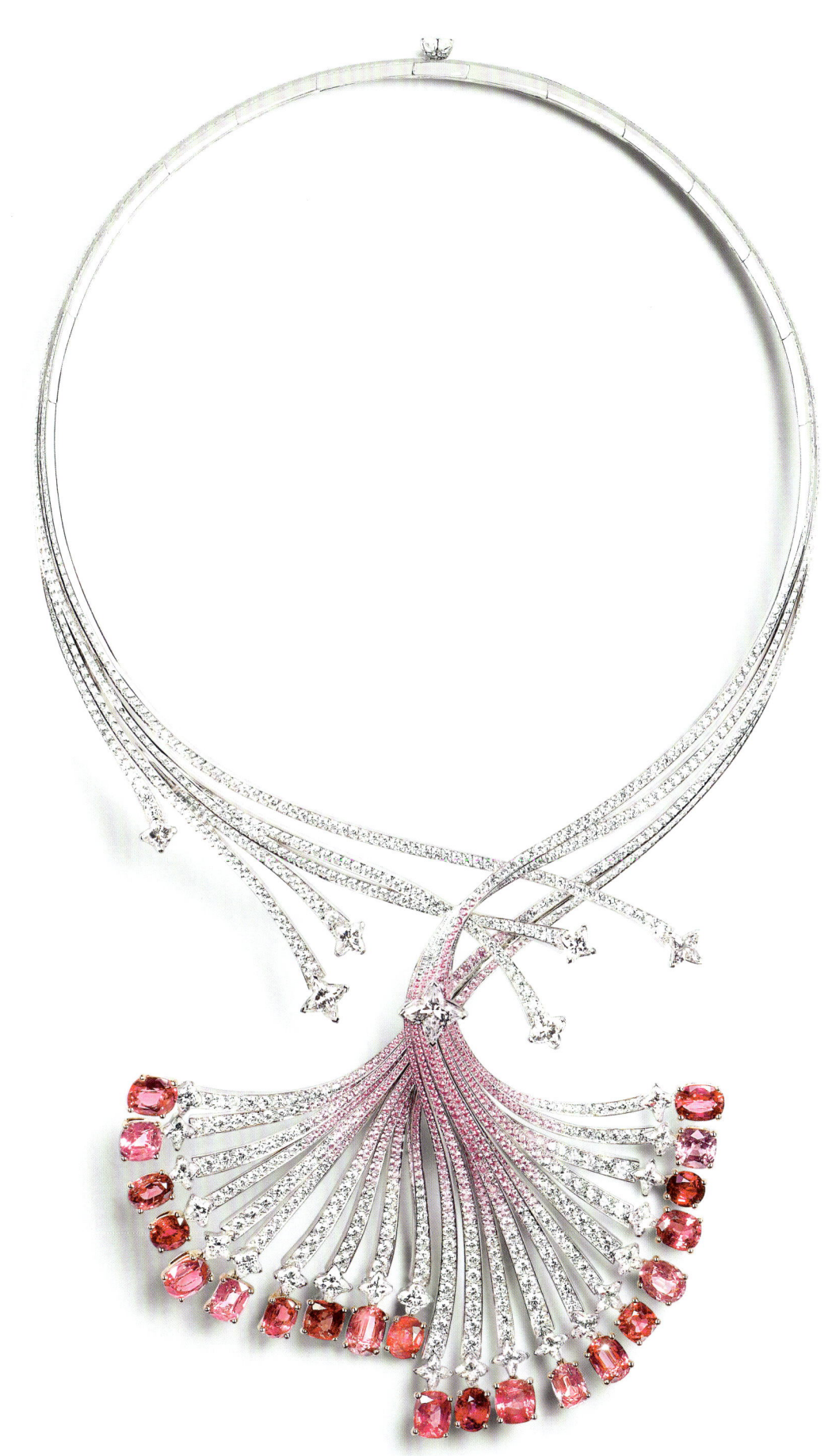

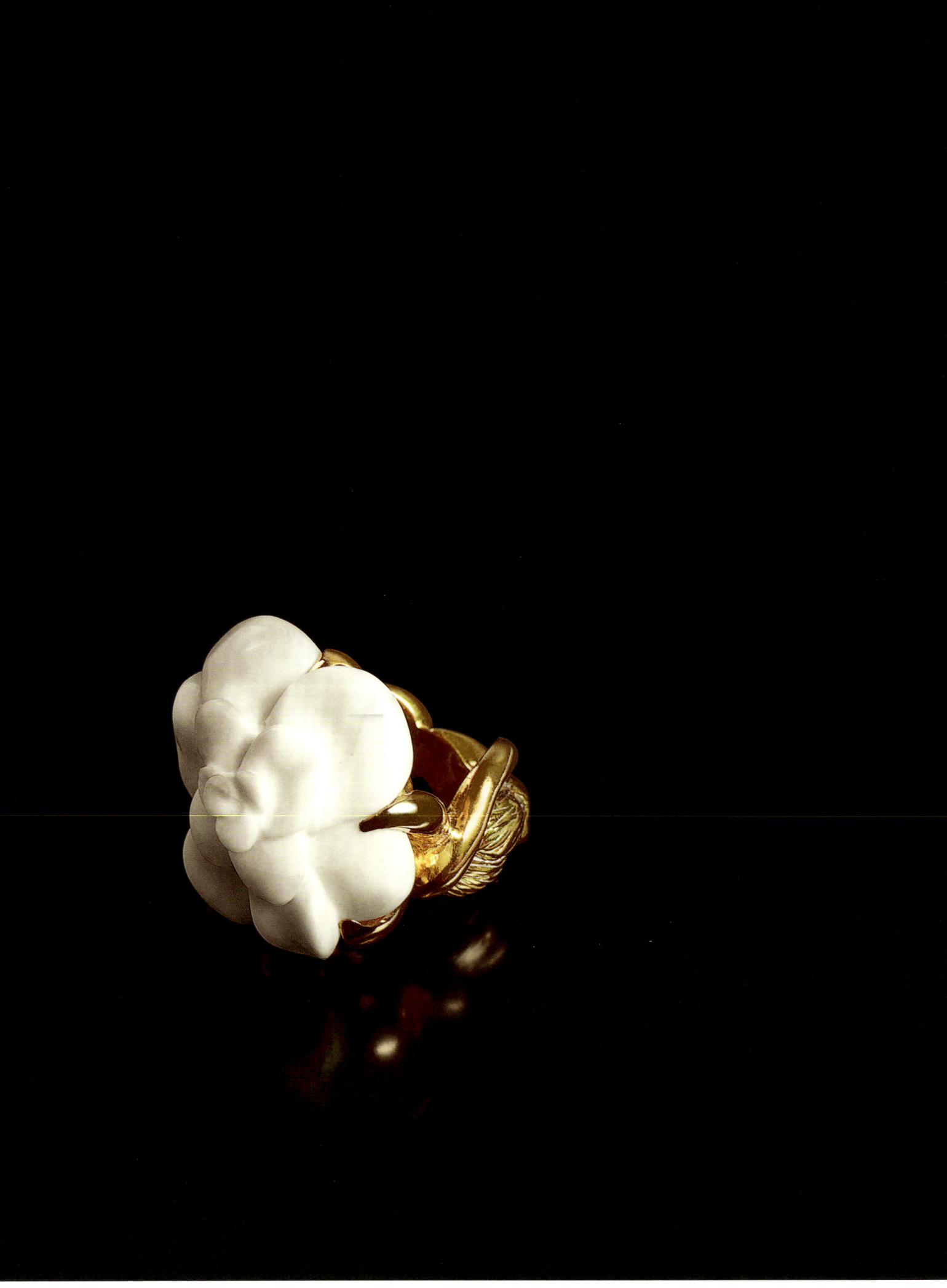

CHANEL

CA ME LIA

I met Lorenz at Nihiwatu on the island of Sumba, Indonesia, where we both go to surf. We immediately hit it off. Being able to talk to another creative in a place that far removed from our daily lives was a pleasant surprise. Lorenz's world is completely different from mine, but we both like to explore the world beyond our disciplines. I really admire Lorenz's ability to improve certain techniques to create new forms and push the limits of certain materials. I always find it fascinating to discover a new form of know-how. I love understanding how others work in fields that are far removed from mine. In Lorenz's work, there is a very palpable desire to always innovate, and this can be seen in the *Camellia* ring he designed for Chanel. The visual effect is very interesting because Lorenz pares the form right back using the monochrome white, all while keeping the subtlety of the natural design. This is then joined, by means of delicate silver lines, by a subtle revelation of the flower's structure in jewelry form, its poetic mechanism.

Yves Béhar
Designer

GUERLAIN

BEE BO TTLE

When I met Lorenz, it was friendship at first sight. I was immediately captivated by his personality, his work, and his world. From a professional standpoint, his ability to simultaneously use both parts of the brain—the generally rational left side and the creative right side open to poetry and imagination—continues to impress me. It is a very rare quality without which some products, such as Guerlain's *Bee* bottle, could have never been developed or produced. Lorenz has the capacity to enchant people with the beauty of his creations and to push artisans to find all the technical solutions needed to make a piece. He involves people, from the very first sketch to the workbench. The same goes for his jewelry. Lorenz is a maker of dreams.

Laurent Boillot
CEO of Guerlain

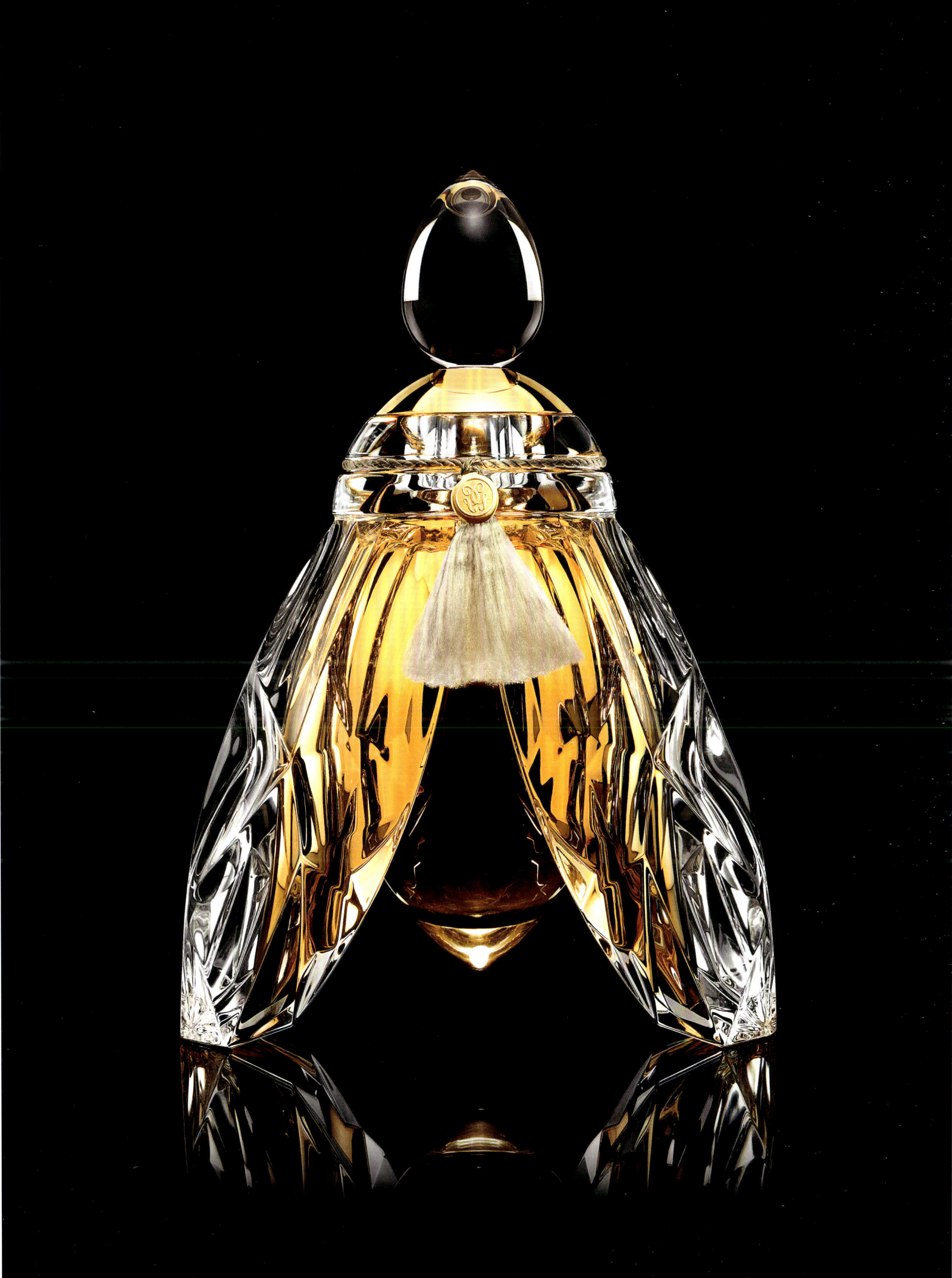

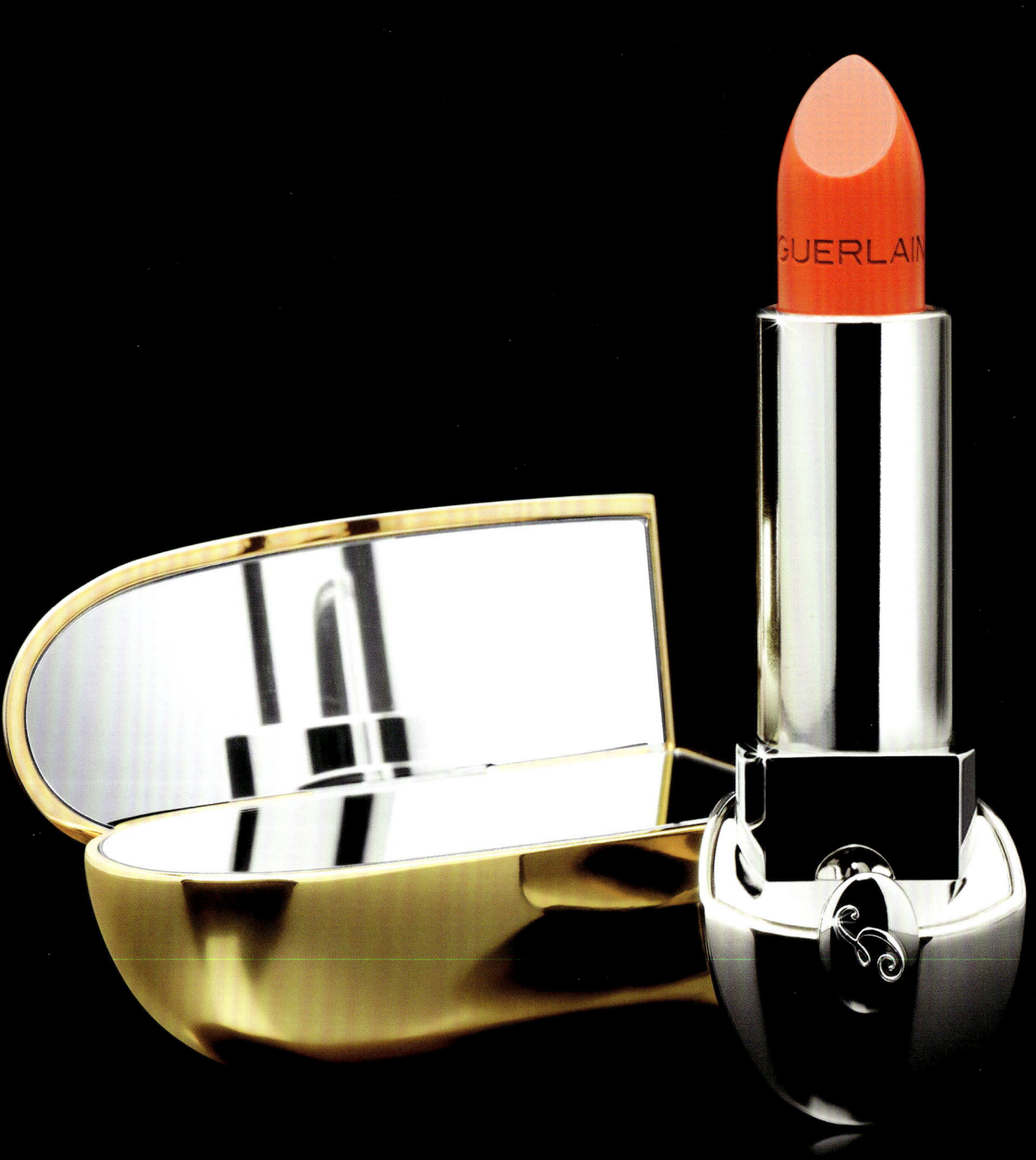

GUERLAIN

ROU GE G

I met Lorenz through an American friend, Josie Natori. I was immediately captivated by the uniqueness of his work, which combines the technical precision of his engineer's eye with his openness to culture. So I suggested we work together to design an object that all perfumers have dreamed of inventing, but never successfully: a combined lipstick and mirror! Lorenz designed the Rouge G, an object that is entirely in keeping with Guerlain's style, with its timeless modernity and wit. The proof is that it immediately became a classic and has aged very well. I believe this object conveys quite an accurate idea of Lorenz's creative genius. He is very inquisitive. He has the ability to look elsewhere to invent completely new things without sacrificing any of the elegance or appeal of his style.

Olivier Echaudemaison
Creative director of Guerlain makeup

HENNESSY
NBA

PARA
DISE
DECANTER

I met Lorenz when he designed this magnificent crystal basketball to celebrate our partnership with the National Basketball Association (NBA). I felt as if I'd known him for twenty years! He is an approachable and generous person. He is conscientious but doesn't take himself seriously. And there is a playful dimension to this contemporary design that I love. It is a beautiful and innovative object that was technically challenging to produce. Baccarat's invaluable expertise helped him push the boundaries in terms of its manufacture without the slightest sacrifice in aesthetics. It expresses a new kind of luxury that combines the useful with the beautiful while completely respecting the product. It is the perfect complement to this wonderful Cognac, which was blended by my great-uncle in 1979.

Renaud Fillioux de Gironde
Master blender at Hennessy

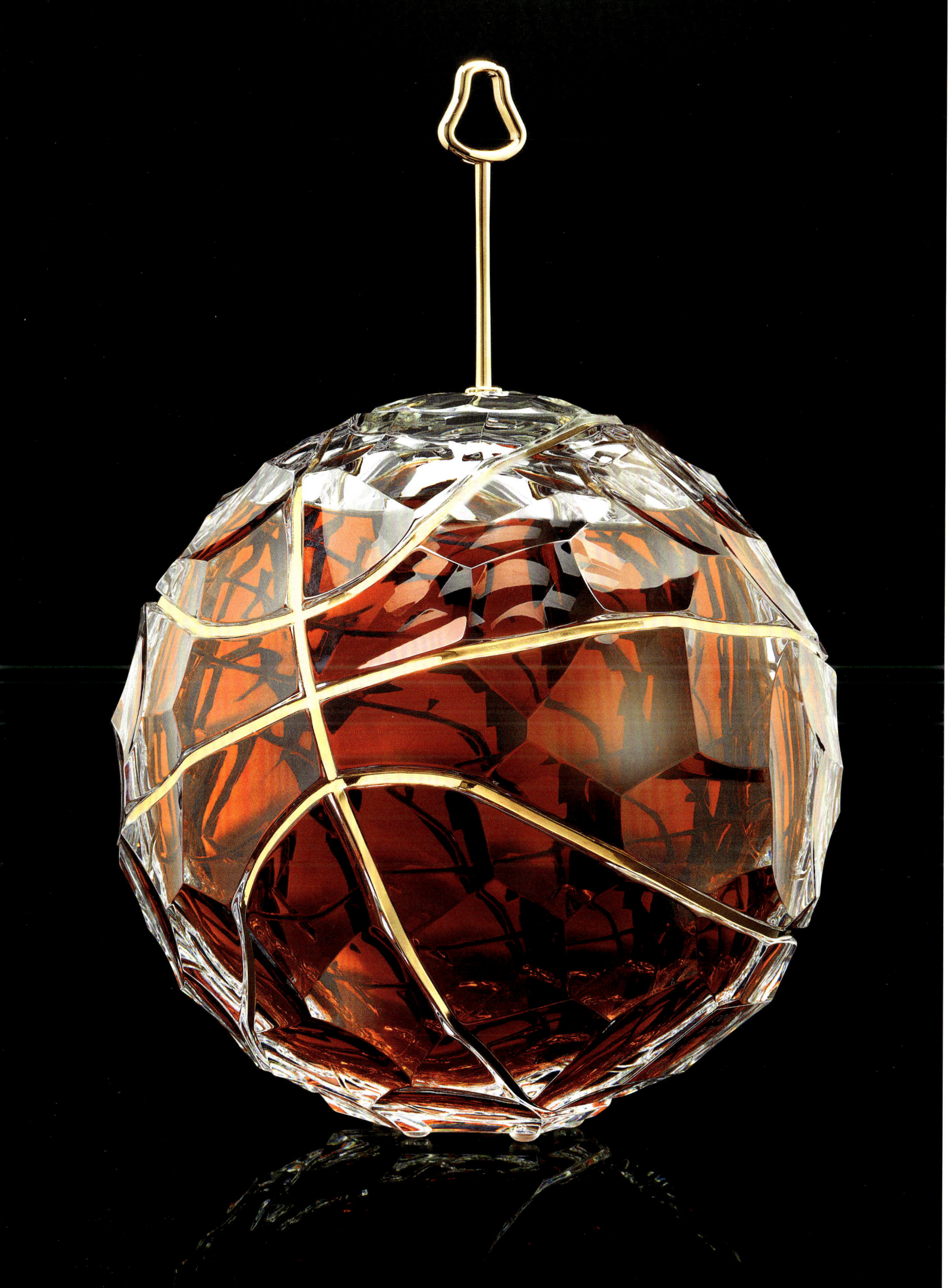

CATALOGUE RAISONNÉ

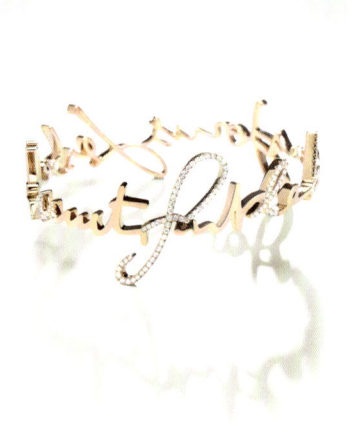

WRITING BRACELET "LES BELLES NUITS…"

White diamonds 1.95 cts;
yellow gold 41.20 g

2009

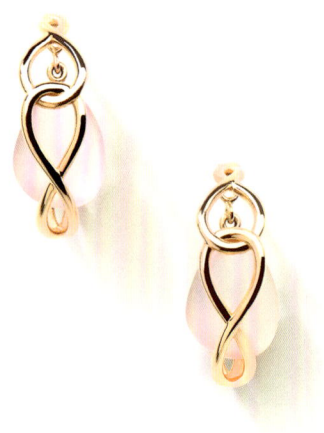

SUMBA HOOPS

Rose gold 7.91 g; rose quartz 14.5 cts

1999

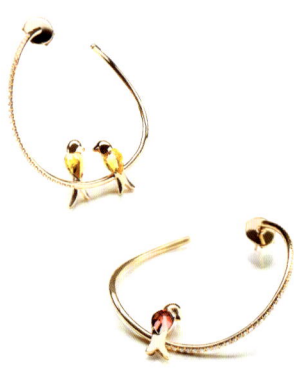

LOVE BIRD HOOPS

Rose gold 11 g; pear-shaped tourmaline
0.60 ct; yellow citrine 0.68 ct; orange
citrine 0.68 ct; white diamonds 0.47 ct

2010

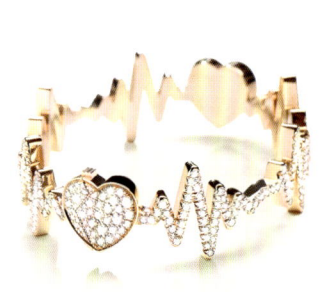

DIAMONDS HEARTBEAT BRACELET

Rose gold 35.98 g; pavé-set white
diamonds 3.59 cts

2006

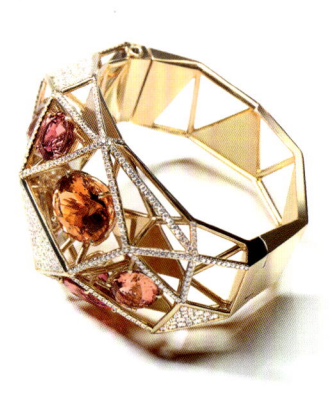

MIKADO ARCHITECT BRACELET

Rose gold; pink tourmaline 10.44 cts;
pink tourmaline 9.02 cts; pink tourmaline
6.29 cts; copper tourmaline 16.51 cts;
copper tourmaline 14.47 cts; pink
spinel 1.99 cts; red spinel 1.40 cts; white
diamonds 8.12 cts; rose gold 122.52 g

2013

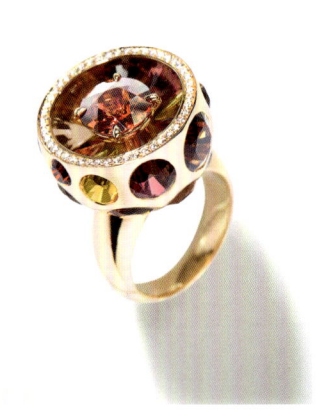

À LA FOLIE RING

Rose gold 18.60 g; pink tourmaline 3.17 cts;
pink tourmalines 2.95 cts; garnets 3.94 cts;
citrines 3.83 cts; smoky quartz 4.57 cts

2007

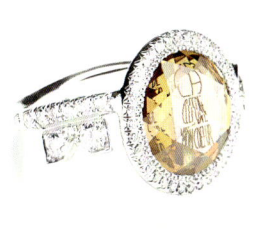

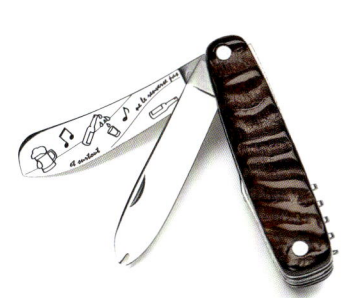

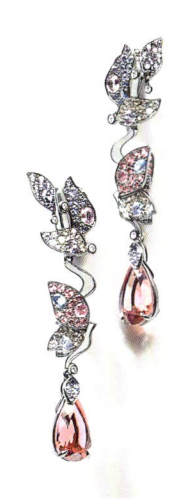

TATOO DIAMOND RING
THE KEY TO MY HEART

Rose-cut white diamond
DVS1 1.82 cts; white diamonds
0.86 ct; white gold 3.70 g

2014

FRIENDSHIP KNIFE

Steel; oryx horn

2020

METAMORPHOSE EARRINGS

White gold 20.11 g; white diamonds
0.35 ct; brown diamonds 0.97 ct;
spinels 1.18 cts; sapphire 0.39 ct;
pink sapphire 0.27 ct; purple sapphire
2.96 cts; pink tourmalines 15 cts

2019

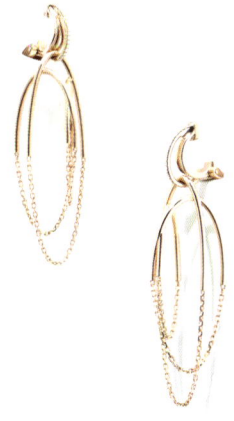

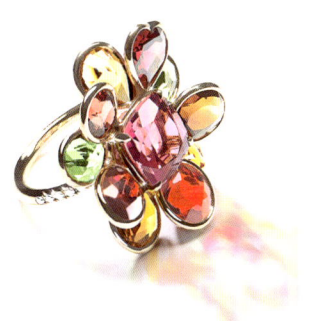

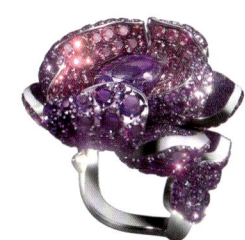

MORSE AMOUR EARRINGS

Rose gold 15.00 g;
white diamonds 0.20 ct

2018

À LA FOLIE BLOSSOM RING

Rose gold 5.85 g; pink tourmaline 7 cts;
red spinels 5.31 cts; peridot 2.06 cts;
citrines 1.95 cts; garnet 0.94 ct; pink
spinel 0.73 ct; white diamonds 0.24 ct

2016

DAMASCUS ROSE NFT RING

Blackened white gold;
purple sapphire; amethyst

2023

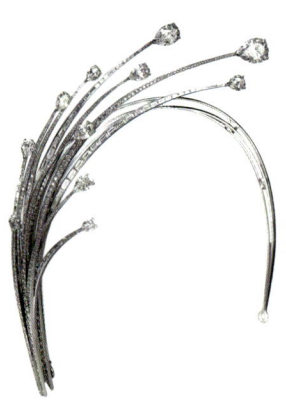

DIAMONDS FOAM TIARA

11 pear-shaped diamonds for
a total of 28.27 cts; 31.03 cts of white
diamonds; 196 g of white gold

2011

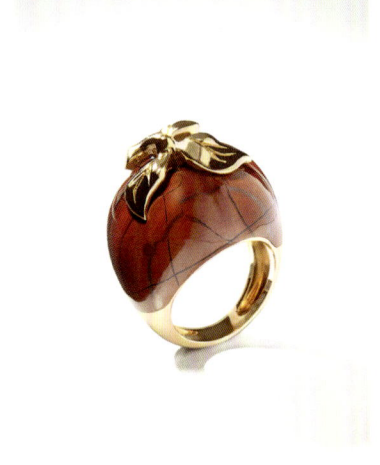

GOURMANDISE
RED JASPER RING

Gold rose 23 g; red jasper 32 g

2001

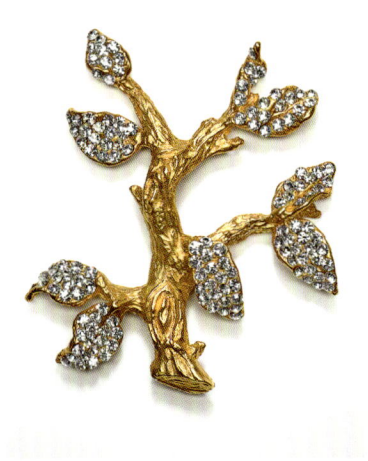

TREE OF LIFE COSTUME
JEWELRY BROOCH

Gold pewter; rhinestones

1993

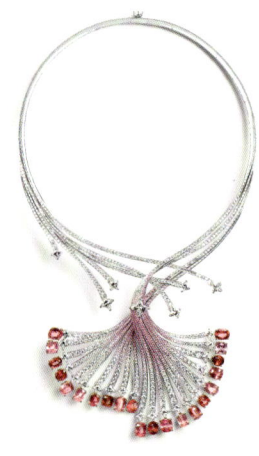

LOUIS VUITTON,
SOUL OF THE JOURNEY
NECKLACE

White gold 259.30 g; 34 Louis Vuitton
diamonds 20.98 cts; 3,417 diamonds
21.56 cts; 19 padparadscha sapphires
23.56 cts; 361 pink sapphires 2.28 cts

2009

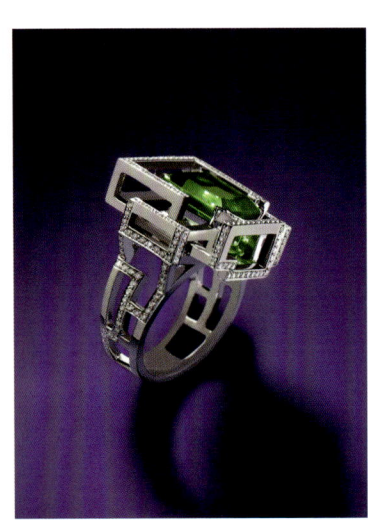

CUBIST GARDEN RING

White gold 18.85 g; green tourmaline
3.92 cts; chalcedony 1.40 cts; turquoise
1.15 cts; blue sapphires 0.25 ct; white
diamonds 0.31 ct; tsavorites 0.50 ct

2014

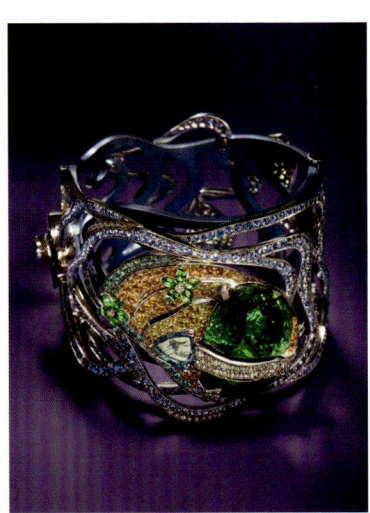

TREASURE ISLAND BRACELET

Green tourmaline 55.38 cts; aquamarines
10.19 cts; green tourmalines 1.92 cts;
tsavorites 1.28 cts; white diamonds
1.26 cts; blue sapphires 19.21 cts;
orange sapphires 1.35 cts; yellow
sapphires 4.05 cts; paraiba tourmalines
1.70 cts; tsavorites 0.11 ct; white
gold 179.49 g; titanium 20.67 g

2013

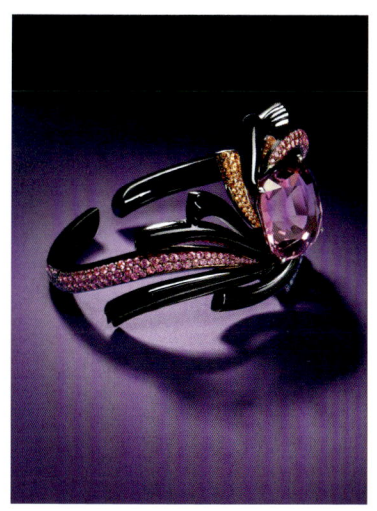

BLACK MAGIC NÉBULEUSE BRACELET

Purple tourmaline 32.29 cts; pink sapphire 2.85 cts; orange sapphire 1.87 cts; blue sapphire 0.71 ct; black lacquer

2018

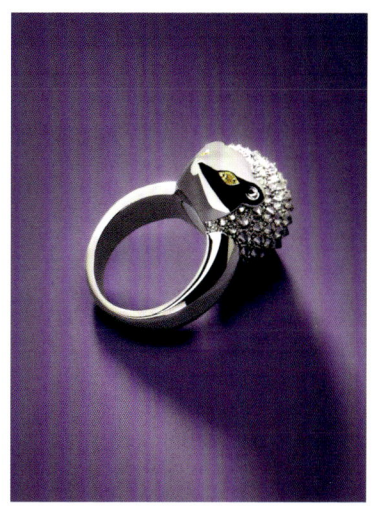

HEDGEHOG RING

White gold 22 g; white diamonds 3.902 cts; yellow diamonds 0.038 ct

2002

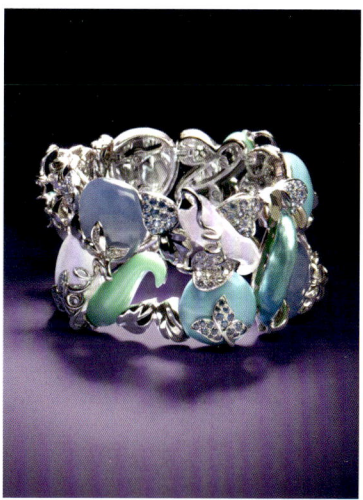

GOURMANDISE WINTER BRACELET

Chalcedony; rock crystal; chrysoprase; turquoise; amethyst; white diamonds 4.07 cts; blue sapphires 9.98 cts; white gold 168.51 g; lacquer

2004

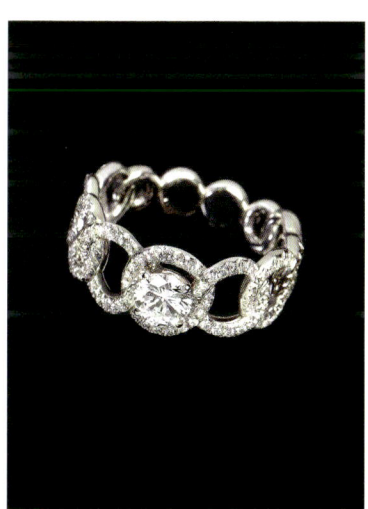

ELLIPSE SOLITAIRE

White diamond DIF2 0.5 ct; white diamonds 0.45 ct; white gold 6.34 g

2016

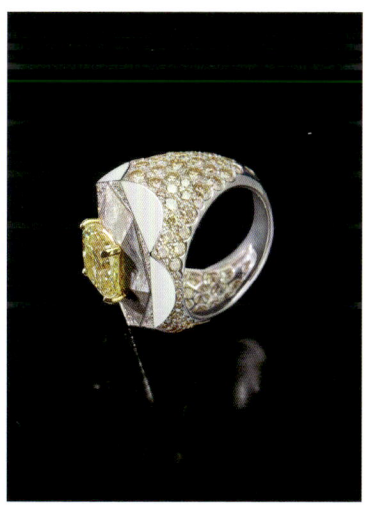

METEORITE YELLOW DIAMOND RING

White gold 22.3 g; canary diamond 4.34 cts; white diamonds 0.31 ct; chocolate diamonds 4.39 cts; meteorite 3.73 g

2015

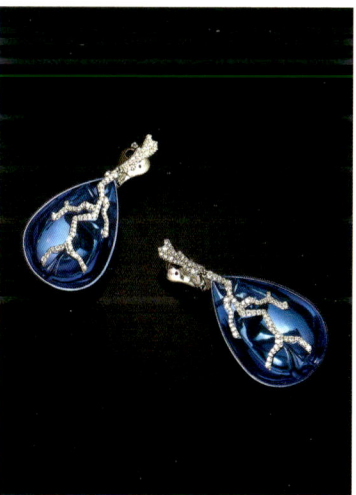

TITANIUM OCEAN CRUSH EARRINGS

White gold 13.25 g; white diamonds 1.37 cts; titanium 18.74 g

2005

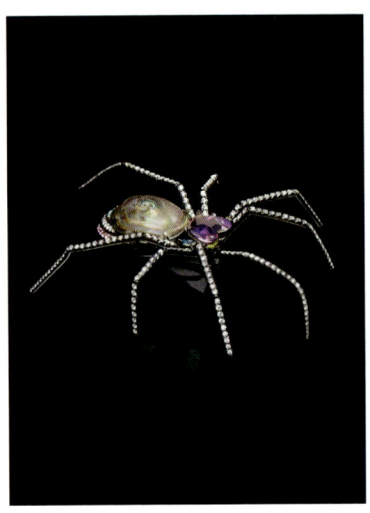

SPIDER BROOCH

Black rhodium-finished white
gold 41.70 g; abalone pearl 38.84 cts;
amethyst 5.51 cts; peridots 0.47 ct;
white diamonds 2.66 cts; purple sapphires
0.4 ct; paraiba tourmalines 0.05 ct;
aquamarines 0.37 ct; amethysts 0.41 ct

2017

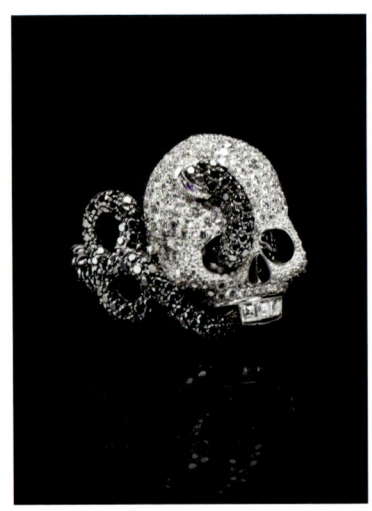

VANITAS DIAMONDS RING

White gold 18.20 g; white diamonds
2.90 cts; black diamonds 2.35 cts;
purple sapphires 0.02 ct

2008

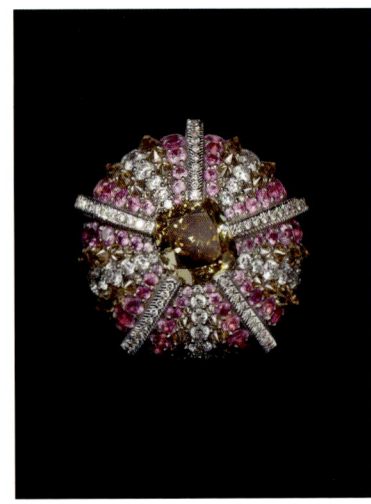

SEA URCHIN RING

White gold 23.8 g; chocolate
diamond 3.01 cts; chocolate
diamonds 4.65 cts; pink sapphires
3.97 cts; diamonds 1.81 cts

2006

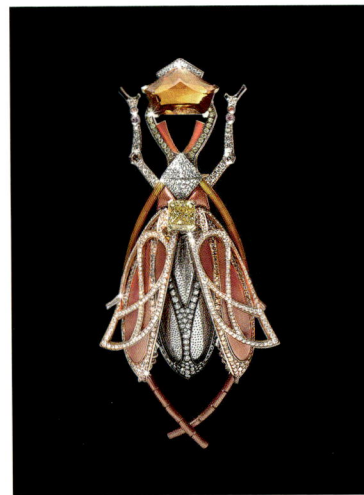

SCARAB BROOCH

White gold 65.77 g; emerald-cut yellow
diamond 2.05 cts; citrine 9.31 cts;
white diamonds 2.60 cts; chocolate
diamonds 3.84 cts; pink sapphire 0.24 ct;
orange sapphires 0.04 ct; lacquer;
aluminum (olfactory material) 0.08 g;
total weight of 70 g; 543 stones

2012

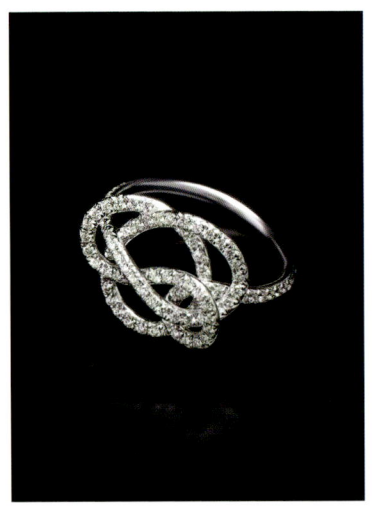

PENSE À MOI
DIAMONDS RING

White gold 4 g;
white diamonds 0.53 ct

2009

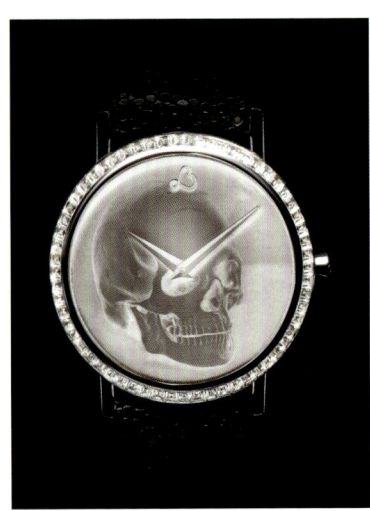

VANITAS DAGUERREOTYPE
WATCH

Skull daguerreotype, limited edition,
self-winding; diamonds 1.60 cts;
rose gold 54.33 g; pin buckle;
camel crocodile strap

2003

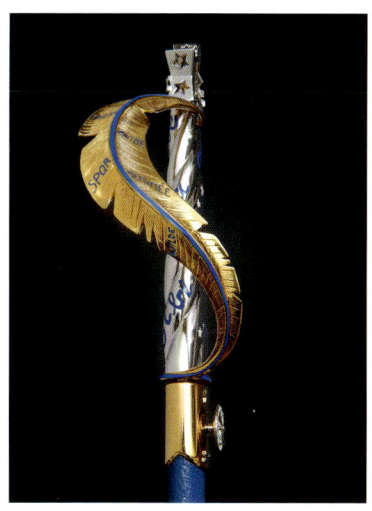

ACADEMICIAN'S SWORD

Steel; silver; gold rose 18 cts;
enamel; leather

2004

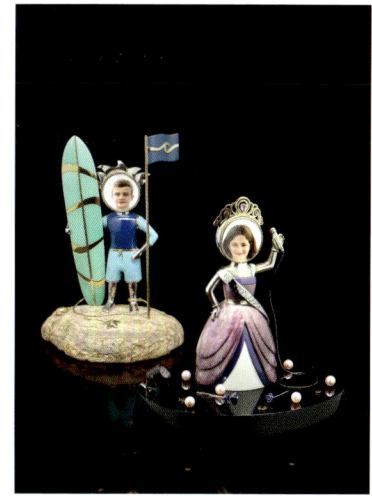

SURFER FRAME

Jasper; malachite 358 cts; lapis lazuli
108 cts; yellow sapphires 2.91 cts;
yellow gold 26.36 g; silver 389.10 g

PRINCESS FRAME

White diamonds 0.19 ct;
amethysts 1.39 cts; black obsidian
5124.30 cts; lavender jasper;
yellow gold 14.82 g; silver 212.04 g

2000

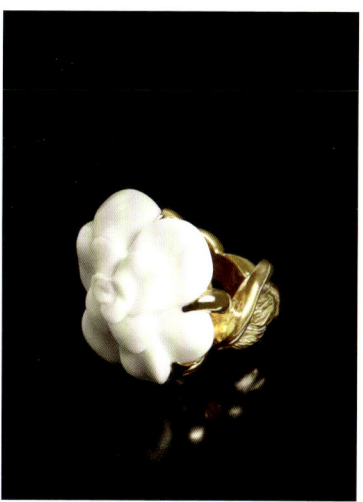

CHANEL,
CAMELIA RING

Yellow gold 23 g; cachalong

1990

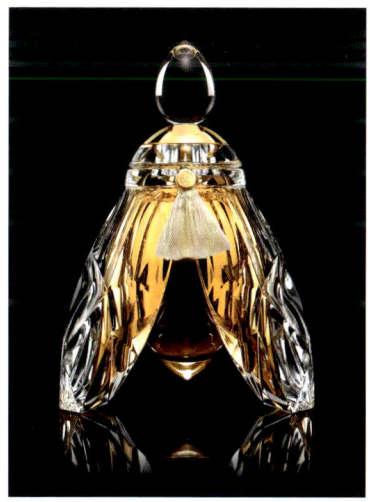

GUERLAIN,
BEE BOTTLE

Baccarat crystal; silk; perfume

2010

GUERLAIN,
ROUGE G

Brass; mirror; raisin

2009

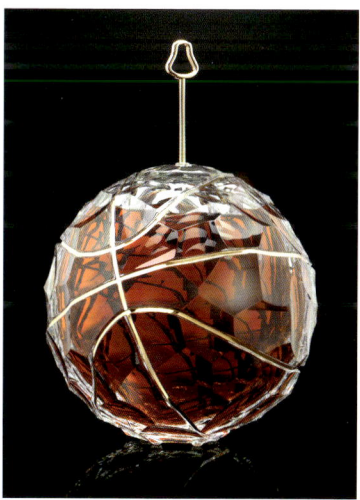

HENNESSY NBA,
PARADISE DECANTER

Baccarat crystal; gilded brass; cognac

2022

LORENZ BÄUMER BY PATRICK BAILLY-MAÎTRE-GRAND

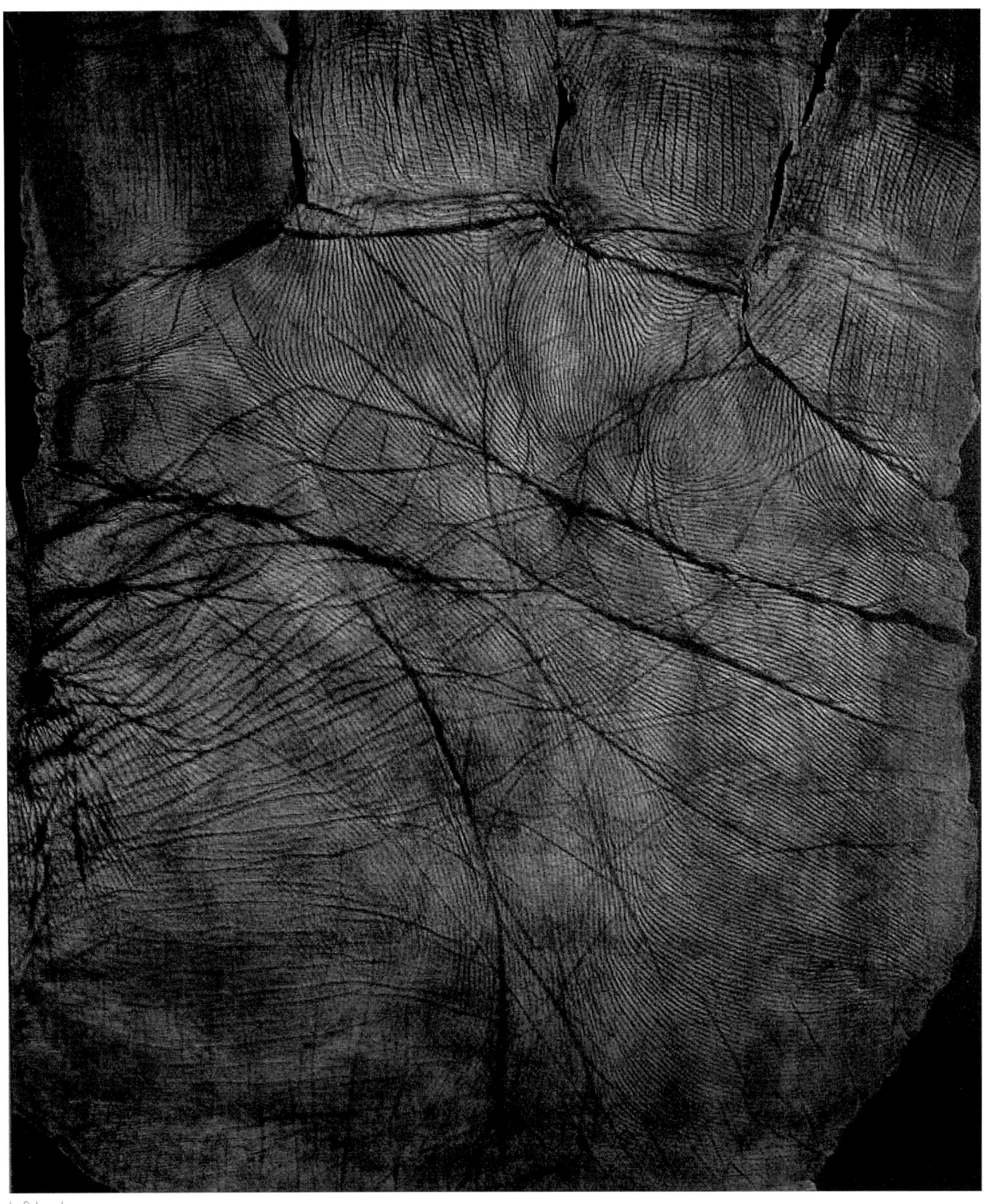

Left hand.

Right hand.

LORENZ BÄUMER'S HAND LIFE LINES BY PATRICK BAILLY-MAÎTRE-GRAND

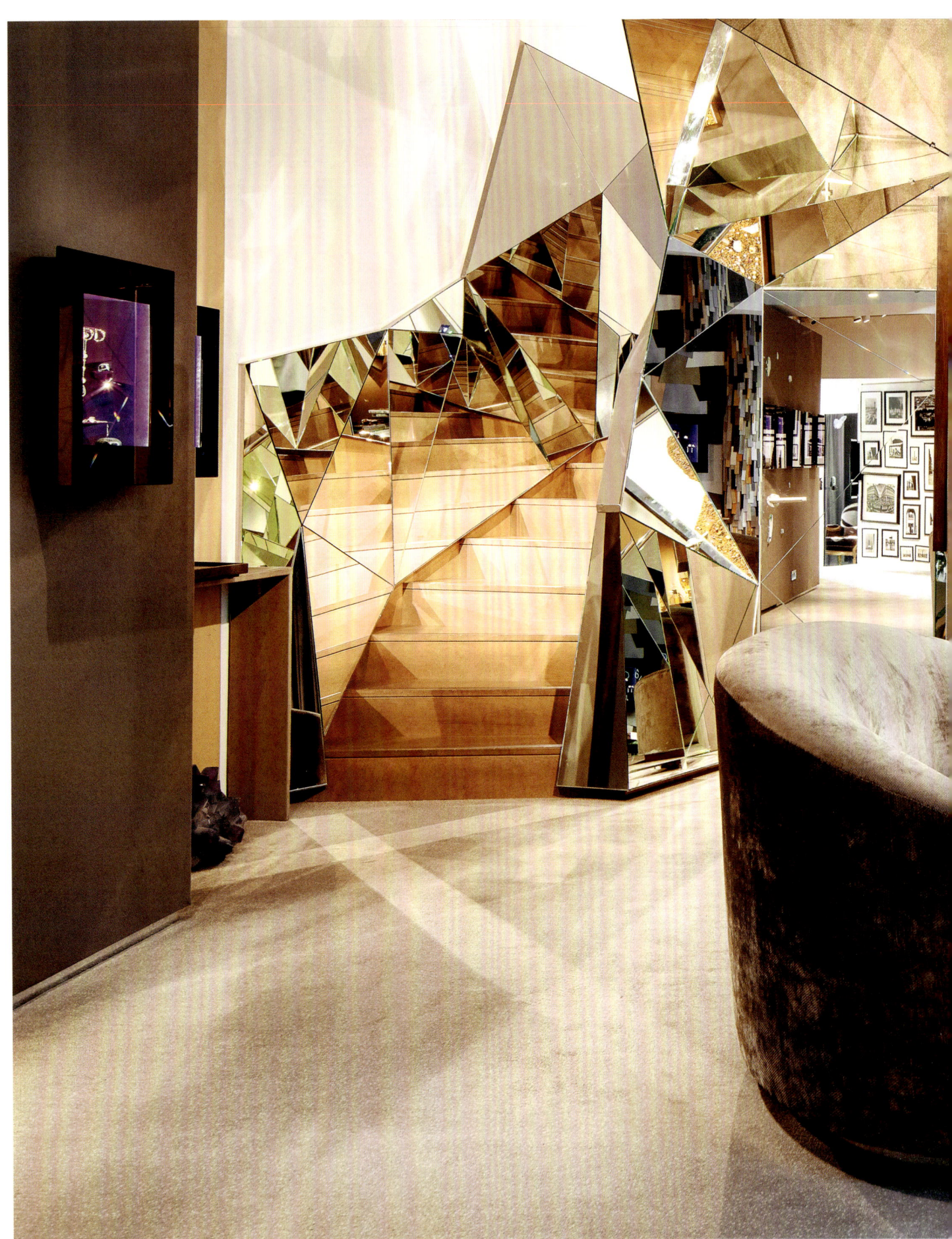

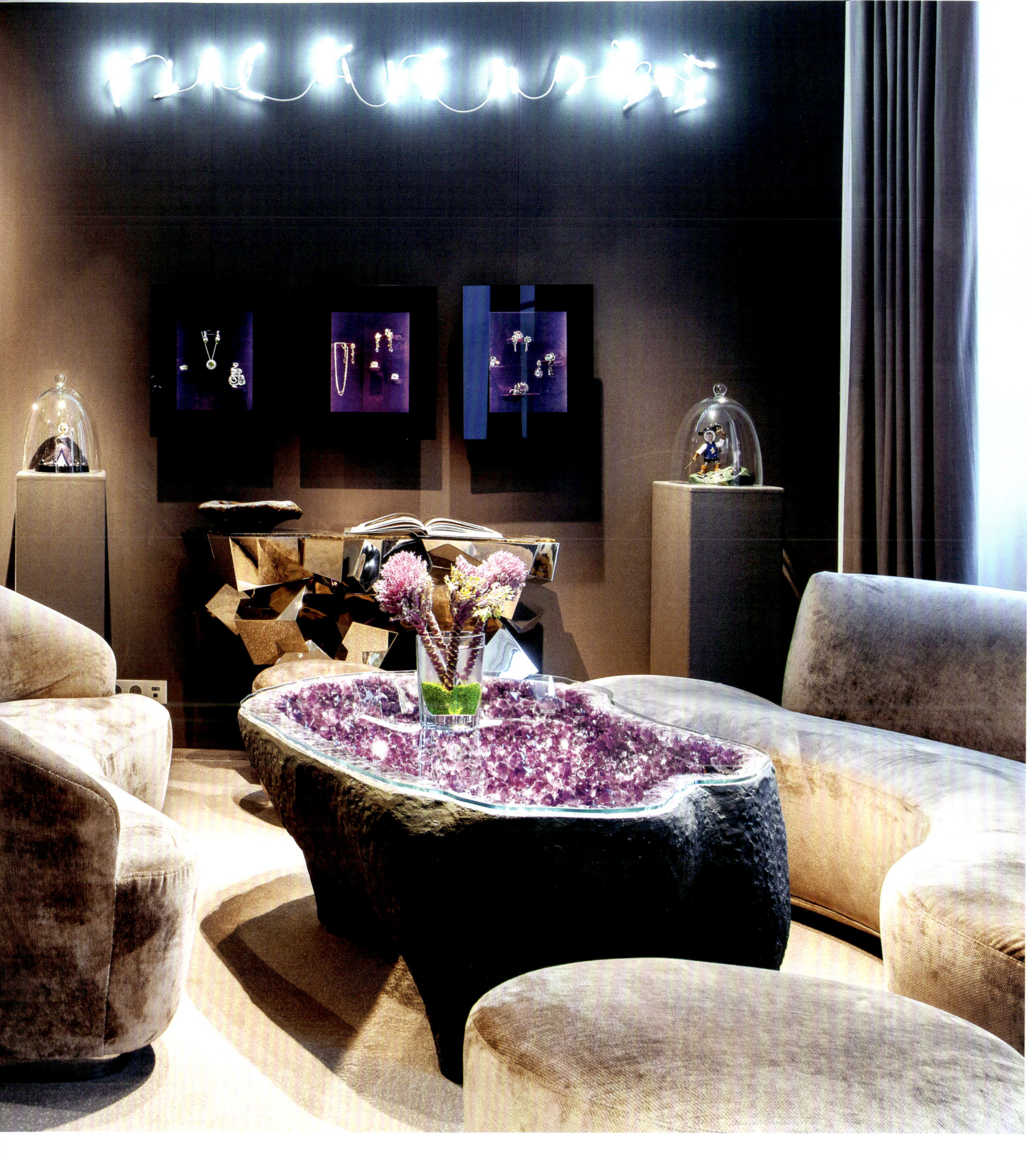

THE BOUTIQUE AT 19, PLACE VENDÔME, PARIS

Editorial: Virginie Mahieux
Graphic design: Élisabeth Welter

Texts: Paul-Henry Bizon
Photographs: Philippe Garcia

With exception of: © Lorenz Bäumer
for "Damascus Rose," "Diamonds
Foam Tiara," Photograph of H.S.H.
Princess Charlène of Monaco,
"Soul of the Journey"; © Fabien
Sarazin for "Guerlain bee boottle";
© Virginie Garnier for the
19 Place Vendôme, in Paris.

Retouching: Brigitte Carasco
Translation from French: Ubiqus
Proofreading: Rachel Zerner

The worn jewelry photographs
were taken on works displayed in
various museums, the casts for which
were produced by the Ateliers d'Art
des Musées Nationaux (national
museum art studios). Each photograph
shows a detail of these works.

By order of appearance in the book,
the portraits of Lorenz Bäumer
were created by the following artists:
Vik Muniz, Nathalie Boutté, and
Patrick Bailly-Maître-Grand (as well
as the works depicting the palms
of Lorenz Bäumer). Thank you
for your contributions.

Editorial Partnership: Corinne Schmidt
and Charlotte Court

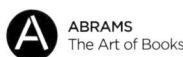

ABRAMS
The Art of Books

Printed and bound in Italia
Legal deposit: October 2023
ISBN : 978-1-4197-7169-9

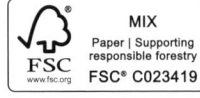

MIX
Paper | Supporting
responsible forestry
FSC® C023419

$50 US / $63 CAN / £35 UK / €50
ISBN 978-1-4197-7169-9

55000